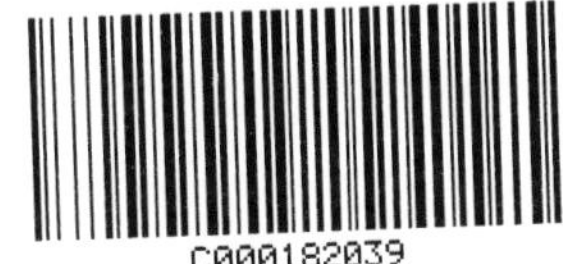

Management & Cost Accounting FOR DUMMIES

A Wiley Brand

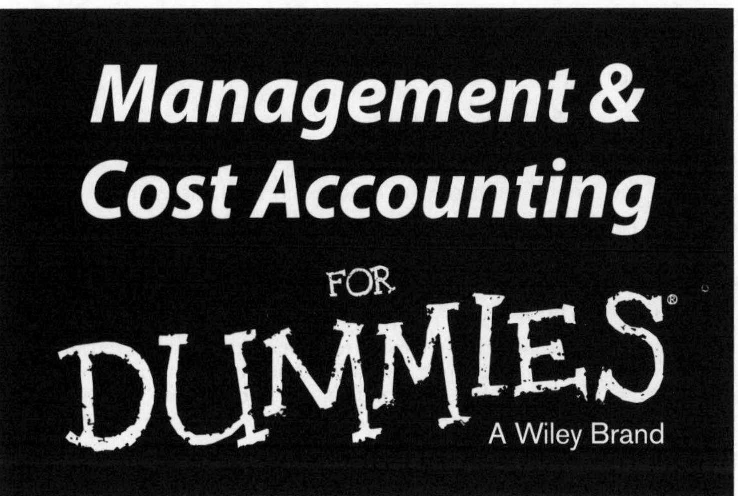

by Mark Holtzman and Sandy Hood

Management & Cost Accounting For Dummies®

Published by: John Wiley & Sons, Ltd., The Atrium, Southern Gate, Chichester, www.wiley.com

This edition first published 2013

Registered office

John Wiley & Sons Ltd, The Atrium, Southern Gate, Chichester, West Sussex, PO19 8SQ, United Kingdom

For details of our global editorial offices, for customer services and for information about how to apply for permission to reuse the copyright material in this book please see our website at www.wiley.com.

For general information on our other products and services, please contact our Customer Care Department within the U.S. at 877-762-2974, outside the U.S. at (001) 317-572-3993, or fax 317-572-4002. For technical support, please visit www.wiley.com/techsupport.

For technical support, please visit www.wiley.com/techsupport.

A catalogue record for this book is available from the British Library.

ISBN 978-1-118-65049-3 (pbk), ISBN 978-1-118-65046-2 (ebk), ISBN 978-1-118-65047-9 (ebk)

Printed in Great Britain by TJ International Ltd, Padstow, Cornwall

10 9 8 7 6 5 4 3 2 1

Contents at a Glance

Table of Contents

Introduction

Language is a funny thing, necessary but full of pitfalls. After all, as humorist Franklin P. Jones wrote, 'skating on thin ice can get you into hot water'! But if, as people say, accounting is the language of business, management accounting is the language inside a business. Accountants establish specific definitions for terms such as *revenue*, *expense*, *gross profit*, *assets* and *liabilities*. Everyone uses these same definitions when they announce and discuss these attributes, so that when a company reports sales revenue, for example, investors and other businesspeople understand how that figure was calculated. This way, companies, investors, managers and everyone else in the business community speak the same language – a language for which accountants wrote the dictionary.

Management accounting allows a company's managers to understand how their business operates, and gives them the information needed to make decisions. It helps them plan their business's activities and control its operations. For example, suppose that a marketing executive needs to set a price for a new product. To do so, that person needs to understand how much the product costs to produce, which is where management accounting comes in. Furthermore, the price needs to be set at an appropriate level so that at the end of the year (after the company sells all the products it's supposed to sell at whatever prices it sets), the firm earns the profit and cash flow that it projected. Here, too, management accounting proves its usefulness.

We often take management-accounting classes, and we always like to point out to students who the users of management-accounting information usually are: the managers, marketing professionals, financial analysts and information systems professionals working within a company. All have a role not only in developing management accounting information, but also and more importantly in using it to make better business decisions.

About This Book

If you accept that management accounting is the language inside a business, clearly running a business without understanding this topic is pretty difficult. Therefore, we've written this book for businesspeople – present and future – who want to better understand how to use management accounting to make decisions and how management accountants develop the information in reality.

We have a confession to make: we really love to do accounting, especially management accounting. And better yet, we love to convey our knowledge and enthusiasm for it. We believe that contribution margin (see Chapter 9) is the greatest thing since sliced bread and that the theory of constraints can solve most of life's problems (see Chapter 19).

In our view, an urgent need exists to redress the balance – to counter the bad rap that accounting gets for being boring (even financial accountants, of all people, trash their poor management brethren for being the most boring of all accountants). We want to show what we believe makes management accounting engaging and (yes) exciting, right here in this book.

Therefore, when you start reading our handiwork and find that you can't put this book down, don't blame us and our lame little puns. Instead, appreciate that after you start discovering accounting, it can be quite difficult to stop.

What You're Not to Read

We tried to write this book so that it spellbinds you, so that you can't stop reading until you've consumed every last word (though we don't mind if you're tempted to peek at the last few pages to see how it ends!).

That said, if you're very busy, feel free to focus on the most important stuff that you need to know and skip some of these less important elements:

- **Technical stuff:** Anything marked with this icon is especially interesting to management-accounting geeks like us. But if you're in a rush, you can skip these paragraphs safe in the knowledge that you aren't missing anything essential.
- **Sidebars:** These fascinating grey-shaded boxes include additional information that we think you may like, but you can pick up management accounting just fine without reading them.

Foolish Assumptions

We assume that you're one of the following:

- A college student taking a management-accounting course who needs some help understanding the topics you're covering in class. Specifically, you'll certainly find this book helpful supplementary reading if you're taking the level 3 and 4 AAT courses, or operational or managerial level CIMA courses, or the fundamental ACCA courses.

- A businessperson or entrepreneur who wants to know more about how to collect accounting information to make better business decisions.
- A recent college graduate interested in pursuing a career in management accounting, perhaps as a chartered management accountant.
- A professional accountant or bookkeeper looking for a straightforward refresher in the basics of management accounting.

How This Book Is Organised

Each of the five parts of this book tackles a different aspect of management accounting. The following sections explain how we organise the information so that you can find what you need quickly and easily.

Part I: Getting Started with Management and Cost Accounting

Part I gives you a taste of what management accounting is and why it's important. The chapters also review some important aspects of accounting that every businessperson needs to know. We hit profitability, efficiency, productivity and continuous improvement especially hard.

Part II: Understanding and Managing Costs

At its crux, management accounting is all about costs – be they direct, indirect, overhead or whatever – and how they behave. Part II explores the world of costs – what drives them up, down or sideways.

Part III: Planning and Budgeting

An important part of managing an organisation is planning for the future, and management accountants play a critical role in this process by preparing budgets, the topic of Part III. These budgets integrate information from every part of an organisation to develop a plan to meet managers' goals.

Part IV: Using Management Accounting for Evaluation and Control

Accountants have a reputation for being control freaks, but it's part of the job. Managers and management accountants not only plan but also need to control. This duty means that they monitor a company's performance carefully and compare that performance to their budgets. In this way, managers can identify and address problems quickly, before they become crises. We describe how managers can *flex* their budgets – that is, prepare budgets that can adapt to changing facts and circumstances. Part IV also explains how to evaluate and control the activities throughout an organisation, including using responsibility accounting, variance analysis and two techniques that managers use to run their companies: the balanced scorecard and the theory of constraints.

Part V: The Part of Tens

The chapters in this part provide you with a quick reference to the most important formulas in the book. We also share some career options for management accountants.

Hop online and visit `www.dummies.com/extras/managementcostaccountinguk` for a bonus Part of Tens chapter 'Ten Ratios to Know for Management Accountants', which includes helpful exam practice.

Icons Used in This Book

Throughout the margins of this book, we use certain symbols to emphasise important points. Watch for these icons:

This icon marks simple hints that can help you solve problems on tests and in real-life management accounting situations.

We use this icon to highlight information that's especially important to keep in mind. Tucking these facts away helps you keep key concepts at your fingertips.

This icon pops up alongside examples (surprise, surprise!) that show you how to apply an idea to real-world accounting problems.

Like building *Titanic II,* not every idea is a good idea. This icon alerts you to situations that require caution. Iceberg ahead!

We just had to share these interesting snippets of knowledge with you. If you're in a hurry, however, don't panic; just skip them.

This icon shows where we provide an exercise for you to try, so that you get to put some of your recently acquired expertise into practice.

Where to Go from Here

All the chapters in this book are modular, and so you can study and understand them without reading other chapters. Just go through the table of contents and select a subject that you want to know more about. We provide cross references to topics in other chapters where appropriate, so that if you skip a foundational concept crucial to what you're reading about, you know where to find what you need.

If you're looking to discover management accounting from scratch, or to unlearn some aspect that you fear you've got wrong, start with Part I to get the basics under your belt. We take special care to explain all the fundamentals that some management accounting texts skip. If you're a student with little or no background in accounting, make a point to read Chapter 2.

Management accounting itself is built on a few basic principles. In our experience, most students who have trouble with management accounting usually improve their performance after becoming more familiar with these basics. Therefore, to better understand these foundations, take a look at Chapter 3 (cost principles), Chapter 8 (cost behaviour) and Chapter 9 (contribution margin).

If you're studying for an accountancy exam, make sure that you know the relevant key formulas in Chapter 20.

Where to Go from Here

Part I
Getting Started with Management and Cost Accounting

getting started
with
management
and
cost accounting

For Dummies can help you get started with lots of subjects. Visit www.dummies.com to learn more and do more with *For Dummies*.

In this part . . .

- Discover what management accountants do and why they do it.
- Find out what you can do to become a management accountant.
- Learn how different kinds of companies operate.
- Know how accountants measure profits, efficiency and productivity.
- Find out how managers apply continuous improvement.

Chapter 1

Planning and Control: The Role of Management Accounting

In This Chapter

- Appreciating the importance of management accounting
- Costing business activities
- Planning for profits and cash flow
- Monitoring and evaluating company performance

Before embarking on a journey, you need a clear plan. Even if you're driving a familiar route and know where you're going and how you intend to get to your destination, you may well have landmarks along the way in mind. Perhaps you plan to take an hour to reach the motorway, spend another hour on it and allow 20 minutes for the final section of your trip.

When you have a plan, you can monitor it and revise your arrival time based on the times you achieve for each section. You can also check that your passengers are comfortable and happy with your driving.

These types of duties are central to *management accounting:* the collecting and monitoring of information about a venture to make sure that it's on track to meeting its goals. For the journey analogy, setting up the route and arrival time, considering the level of comfort for the passengers and adhering to the speed limit are goals within the plan. Monitoring how the journey is progressing and modifying the expected arrival time is control.

This chapter explains what management accountants do (in essence, planning and control) and why they do it. We explain what costs are and investigate different ways of measuring them. We also explore management planning, budgeting, and monitoring and evaluating operations, and discern the differences between management accounting and financial accounting.

Understanding What Management Accountants Do, and Why

Management accounting is at the heart of running a business. It provides the valuable information about the business that can help managers make important decisions. As we describe in this section, the process of gathering information involves the following aspects:

- Identifying different types of costs based on how they're used to provide the products or services of the business.
- Analysing costs to understand how they behave and how they'll respond to different activities.
- Planning and budgeting for the future.
- Evaluating and controlling operations by comparing plans and budgets to actual results.

For much more on the benefits that management accounting brings to businesses, turn to Chapter 2.

Distinguishing management from financial accounting

We want to clarify one issue here and now, and that's to explain the different aims and duties of management and financial accountants. In essence:

- **Management accounting** provides internal reports tailored to the needs of managers inside the company.
- **Financial accounting** is concerned with providing external financial statements for general use by people with a vested interest in the business.

Management accountants report the facts and figures they collect. Financial accountants need the management accountants' cost information for financial reports on past activities produced for shareholders, tax authorities and other stakeholders. Managers need the management accountants to provide the best quality information as a basis for decisions about future activities.

Table 1-1 compares the differences between management and financial accounting based on the information prepared.

Table 1-1 Contrasting Management and Financial Accounting

Preparing Information	*Management Accountants*	*Financial Accountants*
What info?	Internal reports	Financial statements
Who uses info?	Managers who work for the company	Stakeholders, such as shareholders, suppliers and government regulators
When is it prepared?	Whenever needed	Quarterly and annually
How detailed is it?	Very detailed, to address specific decisions to be made by managers	Very general, pertaining to the whole company
How is it prepared?	In accordance with the needs of managers and officers	In accordance with accounting standards depending on where the company is based
How is it verified?	By internal controls among management accountants	By external auditors

Identifying costs

Management accountants need to know what things are used for, to enable the calculation of the cost of the products the business makes.

Some costs are *direct* in that they belong to the product being made. Other costs are *indirect:* they may well be just as essential but they aren't specific to the product.

For example, to produce marmalade you need oranges, sugar, a clean kitchen and skilled labour, among other key inputs. The oranges are a direct cost; having a clean kitchen is indirect.

When the Financial Reports are produced at the end of the accounting period, the company has to know how much revenue was generated and what costs were incurred. Management accountants provide this information. They also organise it for internal reporting, such as showing the revenues, costs and profits of products and departments.

For loads more on direct and indirect costs, flip to Chapter 3.

Analysing costs

Business costs differ in the way they behave. If you make more marmalade, you need more oranges. Therefore, the total cost of oranges varies depending on the number of jars of marmalade that you make.

In this sense, the total cost of oranges is a *volume-based* cost: it varies depending on the volume of jars produced. Other costs may not change at all, whether you make 60 jars or 6,000 jars. For example, the annual fee for hosting the website advertising the marmalade doesn't change even if you make 600,000 jars! So this isn't a volume-based cost.

Management accountants collect the information necessary to discover how costs behave, and provide this info to management. Understanding cost behaviour is extremely useful when deciding how many items you need to sell to make a profit.

Planning and budgeting

Management accountants are involved in a business's planning and preparation for the years ahead. While managers look into the possible activities, management accountants add the numbers.

Within a business, employees and supervisors may suggest improvements to the business. Managers then select the ones that look viable and/or fit the strategic plan and management accountants draw up a budget to add values to the forecasts.

Flip to the later section 'Accounting for the Future: Planning and Budgeting' for more on this subject.

Evaluating and controlling operations

Planning is one thing, but execution is another. Management accountants are responsible for continuously monitoring performance, evaluating it and comparing it to the budget. This control allows managers to see how the business has progressed and where attention needs to be focused to ensure continued progress to the final goals. Evaluating and controlling operations keeps the business on track and also allows management to carry out comparisons between different branches.

Suppose that a chain of pizza restaurants wants to look at the respective performance of the restaurant managers. The management accountant can show all the financial aspects and highlight the cost and revenue differences (called *variances*) from one to another and against the budget. This process gives senior management key information they can use to enable successful practices to be adopted in all the restaurants where they'd be beneficial.

The later section 'Exercising Control' provides more information in this area.

Gathering information needed for decisions

Good managers look to management accountants when they carry out key management activities. The numbers part of planning or control and of decision-making all comes from the management accountant. They gather the data, process and analyse it, and convert it into the sort of information that enables prompt and accurate management decisions.

We discuss helping with short-term decisions in Chapter 10 and long-term ones in Chapter 11.

Concentrating on Costs

Management accountants are often called *cost accountants* because they focus primarily on costs. They collect information about costs, analyse that information, predict future costs and use many different techniques to estimate how much different products or processes are going to cost.

A given product may even have several different costs, depending on how managers plan to use the information. For example, Tom's Taxi service estimates that driving from Tanta Mount to the airport costs £20 in diesel plus £10 in wages, a total of £30, and so a round trip costs the company £60. A taxi picks up passenger Pearl, who pays £100 to travel from Tanta Mount to the airport. Expected profit comes to £40 (£100 – £60).

After dropping Pearl off at the airport, another passenger, Tex, hails the taxi to drive him back to Tanta Mount. However, Tex only has £20 to pay for the taxi ride. Should the driver give Tex an £80 discount and drive him for only £20? The taxi driver might not call himself a management accountant, yet this is a management accounting decision. When Tex is allowed to pay £20 for a taxi ride that is normally £100, the taxi driver recognises a key concept. His taxi is heading exactly where Tex wants to go, and will travel there with no passenger for £0 or with Tex for £20.

This scenario also begs the question of how much Tex's journey costs the taxi company, which you can address and answer in several different ways:

- You can say that it doesn't cost anything, because Pearl has already paid for a round trip and the taxi needs to be driven back to town anyway.
- You can also say that it costs £30: the cost of diesel and wages for driving from the airport back to Tanta Mount.
- You can say that Tex's journey back to town costs £60, just like Pearl's trip to the airport (for which she paid £100).

But wait: what if taking Tex to town prevents the taxi from picking up another passenger on the way back to Tanta Mount? This passenger would pay £50. Tex is becoming expensive: in order to drive him back from the airport, you may lose £50 from the lost business of the other passenger. Was that part of the cost of driving Tex?

As this example indicates, determining how much something costs demands a lot of judgement and plays a very important role in the decisions you make as a management accountant.

In the following sections, we look at what a cost is and describe some of the techniques accountants use to understand how costs behave. We also discuss how to cost products, including how to incorporate overhead costs into product cost. In addition, we examine the idea of relevant and irrelevant costs: when managers make decisions, some cost information needs to be part of the decision but other costs are – quite frankly – irrelevant.

Defining types of costs

A *cost* is the financial sacrifice a company makes to purchase or produce something. Managers accept this necessary evil with the expectation that costs provide some kind of benefit, such as sales and profit.

Costs can have many components. Consider the example of manufacturing a chair:

- **Raw material costs:** Costs of tubular steel, padding and other materials.
- **Labour costs:** The chair factory has to pay workers to sew up the cushion for the base and attach it to the frame.
- **Overhead:** The general expense of running the chair factory.

Chapter 5 looks into product cost calculations and the different approaches that management accountants take to suit different conditions.

Predicting cost behaviour

To make decisions, managers need to understand how certain choices affect costs and profitability. For example, suppose that a firm's managers are trying to decide whether to pay employees overtime (time-and-a-half) in order to increase factory production. On one hand, more production may well increase sales. On the other hand, overtime wages increase costs. Which choice is going to result in higher profits?

To answer these types of questions, management accountants focus on cost behaviour, which can be variable or fixed:

- **Variable costs** change with volume made or sold: the more you sell, the higher the cost.
- **Fixed costs** don't change with volume: regardless of how many items you make or sell, the cost stays the same.

Management accountants who know which costs are variable and which are fixed can use that information to predict how changes in volume affect total costs and the profit per unit of the product sold.

That said, management accountants don't know everything about cost behaviour. They develop their understanding from what the company has experienced in the past. Radical changes push management accountants out of their comfort zones and make predicting how costs are going to react very difficult. For example, if a factory shuts down and then retools to make a new product, management accountants have very little experience from which to make predictions. Similarly, if a factory doubles its production, hiring many more workers, cost behaviours are also likely to change in unpredictable ways.

We discuss cost behaviour in greater detail in Chapter 8.

Driving overhead

Management accountants have to look at costs in different ways. Cost behaviour focuses on what happens when the volume of production changes, with direct and indirect definitions focusing on what the cost is used for.

Overheads are indirect costs. *Production overheads* are those essential costs incurred while producing the products in the factory but that can't be traced to products: examples may be heat and electricity, or the cleaning costs after production is finished. If you make marmalade, how much of the cost of a food-hygiene certificate should you charge to each jar?

Don't dismiss the importance of this question. A chain is only as strong as its weakest link (to read about overheads and bottlenecks, flip to Chapter 19), and an inaccurate overhead allocation over- or under-costs your product. It may even cause the product to be mispriced. As factories become more automated and products become more complex to manufacture, companies use less and less labour but more and more overhead, making accurate costs all the more dependent on accurate overhead allocations. Getting overheads right can be critical to business success. Management accountants who can achieve this aim successfully are incredibly valuable to a business. Chapter 4 investigates the different factors that drive overhead.

In the past factories were very labour intensive; overhead seemed to follow the hours of labour worked. Think about the classic sweatshop with underpaid workers operating sewing machines in a hot and crowded room. Overhead includes supervisor wages and rent, which are the costs of supporting workers. After all, the more workers you have, the more supervisors and rent you need to pay, and so direct labour hours or wages drive overhead in this scenario. If Product X requires 30 minutes to make and Product Y requires one hour, a single unit of Product X brings on half the overhead that Product Y does. Note that because the amount of labour that goes into each product is easy to measure, labour itself is usually treated as a direct cost.

These days, with robots running factories, figuring out what drives overhead isn't simple. Some factories have no direct labour. Therefore, management accountants have to look more carefully when deciding how to allocate the cost of overhead to units produced. Many now use a system called *activity-based costing* to identify a set of overhead cost drivers for overhead. (To read about activity-based costing (ABC), flip to Chapter 4.)

Costing jobs and processes

As we describe in this section, factories usually use one of two approaches to manufacturing products:

- **Job order costing:** Some products are manufactured to meet customer specifications. These products are usually ordered directly by the customer, made especially for that customer and follow this system of job order costing.
- **Process costing:** Some products are mass-produced, with the factory making many identical or near-identical units. Mass production factories follow the process costing system.

Job order costing

When manufacturers make goods to order, they accumulate the cost of each order separately. For example, if an expensive tailor custom-makes shirts, he computes the cost of materials, labour and overhead needed to make each shirt. Some shirts require more materials or labour than others and therefore cost more. Chapter 6 explains the fundamentals of job order costing.

Process costing

When manufacturers make many homogeneous products simultaneously, they usually use process costing. Each unit has to go through several different manufacturing departments. Therefore, management accountants first assign costs to the departments and then assign the costs of the departments to the products made. Chapter 7 explains how to make these allocations.

Distinguishing relevant costs from irrelevant costs

The fact is that some costs make a difference and some don't. When you're faced with a decision, pay attention to the costs that make a difference and ignore the others.

For example, suppose that you're trying to decide whether to eat at home or in a restaurant. You want to do whatever option is cheapest. Here are some relevant costs:

- Cost of food in the restaurant.
- Cost of petrol to drive to the restaurant.
- Extra money you pay if you split the bill among friends who order more expensive food or drinks than you.
- Extra groceries you'd have to buy in order to eat at home.
- Cost of paying a tip to the waiter.

All these costs depend on your decision and so you need to focus on them. Certain costs, however, aren't relevant and can be safely ignored:

- **Your car's lease payments:** You may think that because you have an expensive lease payment you need to justify it by driving your car. But eating in a restaurant doesn't bring down your lease payments (sorry).

- **Cost of food spoiling in your fridge:** Perhaps you think that you should eat at home so that the food in your fridge doesn't spoil. However, you've already paid for the food in the fridge, and so eating at home doesn't get you a refund. Choosing to eat in the restaurant doesn't mean that you have to pay for the spoiled food twice.
- **Your council tax payment:** Perhaps your council tax charge is so high that you feel it commits you to spending more time at home (and less time in restaurants). But staying at home doesn't lower your council tax bill.

Accounting for the Future: Planning and Budgeting

When you understand how costs behave, you can then apply that understanding to develop realistic goals and strategies for the future. Knowing that fixed costs stay fixed and that variable costs change with volume allows you to predict accurately likely costs, income and cash flow for coming periods.

Check out Chapter 18 on creating a balanced scorecard for your business's strategy.

Analysing contribution margin

A product's *contribution margin* measures how selling that product impacts your overall profits. Analysis of contribution margin provides a simple and powerful approach to planning.

For example, selling jars of marmalade for £3 apiece, when each jar costs £1 per jar to make, earns a contribution margin of £2 per jar. That is, every jar sold increases profits by £2. Contribution margin also becomes very useful in calculating the number of units of a product a business needs to sell to break even.

We talk more about this approach in Chapter 9.

Budgeting capital for assets

Capital budgeting is an important planning technique. When faced with a decision about whether or not to invest in long-term assets, such as a building or a piece of machinery, *capital budgeting* analyses the future cash flows from the investment in order to tell decision-makers whether the investment is going to have a good return for the company.

Chapter 11 explains this technique in more detail.

Choosing what to sell

Most companies don't have the resources to make or buy every product they can possibly sell. Therefore, they have to choose the mix of products that yield the highest profit.

Sofi makes cupcakes, but doesn't have enough time to make all the different types of cupcakes she knows her customers want to buy. Using a management-accounting technique that builds in demand, price, ingredient costs and her time, she's able to identify the combination of types of cupcakes that maximise her profit.

Chapter 10 provides you with the tools for making this kind of decision.

Pricing goods

Managers need to take special care when pricing goods. After all, if you price your product too high, customers don't buy it; if you price it too low, you sacrifice sales revenue and profits. Therefore, setting prices requires a measured understanding of how costs behave.

A theatre offers tickets at £100 each, to cover the cost of staging a play and make a reasonable profit. The price is neither too high nor too low and half an hour before the play starts the theatre is almost full. Ten seats are left, which look unlikely to be sold.

A customer walks in and offers £10 for a seat that usually sells for £100. Should the theatre accept the offer?

Probably, yes. One way or another, the cost of the remaining seat is virtually nil; in half an hour (or less by now) the curtain will rise with no one sitting in that seat, whereas the £10 offer is £10 more than the theatre would otherwise receive. In fact any payment is better at the 'last minute'; it fills the theatre and adds to the atmosphere for the other theatregoers.

We provide further examples to help explain pricing in greater detail in Chapter 12.

Setting up a master budget

The planning process climaxes with the master budget. To prepare this important document, management accountants collaborate with managers throughout the organisation to develop a realistic plan, in numbers, for what will happen during the next period (see Chapter 20 for a summary of ten useful management accounting formulas). As we explain in Chapter 14, the master budget counts on your understanding of cost behaviour, the results of capital budgeting, pricing and other management accounting information in order to plan a concrete strategy to meet sales, profit and cash-flow goals for the coming year.

Budgeting can get frustrating because decision-makers throughout the organisation need to agree to a single plan: the master budget. In addition, the master budget they agree to must work in the real world; it has to result in sustainable cash flows and meet the company's profitability goals.

Suppose Sally in the Sales department expects to sell 1,000 widgets for £20 each. Peter says that the Production department can produce a maximum of 900 widgets, costing £21 each. Cath in Cash Management says the company has £500 in cash. Combining all this information, as shown in Figure 1-1, results in a train wreck.

Projected Cash Flow

Sales revenue (900 widgets selling for £20 each)	£18,000
Cost of units sold (900 widgets costing £21 each)	(£18,900)
Net loss	(£900)

Projected Cash Flow

Beginning balance	£500
Cash received from sales	£18,000
Cash paid for units produced	(£18,900)
Ending cash balance (overdraft)	(£400)

Figure 1-1: A budget that doesn't work.

First of all, even though the Sales department projects selling 1,000 units, it can only sell as many units as the Production department makes: in this case, 900 units. Therefore, the company is probably not going to meet customer demand.

Also, the sales price is too low. The company spends £21 to make each widget but only sells each one for £20, and so it loses £1 on every widget, resulting in a projected net loss of £900.

Making matters worse, the company doesn't have enough cash. It has £500 in the bank at the beginning of the year, which is likely to turn into a £400 overdraft by the end of the year.

In short, the company doesn't produce enough goods to sell, it sets the sales price too low, its production costs are too high and it has insufficient cash flow. Things don't look good and changes are needed.

Managers and management accountants need to work together to develop a budget that works. Suppose that, after some negotiation, the Sales department finds a way to raise its price to £22 per widget. The Production department realises that it can produce 1,000 units if employees reconfigure their equipment. This equipment change also reduces the cost per unit to £19. Figure 1-2 shows what can happen under these new circumstances.

Projected Cash Flow

Sales revenue (1,000 widgets selling for £22 each)	£22,000
Cost of units sold (1,000 widgets costing £19 each)	(£19,000)
Net income	£3,000

Projected Cash Flow

Beginning balance	£500
Cash received from sales	£22,000
Cash paid for units produced	(£19,000)
Ending cash balance	£3,500

Figure 1-2: A reworked budget.

As a result of close co-ordination (and perhaps a little arm-twisting), the company now projects to meet customer demand fully, producing 1,000 units. In doing so, it projects (positive) net income of £3,000 and an ending cash balance of £3,500.

If management had taken the department's plans at face value without preparing a budget, it would have manufactured too few units at too high a cost and sold them at too low a price, incurring a loss. The budgetary process helps avoid this mess and so is a critical step to help a company meet its goals.

Flexing your budget

Unfortunately, things usually don't go as planned. A *flexible budget* allows you to plug different scenarios into next year's master budget.

For example, if you expect sales to range between 10,000 and 15,000 units, you need to prepare a budget that projects what would happen across this entire range, laying out what happens to profits and cash flow if you sell 11,000 units, 12,000 units, and so on. A flexible budget helps prepare your company for a broad range of possibilities. You can read more about flexing budgets in Chapter 15.

Exercising Control

A budget is a great planning tool for reaching your goals, as long as everyone in the company follows it. If people do whatever they want, the result is chaos.

Management accountants ensure that the organisation follows its budget by continuously monitoring actual performance and comparing the budget to what actually happens. Making sure that the company is on course, following its plan, is called *control.*

In this section, we introduce you to the important aspects of controlling departmental responsibility, discerning reasons for good and bad performance, and striving for improvement.

Allocating responsibility

Companies are usually made up of many parts or departments, each of which takes responsibility for different aspects of operations. Consider the following typical departments:

- **Finance:** Responsible for managing cash activities and keeping records.
- **Maintenance:** Responsible for keeping buildings and equipment clean and in working order.

- **Manufacturing:** Responsible for production.
- **Purchasing:** Responsible for purchasing raw materials to be resold.
- **Quality control:** Responsible for ensuring that the goods produced meet benchmark quality levels.
- **Sales:** Responsible for selling goods.

Responsibility accounting requires attributing performance in different parts of the company to the department that's responsible. For example, suppose that you budget to purchase raw materials for £100 per unit and the company actually pays £95 per unit. Credit for this achievement goes to the Purchasing department.

Now suppose that, even though you budget to sell 105,000 units, the company sells only 99,000. To discover what went wrong, go and ask the Sales department.

Chapter 17 describes responsibility accounting in greater detail.

Analysing variances

Responsibility accounting in a factory requires untangling many different causes and effects. *Variance analysis* extricates these different factors to reveal who was responsible for what.

For example, say that a single factory, in a single month, has to deal with the following surprises:

- Raw materials cost an extra 5 per cent.
- A shipment of raw materials doesn't arrive on time, delaying production.
- A machine breaks down, requiring unexpected repairs costing £100,000.
- Four employees unexpectedly resign.
- The company can raise prices by 10 per cent.

Some of these events increase costs (the first three), the employees who leave cut costs and the price increase should boost profits.

Imagine that when you reach the end of your accounting year, you discover that profits are up by 4 per cent. Variance analysis can reveal how each of these factors impacted profits. For example, how much did the 5 per cent increase in raw materials hurt profitability? As we explain in Chapter 16, variance analysis considers a broad range of factors and can reveal who's responsible for them.

Producing a cycle of continuous improvement

Management accounting runs in cycles of different lengths, with certain sales reports and controls being repeated every day. Some reports may be prepared every month or each quarter, whereas others may be prepared just once a year.

As a result, businesses need to develop an approach for continuous improvement.

W. Edwards Deming, the American professor and business consultant whose ideas on Quality Management were used to improve businesses all over the world, popularised a tool called the PDCA (Plan, Do, Check, Act) cycle for continuous improvement, as shown in Figure 1-3. Deming's PDCA cycle comes from the scientific model of forming hypotheses and then testing them, and it follows these steps:

1. **Plan:** Establish your objectives and how you plan to achieve them. In the scientific method, the equivalent step is creating your hypothesis and prediction.

   Ripe OJ's orange juice processing plant intends to experiment with new technology (the plan) to squeeze more juice out of oranges (the objective).

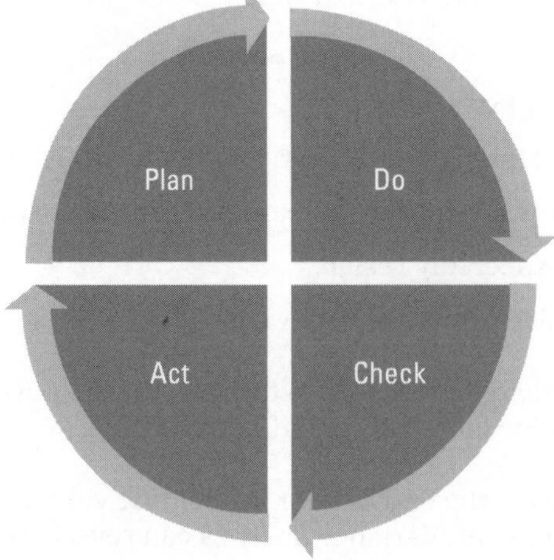

Figure 1-3: Deming's PDCA cycle.

2. **Do:** Implement the plan – making it happen. In the scientific method, this step is the test of your hypothesis.

   Ripe OJ's processing plant sets up the new technology and tries it out on real oranges.

3. **Check:** Measure to determine what happened. The scientific method calls this step the analysis.

   Ripe OJ's managers measure how much orange juice the new technology produced. Did the new technology squeeze more juice out of the oranges? Unfortunately, no. It squeezed less. The plant can usually produce 600 gallons in one batch and it expected the new technology to yield 700 gallons. Instead, the process yielded only 550.

4. **Act:** Think about root causes that may explain the differences between actual and planned results. To close the cycle of improvement, act on a new plan to implement and test these root causes. This stage reflects the scientific method's commitment to evaluation and improvement.

   Ripe OJ's managers call in the engineers to try to figure out why the plant produced so little orange juice. After much discussion, the engineers and managers believe that the shortfall was caused by a junior engineer forgetting to plug the big contraption into the wall outlet. They plug it in and try again, returning to the plan stage (Step 1).

Getting Certified

In accounting (as in other professions, such as medicine or law), professionals are people who demonstrate mastery of a certain field and who agree to accept personal responsibility to practise their work according to established standards. In other words, they're certified (you may think that anyone deciding to become an accountant needs certifying, but this is in a good way!).

Like other professionals, most management accountants accept a code of ethics, established by the Chartered Institute of Management Accountants (CIMA). Agreeing to practise by this code is one of the requirements for becoming a Chartered Global Management Accountant (CGMA). All professional accounting bodies include management accounting exams within their qualifications. The Association of Accounting Technicians (AAT) and The Association of Chartered Certified Accountants (ACCA) test exam candidates' management accounting.

Following the code of ethics

CIMA's code of ethics comprises five fundamental principles: integrity, objectivity, professional competence and due care, and professional behaviour. The code explains these principles and gives examples of their use for management accountants. Membership of CIMA provides employers and clients with a badge of quality.

Failure to comply with the standards can result in disciplinary action by CIMA.

Becoming a chartered global management accountant

CGMA is the global designation for management accountants. It's powered by AICPA (the American Institute of Certified Public Accountants) and CIMA, two of the world's leading accounting organisations.

On completion of the CIMA qualification and becoming a CIMA member, you're automatically entitled to the CGMA designation. This adds global power to your CV, showcases your value around the world and demonstrates your business acumen, ethics and commitment.

To complete the CIMA qualification applicants are required to have completed the CIMA professional examinations and have demonstrated three years of relevant practical experience. *Management & Cost Accounting For Dummies* provides you with the fundamentals of management accounting, which you can use as foundation stones. This book helps you to understand key concepts. You can build on this knowledge to become a Chartered Management Accountant.

Chapter 2

Using Management Accounting in Your Business

In This Chapter

- Understanding the different kinds of businesses
- Dealing with profits
- Using assets efficiently and productively
- Examining income-producing assets

A tremendous amount of flair and ingenuity goes into entrepreneurial successes, such as the empires built by Richard Branson and Alan Sugar. But continued success and avoiding pitfalls and disasters demands the help of management accountants. In many cases, the difference between maintaining and blowing a fortune boils down to how well high-rollers manage their money.

In this chapter we explore the benefits of management accounting to all types of business. We outline some of the fundamental accounting principles every business needs to follow and explain how those criteria work, such as knowing what sort of business category you're in, handling your profits and assets effectively, and dealing with income-producing assets efficiently. Believe it or not, success or failure in many different areas of business comes down to a few basic principles.

Classifying Companies by Their Output

Most businesses fit into one of three basic categories:

- **Service companies:** These companies do things for their customers.
- **Retailers:** These companies sell products.
- **Manufacturers:** These companies make products.

Often firms provide many different services and products to their customers, which means that some companies fit in more than one of these categories. For example, restaurants are manufacturers and service companies; they prepare meals and serve them. Some retailers are also manufacturers, selling products that they make. A few organisations don't naturally fit into the three basic categories; perhaps they extract products to sell or rely on more of a co-operative arrangement with customers rather than straightforward transactions. They're important too, but we don't discuss them here.

Figure 2-1 illustrates how manufacturers, retailers and service companies make and sell physical products and provide services for end-user customers.

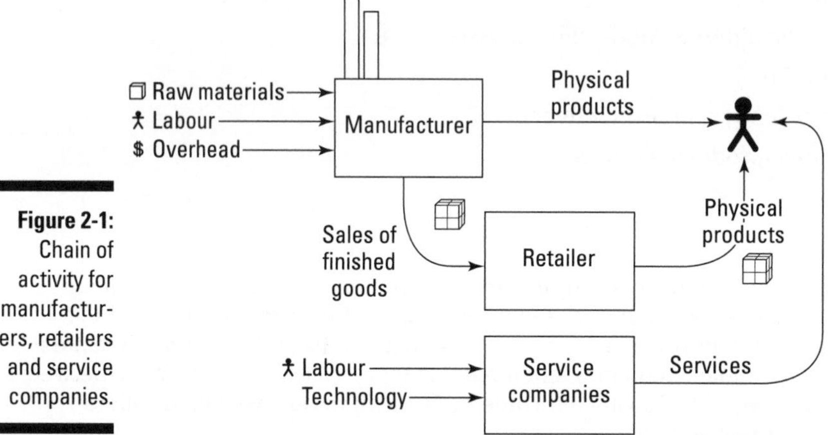

Figure 2-1: Chain of activity for manufacturers, retailers and service companies.

Checking out service companies

Simply put, *service companies* do things for their customers. Here are just a few examples of the wide range of service companies you may encounter:

- Banks and accounting firms
- Doctors, dentists and opticians
- Dog walkers
- Mobile phone, Internet and TV providers
- Power utilities
- Universities

Although companies can be part of more than one business category, service companies that sell or give customers physical products incidental to their basic services don't necessarily qualify as retailers. For example, even though a university may sell books and supplies, its main business is a service – to educate.

Service companies earn money by providing services to customers and so they usually rely on having highly skilled workers or some technology that their customers value. Accounting firms, universities, hospitals and dog-walking services have to hire trained and well-qualified professionals.

Perusing retailers

Retail companies buy products with the intention of selling them to customers for a higher price. Some of the businesses that comprise this category include:

- Car dealers
- Convenience stores
- Department stores
- Internet retailers
- Mail-order catalogues
- Supermarkets

Retailers typically create *distribution channels,* ways to get their products to customers. For example, an Internet retailer or a mail-order catalogue usually packs and ships products to customers. A supermarket, on the other hand, lets customers physically pick out the products they want to buy and then take them home themselves.

Retailers need to know their customers and the types of products they want to buy. For example, a clothing retailer has to predict which colours and styles its customers are going to like in order to buy and stock saleable inventories.

Looking at manufacturers

Manufacturers produce goods and then sell them to retailers or to end-users. Check out a few examples:

- Bakeries
- Car manufacturers
- Farms
- Oil refineries
- Soft-drink bottlers

To make products, manufacturers need long-term assets, such as a factory with equipment, and raw materials – inputs into the production process. For example, a car manufacturer needs steel. Manufacturers also need labour (that is, employees who work to produce the products), and they have to pay *overhead,* the essential general costs of running their factories. (Head to Chapter 4 for more on overhead.)

Many companies manufacture and retail the same goods. For example, independent bakeries often bake bread and cakes on the same premises where they sell them. Some petroleum companies own refineries and petrol stations. Other manufacturers choose to wholesale their goods to retailers. For example, a soft-drink bottler may produce and bottle fizzy drinks and sell them to convenience stores and supermarkets. The soft-drink bottler's customer – the corner shop or supermarket – retails the drinks directly to end-users.

Measuring Profits

To earn money and succeed, all businesses – whether they're service companies, retailers or manufacturers – need to create profits. To generate profits, companies have to generate incomes from sales to customers that exceed the costs they incur. In this section we look at the three key components of profits: Sales Revenues, Cost of Sales and other types of expenses. The Net Income is the profit that's left.

Earning revenues

Revenues are inflows from customers. They're the amounts of money that your customers pay or, in some cases, promise to pay. Sometimes the term *Sales Revenue (or Sales Value)* is used to distinguish the value of sales from the physical volume of units sold.

For example, an airline's revenues come from selling tickets (and charging baggage fees, handling fees, boarding fees, carry-on fees and late-arrival fees). A bakery's revenues come from getting tasty treats to hungry customers.

Typically, the Sales Revenue needs to be recorded when a sale takes place, even if the sale allows a period of credit before payment is due.

Revenues come only when you sell whatever you usually sell to your customers. If you sell a product you normally don't sell, such as equipment or machinery, the records need to show that as a disposal of an asset rather than as revenue.

Computing Cost of Sales

Cost of Sales is the cost of buying or making the products that you sell. For example, suppose that a soft-drink bottler sells a can of cola for 50p. Consider what goes into producing that can of cola:

- Water
- Caramel colour
- Carbonation
- Sweeteners
- Natural flavours
- Caffeine
- Various preservatives
- Aluminium
- Labour
- Overhead (other costs)

Given all these (inexpensive) ingredients and costs, consider how much it probably costs to produce a can of cola. It's likely to be only a fraction of the selling price of 50p.

Retailers don't manufacture the goods themselves, and so when they measure Cost of Sales they base it on their cost to purchase the goods from a supplier.

Many manufacturers and retailers use the term *Cost of Goods Sold* instead of Cost of Sales. Chapter 5, which discusses only retailers and manufacturers, uses that wording. Just know that regardless of the name, these two terms mean the same thing.

Integrated cost accounting system

In an integrated cost accounting system, the purchase of inventory triggers accounting entries to record the transaction:

1. **On 10 January 2013, the Barnham Marmalade Company purchases 2 boxes of Seville Oranges by paying £40 in cash.**
2. **On 12 January, 1.5 boxes are issued from inventory to production (1.5 × £20 per box = £30).**
3. **On 13 January, 300 jars of marmalade are produced and placed in the inventory of Finished Goods.**
4. **Over the next two weeks, 250 jars are sold at £1.20 each for cash.**

For this example, we ignore all other costs in order to show you how the transactions are recorded (see Figure 2-2).

Date	*Account (or Code)*	*Debit*	*Credit*
10 Jan 2013	Orange Inventory	£40.00	
10 Jan 2013	Cash		£40.00
Narrative: The purchase of 2 boxes of oranges for cash			
12 Jan 2013	Production	£30.00	
12 Jan 2013	Orange inventory		£30.00
Narrative: The issue of 1.5 boxes of oranges from inventory to production			
13 Jan 2013	Finished Goods	£30.00	
13 Jan 2013	Production		£30.00
Narrative: 300 jars of marmalade transferred from production into Finished Goods			
January 2013	Cash	£300.00	
January 2013	Sales		£300.00
Narrative: 250 jars of marmalade sold for cash			
January 2013	Cost of Sales	£25.00	
January 2013	Finished Goods		£25.00
Narrative: 250 jars of marmalade taken from Finished Goods inventory and sold to customers			

Figure 2-2: Integrated Cost Accounting System: Example Journal Entries for Barnham Marmalade.

The Barnham Marmalade Company buys oranges, turns most of them into marmalade and sells most of the marmalade. This process leaves two types of closing inventory and some cash. The integration of the cost accounting system with production means that management can produce key reports very easily. For example, the top part of an income statement appears as in Figure 2-3.

Figure 2-3: Integrated Cost Accounting System: Example Income Statement for Barnham Marmalade, January 2013.

			£
Sales Revenue			300.00
Cost of Sales			(25.00)
Gross Profit			275.00

The system also provides the information needed for a statement of financial position at the end of January (see Figure 2-4).

Figure 2-4: Integrated Cost Accounting System: Example Accounting Statement of Financial Position for Barnham Marmalade, 31 January 2013.

		£	£
Assets			
Inventories:			
Oranges	(0.5 of a box)	10.00	
Marmalade	50 unsold jars	5.00	15.00
Cash			260.00
Total Assets			275.00
Equity and Liabilities			
Profit			275.00

The inventory values for the oranges and the jars of marmalade can only be recorded if they retain their value at 31 January. Barnham Marmalade freezes its oranges so that it can use them to make marmalade later in the year. Therefore, including the value of oranges as a closing inventory is perfectly legitimate. Another business selling, say, freshly made sandwiches, in which any left at the end of a day can't be sold, has to include this cost in the Cost of Sales. The sandwiches are waste and this fact reduces the profit.

Financial accounting system

When an integrated cost accounting system isn't in use, a business needs to rely on records kept for financial accounting purposes. In this case, stock purchases have very few credit entries, possibly purchase returns, and build up a total throughout the accounting period. Only at that point is a value attached to the inventory of raw material and a closing inventory value determined. If Barnham Marmalade Company used that approach, the journal entries would be as shown in Figure 2-5.

Date	*Account (or Code)*	*Debit*	*Credit*
10 Jan 2013	Purchases	£40.00	
10 Jan 2013	Cash		£40.00
Narrative: The purchase of 2 boxes of oranges for cash			
January 2013	Cash	£300.00	
January 2013	Sales		£300.00
Narrative: 250 jars of marmalade sold for cash			

Figure 2-5: Financial Accounting System: Example Accounting Journal Entries for Barnham Marmalade.

A physical count of the inventories at 31 January 2013 would show:

Raw Materials 0.5 of a box of oranges at £20 per box = £10

Finished Goods 50 jars of marmalade at a cost of £0.10 each = £5

Figure 2-6 shows how the accounts are constructed.

The statement of financial position, as shown in Figure 2-7, is the same as before (see the earlier Figure 2-4).

Figure 2-6: Financial Accounting System: Example Income Statement for Barnham Marmalade, January 2013.

		£	£
Sales Revenue			300.00
Opening Inventories		0	
Purchases		40.00	
Closing inventories			
	Raw materials	(10.00)	
	Finished goods	(5.00)	
Cost of Sales			(25.00)
Gross Profit			275.00

Figure 2-7: Financial Accounting System: Example Accounting Statement of Financial Position for Barnham Marmalade, 31 January 2013.

		£	£
Assets			
Inventories:			
Oranges	(0.5 of a box)	10.00	
Marmalade	50 unsold jars	5.00	15.00
Cash			260.00
Total Assets			275.00
Equity and Liabilities			
Profit			275.00

Plugging in the Cost of Sales formula

The second layout of the Gross Profit in Figure 2-6 gives the Cost of Sales formula:

> Opening inventories + Purchases – Closing inventories = Cost of Sales

We explore this formula further in Chapter 5 and it becomes useful in budgeting production levels in Chapter 14.

Incurring operating expenses

Unfortunately for businesses, sales don't just materialise by themselves. To bring in sales, you have to pay employees, advertisers and other marketers, and that's just the beginning. Typical expenses for a company include the following:

- **Selling, general and administrative expenses:** Costs such as sales commissions and managerial salaries needed to generate sales and run the company.
- **Research and development expenses:** Costs of finding and advancing innovative technologies needed to create new products.
- **Interest expenses:** Costs of borrowing money, which companies have to pay to their lenders.
- **Income tax expenses (also known as *provision for income taxes*):** The portion of profits companies are usually required to pay to government authorities.

Although Cost of Sales is always an expense, not every expense qualifies as Cost of Sales. Cost of Sales is the actual cost of producing or buying the item you sell. But your company may need to pay additional expenses, such as sales commissions and advertising, to sell this item.

The distinction between Cost of Sales and other expenses is important for determining *Gross Profit,* the difference between revenues and Cost of Sales. When calculating Gross Profit, you deduct Cost of Sales but not the other expenses. Gross Profit less these other expenses produces a profit value for the accounting period.

Measuring Net Profit

Net Profit is the difference between revenues and all expenses, including Cost of Sales. Investors and managers often refer to profit for the year because it provides a single bottom-line number to measure a company's performance. (Of course, that figure is only considered profit when it's a positive number; it can also be a loss for the year.)

Within financial reporting three stages lie between Gross Profit and Profit for the Year. Management accounting doesn't have a major involvement in the presentation, but we provide the layout in Figure 2-8. Management accountants are involved in providing the information that's subsequently entered into the income statement.

	£
Sales Revenue	
Less Cost of Sales	
= Gross Profit	
Less Distribution and Administration Costs	
= Profit from Operations	
Less Finance Costs	
= Profit Before Tax	
Less Tax	
= Profit for the Year	

Figure 2-8: Income Statement Layout.

Management accountants are interested in all aspects of the income statement, but confusion can arise when referring to net profit; after all, no value for net profit is present in the income statement.

In this book, generally we use *profit from operations* as a net profit. When the other values are needed, we signpost them clearly and accompany them with an explanation. Management accounting has a primary focus on the Cost of Sales and the distribution and administration costs.

Cash flow and profit aren't necessarily the same. Some cash payments aren't treated as costs at the time they're made. Although payments for equipment or vehicles take cash out of the business, accounting rules require these costs to be depreciated over their lives. This means that only the annual charge for depreciation (rather than the cash cost) is treated as an expense on the income statement for that year. Similarly, finance such as loans represents cash coming into the business, but isn't part of the Sales Revenue and so doesn't increase the profit.

Working out the Operating Profit Margin

The *Operating Profit Margin* is a useful figure that shows how much profit the company can earn from sales. This is calculated using the profit from operations on the income statement layout in Figure 2-8. Some companies are deliberate discount retailers, such as Lidl, and deliberately have a low-price, high-volume strategy. They keep profit margins very low so that they can charge customers the lowest prices possible. Because these companies usually yield relatively little profit from their sales, they usually have to make it up in volume to earn a healthy income.

Other companies develop a high-price, low-volume strategy. These companies differentiate their products so that they can charge customers premium prices that yield rich profit margins and fairly high profits from their sales.

Here's the formula for calculating the Operating Profit Margin:

$$\frac{\text{Profit from Operations}}{\text{Sales Revenue}} \times 100$$

Two companies that make and sell blue jeans each earned £1 million in profits last year. The Plain Jeans Company makes jeans costing £20 per pair, which it sells to retailers for £25 per pair. The Designer Jeans Company makes jeans costing £40 per pair, which it sells to retailers for £80 per pair. Here are the calculations:

- Plain Jeans earns £1 million on £20 million in Sales Revenue:

  £1,000,000 ÷ £20,000,000 × 100 = 5 per cent

- Designer Jeans earns £1 million on £2.5 million in Sales Revenue:

  (£1,000,000 ÷ £2,500,000) × 100 = 40 per cent

Even though both companies earn the same amount of Net Income, Plain Jeans' low Operating Profit Margin reflects its low-profit-margin/high-volume strategy. Designer Jeans' high Operating Profit Margin results from its high-profit-margin/low-volume strategy.

People also refer to Operating Profit Margin as *Net Profit Margin* or *Return on Sales.*

Meeting the Three Es of Performance

Management accountants can help out company managers when they need to know how well a business is performing. In some cases managers can confuse inputs and outputs, which is excusable when outputs are hard to measure. As Figure 2-9 shows, businesses take inputs through a process or processes and produce outputs:

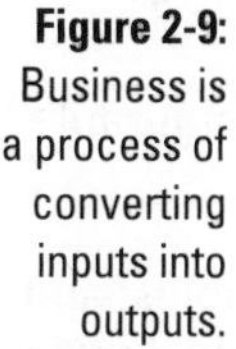

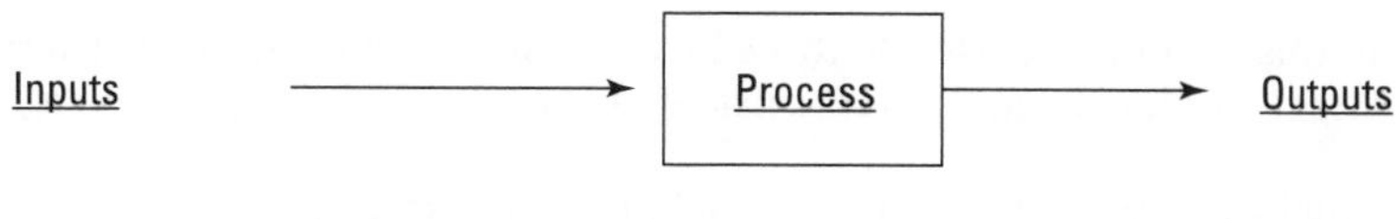

Figure 2-9: Business is a process of converting inputs into outputs.

Here are two simple examples:

- **A stall selling carbonated drinks at a village fete:** The canned drinks are bought in cases of 24 from the cash 'n' carry and then sold individually. Inputs go into the process; outputs come out of the process.
- **Making marmalade:** The inputs are oranges, sugar, jars, labour time and cooking time in a clean kitchen. The outputs are jars of marmalade. (In the earlier section 'Computing Cost of Sales', we describe a marmalade producer's accounts in more detail.)

When assessing the performance of a business, you can use three different aspects of this process, each starting with the letter E:

- **Economy:** This aspect looks at only the input costs. Success is judged by the cost of the inputs, and output is ignored. Good performance is achieved by keeping input costs as low as possible.
- **Efficiency:** This aspect looks at output in terms of input. When this is assessed using money values, one possible measure of efficiency is Sales Revenue divided by Cost of Sales (see the earlier section 'Measuring Profits' for definitions of these terms). It can also be more specific, such as how much money does the process generate per £1 of labour cost? Efficiency is closely related to productivity measures, such as the number of jars of marmalade produced per labour hour.

  Think of efficiency as answering the question: *how well does the company do what it does?*
- **Effectiveness:** This aspect looks at outputs alone. Do the outputs of the process do the job they should do? This raises questions about what the customer wants, and how well the product satisfies the customer. Without any questions about inputs, effectiveness is just concerned with what you do: *is the company doing what it should be doing?*

Making comparisons using the three Es

In this section, we use the three Es to compare two fictional pizza restaurants, which both charge the same price per pizza.

Luigi's keeps costs down by only having two staff to serve all the tables, and cuts back on the toppings to keep the cost of the pizza to a minimum. Luigi's has fewer customers now because it's not providing the sort of pizza or service the customers want. Still, the restaurant carpet is going to last for years, because of too few customers to wear it out.

Enrico's has plenty of staff and is keen to make sure that customers are happy with the food and service. Queues form every night and the restaurant expects to wear the carpet out very quickly.

- **Economy and efficiency:** Luigi's is better than Enrico's in terms of economy because the costs are lower. It would be more efficient if the pizza sales produce more per £1 of the costs incurred.
- **Effectiveness:** Enrico's is better in terms of effectiveness, because it's meeting customers' needs. Although it's less efficient (each pizza sale costs more), the chances are that the restaurant where customer satisfaction is more important than cost savings is going to be in business for longer and ultimately make more money.

Businesses need to consider all these measures of performance, but accountants are often accused of focusing too much on the input costs. These costs can't be more than the business brings in from sales or else the result is no profit. But still, customers must be sold the things they want to buy.

Assessing Asset Turnover

Asset Turnover measures a company's productivity. It looks at the investment and assesses how well the assets were used to generate sales. To calculate Asset Turnover, you divide Sales Revenue by Capital Employed.

Typically, management accountants use the value of all the assets less the value of current liabilities (or non-current assets plus net current assets). The value should be the same as total equity plus non-current liabilities.

Suppose a company earns £100,000 in sales, and Capital Employed during the same year equals £50,000. Here's how to compute Asset Turnover:

$$\frac{\text{Sales Revenue}}{\text{Capital Employed}} \quad \frac{£100{,}000}{£50{,}000} = 2.0$$

Wearing out the carpet

When I (Sandy) was 20, I worked for an American called Mike Hirst. He didn't like accountants much but was prepared to put up with a Brit! I think I may have taught him a thing or two. He certainly taught me two important facts:

- **Firms can go out of business in a very efficient way:** He means that focusing on cost savings can take the manager's eye off the ball, and customer satisfaction is forgotten.
- **Wearing out the carpet:** In the restaurant business, if the carpet needs replacing the business is busy, which means that it's doing the things customers are prepared to pay for. In other words, wearing out the carpet is an approximate measure of effectiveness.

To interpret this result, just say that for every £1 worth of Capital Employed, the company earns £2 in revenue.

The higher the Asset Turnover, the more productive the company has been with the capital. Many companies improve their turnover by taking care to use their scarce assets very carefully. Here are a few ways to do that:

- **Use all assets continuously:** Don't let assets sit around doing nothing. If you run a factory, make sure that your machines manufacture products continuously.
- **Don't buy inventory until you need it:** Maintain just enough inventory to keep your customers happy. Unnecessary inventory increases your assets and lowers your Asset Turnover.
- **Increase your sales without increasing assets:** Expand your hours. Some supermarkets stay open 24 hours to use assets around the clock.
- **Reduce your assets:** Consider ways to cut assets without proportionately reducing sales. You may be able to maintain the level of service without having to pay high rental costs to maintain offices, for example, by allowing staff to work from home.

Putting Profitability and Productivity Together: Return on Capital Employed

Investors can put their money wherever they choose. Thousands of publicly traded companies and other investment vehicles raise money from investors, who often use something called Return on Capital Employed (ROCE) to select from among all the investment options.

Return on Capital Employed provides a simple measure of investment performance that you can apply to many different types of financial investments and to your company's own investments in factories, equipment and other income-producing assets. Return on Capital Employed is a good test of the success of the management to generate profits from the capital that has been invested. Here's the formula to find it:

Return on Capital Employed:

$$\frac{\text{Operating Profit} \times 100}{\text{Capital Employed}}$$

Both profitability and productivity contribute to Return on Capital Employed, which explains how some companies can take a low-profit-margin/high-volume approach to creating income and others take advantage of a high-profit-margin/low-volume method of generating income. The following formula explains how Operating Profit Margin (which we define earlier in 'Working out the Operating Profit Margin') and Asset Turnover (see the earlier section 'Assessing Asset Turnover') feed off of each other to deliver Return on Capital Employed:

Operating Profit Margin	×	Asset Turnover	=	Return on Capital Employed
$\frac{\text{Operating Profit} \times 100}{\text{Sales Revenue}}$		$\frac{\text{Sales Revenue}}{\text{Capital Employed}}$		$\frac{\text{Operating Profit} \times 100}{\text{Capital Employed}}$

Suppose that the Plain Jeans Company and the Designer Jeans Company each earn £1 million in profits last year and that both companies have £5 million in average assets. For each company, the Return on Capital Employed equals 20 per cent (£1 million ÷ $5 million).

Plain Jeans has a low-profit-margin/high-volume strategy and so its Operating Profit Margin is only 5 per cent. However, Designer Jeans' high-profit-margin/low-volume strategy delivers Operating Profit Margin of 40 per cent. (Head to the earlier section 'Working out the Operating Profit Margin' for details on this measurement.)

Both companies have £5 million in assets, such that Plain Jeans has Asset Turnover of 4.0, indicating that it runs a high-volume business. Designer Jeans has Asset Turnover of just 0.5, suggesting a low-volume business. Figure 2-10 shows how both companies' strategies combine so that they provide similar Return on Capital Employed in the end.

Operating Profit × 100 / Sales Revenue		Sales Revenue / Capital Employed		Operating Profit × 100 / Capital Employed	
Plain Jeans Company					
£1,000,000 × 100 / £20,000,000	5%	£20,000,000 / £5,000,000	4 times	£1,000,000 × 100 / £5,000,000	20%
Designer Jeans Company					
£1,000,000 × 100 / £2,500,000	40%	£2,500,000 / £5,000,000	0.5 times	£1,000,000 × 100 / £5,000,000	20%

Figure 2-10: A tale of two companies' Return on Capital Employed.

The numbers tell a fascinating story. Plain Jeans' low prices result in a lower Operating Profit Margin. The company's high-volume management style, however, gives the company a high Asset Turnover. On the other hand, Designer Jeans' high Operating Profit Margin reflects its high-profit-margin approach. Its low Asset Turnover reflects its low-volume strategy.

Part II

Understanding and Managing Costs

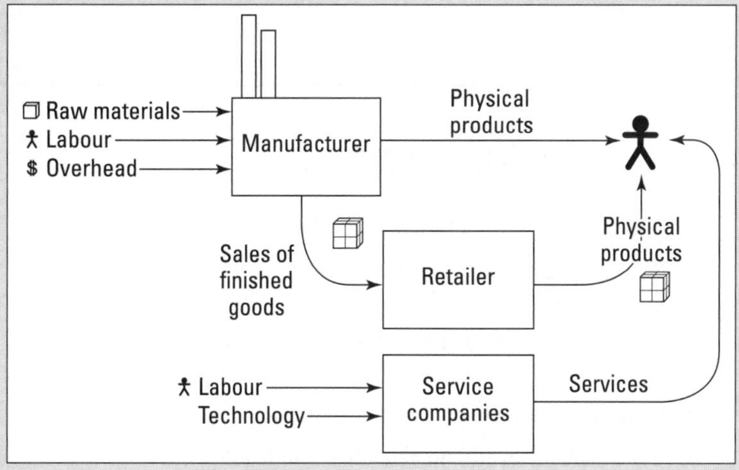

Go to www.dummies.com/extras/managementcostaccountinguk for free online bonus content created especially for this book.

In this part . . .

- Find definitions for different kinds of costs.
- Recognise the costs needed to make products and the costs that affect decision-making.
- Figure out the cost of goods manufactured and the cost of goods sold.
- Distinguish variable costs from fixed costs.
- Get a taste for overhead allocation techniques.
- Apply handy techniques to job costing and process costing.

Chapter 3

Classifying Direct and Indirect Costs

In This Chapter

- Knowing the difference between direct and indirect costs
- Valuing inventory using three popular methods
- Treatment of labour costs within the accounts
- Recognising conversion, product and period costs

In Oscar Wilde's play *Lady Windermere's Fan*, the character Lord Darlington defines a cynic as 'a man who knows the price of everything and the value of nothing'. Management accountants don't need to be quite so cynical, but without doubt a healthy scepticism is an asset. The fact is that they have to know the value *and* the cost.

Management accountants need to understand what costs are (in the sense of the expenditures businesses incur) and be able to view them (or more accurately classify them) in different ways. For example, you can look at something a business sells and then work backwards to find the cost, or you can look at the costs themselves.

In this chapter, you discover how to classify costs in different ways (basically into direct and indirect costs) and why doing so is necessary. We also explain how to handle inventory and labour costs, and guide you through working with conversion costs as well as separating product and period costs.

Distinguishing Direct from Indirect Manufacturing Costs

When manufacturing a product, there are two different sorts of costs incurred:

- **Direct costs:** Costs that you can trace easily to individual products that you make. These costs include direct materials and direct labour, as we discuss in the very next section.
- **Indirect costs:** Costs that you can't trace easily to an individual product, such as the insurance costs of the buildings where the production takes place, and business rates. For more details, check out the later section 'Understanding indirect costs: Production overhead'.

Scrumdiddlyumptious by Sofi makes excellent cupcakes using flour, eggs, caster sugar, butter and other ingredients: these are all direct costs specific to the cakes. If you look at the finished cupcake and then think back in time, all the ingredients listed 'belong' to that cake. Sofi spent time weighing, mixing and baking the cakes. The time spent making the cakes also represents a direct cost. Again, look at the finished product and go back in time.

This aspect is vitally important and not always understood. The things businesses spend money on aren't direct or indirect; how they're used (or what they're used for) is what defines whether they're direct costs or indirect costs.

Indirect costs are just as essential as direct costs; they're called indirect because a specific way of tracing them to the product isn't available. For example, when Sofi attends a wedding fayre to publicise the business and encourage people to order her cakes, when she cleans the kitchen after cooking or does any job except actually making the cupcakes, the cost of her time is indirect. Any costs that you can't trace directly to the product or products being made are indirect costs.

Indirect cost means the same as overhead. In the production departments, if a cost doesn't 'belong' to a specific product then it goes into production overhead (flip to the later section 'Understanding indirect costs: Production overhead' for more).

Costing direct materials and direct labour

Direct costs fall into two categories:

- **Direct materials:** The raw materials that you can directly trace to the manufactured product. To calculate the cost of direct materials for any product, you add up the cost of all the individual components or ingredients needed to make the product. Doing so requires understanding how your products are made and exactly what goes into each product.
- **Direct labour:** The cost of paying employees to make your products. Companies estimate carefully how much direct labour goes into each product made – that is, how long each worker of each level of skill takes to do the job. Then, to find the total direct labour cost of the product, companies multiply this time period by the hourly cost of paying each worker.

Initially, defining the hourly rate the employee earns is to define the labour cost per hour. This suits accounting classrooms. At work it may be necessary to reassess this and build in other costs that are incurred by the business over and above the hourly rate.

Suppose that Scrumdiddlyumptious by Sofi produces a triple-layer chocolate cake based on the following ingredients:

- 500 grams of sugar (£0.80 for a 1 kilogram bag)
- 500 grams of flour (£1.50 for a 1.5 kilogram bag)
- 100 grams of cocoa powder (£3 for 250 grams)
- 4 eggs (£1.20 per dozen)
- 250 millilitres of milk (£0.88 per 2 litres)
- 400 grams of butter (£0.90 per 250 grams)

Table 3-1 shows you how to calculate the total cost of direct materials needed for one cake, adding together the cost of all the individual ingredients used to make it.

Table 3-1 Direct Material Cost for One Triple-Layer Chocolate Cake

Ingredient	*Requirement*	*Cost per Ingredient (£)*	*Cost per Cake (£)*
Sugar	500 grams	0.80 per kilogram	0.40
Flour	500 grams	1.50 per 1.5 kilograms	0.50
Cocoa powder	100 grams	3.00 per 250 grams	1.20
Eggs	4	1.20 per dozen	0.40
Milk	250 millilitres	0.88 per 2 litres	0.11
Butter	400 grams	0.90 per 250 grams	1.44
Total			**4.05**

If a baker at Scrumdiddlyumptious by Sofi is paid £12 per hour and works for 30 minutes on the triple-layer chocolate cake, this cost is added as a direct cost (see Table 3-2).

Table 3-2 Adding Direct Labour Costs for One Triple-Layer Chocolate Cake to Table 3-1

Input	*Requirement*	*Cost per Hour (£)*	*Cost per Cake (£)*
Direct labour	0.5 hours	12.00 per hour	6.00
Subtotal for direct materials (from Table 3-1)			4.05
Total direct cost per cake			**10.05**

Direct costs represent just one part of the total cost of manufacturing goods. Other costs may also be necessary overhead (the cost of lighting and heating the baking area; see the following section for more on overhead).

Understanding indirect costs: Production overhead

Not all costs that a business incurs are direct. You need to keep track of indirect costs too, even though you can't trace them easily to individual manufactured products. In many modern factories the overheads are more than the direct costs of manufacturing. (Accountants sometimes refer to overhead in a factory as *production overhead.*)

Management accountants provide information that financial accountants use in the periodic reports, and so this information needs to meet reporting standards that apply to the business. All the reporting standards we're aware of require that product values include an element of production overhead as well as direct costs. Production overhead forms the main area of concern when looking at product costs. The non-production overheads do need to be monitored and controlled, but they don't form part of the cost of a product.

Overhead consists of the following items:

- **Indirect materials:** The cost of raw materials needed to make products that you can't trace easily to the finished products. The three typical examples are:
  - *Cleaning materials,* used to tidy up after a variety of different products have been made. They're materials and they're essential, but they can't be identified as being specific to any individual products. They're effectively costs of the department (or cost centre) itself.
  - *Equipment-related costs*, such as the lubricants needed to keep machines and equipment running. If that machine is used to produce one product after another, you can't trace the cost easily to batches of products or even to individual items being produced.
  - *Immaterial costs*, as in *not worth fussing about*. For example, a baker spends money on cooking spray to put on the cake trays to prevent the cake mixture from sticking, but dividing up this cost for each cake isn't worthwhile and would be a waste of time. Therefore, you classify the cost of the cooking spray as an indirect cost. It's almost a riddle: what material isn't material! Certainly not material enough to be a direct cost.

- **Indirect labour:** The cost of labour that you need to make products, but which you can't trace easily to the finished products; for example, maintenance workers and cleaners.
- **Other costs needed for operations:** The cost of items such as factory rent, electricity, business rates, insurance and depreciation of factories and equipment.

As factories automate, in essence they replace human workers with machines. Therefore, as they implement new manufacturing technologies, factories rely less on direct labour and more on overhead. In a modern factory, direct labour can account for 5 per cent or less of total manufacturing cost. A completely automated factory doesn't need any direct labour at all.

To check that you can distinguish direct materials, direct labour and production overhead, think about a factory that makes trainers and come up with what falls under each group.

Start from the trainers and look at them:

- **Direct materials:** The cost of the leather, rubber, cotton, paper and plastic used to make and package the trainers all form part of them; they 'belong' to the trainers.
- **Direct labour:** The time taken to assemble the shoes.
- **Production overhead:** All other costs, such as electricity, heat, insurance, security, depreciation, maintenance and even the cost of supervisory managers who run the factory are essential but not directly traceable to the trainers.

Valuing Inventory of Materials and Finished Goods

Typically, manufacturing companies hold material inventories in stores and issue materials to the production departments as they are requested. A requisition note is produced by the department and sent to the stores in much the same way that the stores place a purchase order with an outside supplier. You refer to the internal request as a *requisition* and the external request as an *order*.

Issues from the stores are classified as direct materials or as indirect materials depending on how they'll be used. How the issue is valued depends on the accounting policy of the company. There are three common methods tested as part of accountancy qualifications.

In many businesses, finished goods are also held before being sold to customers. This inventory is valued at production cost and issued to sales using the company's inventory valuation policy.

Note that:

- In the long run, profits are the same whichever valuation method is used.
- In the short run, profits can be different depending on the valuation method chosen.

Inventory values are dependent on the amount of each type of inventory held, as you'd expect, but they're also dependent on the company's valuation policy.

Whichever method is used, they're all issue-based approaches. The three key methods are:

- **First-In First-Out (FIFO):** Material is issued at the earliest prices paid for the inventory held.
- **Average Cost (AVCO):** Material is issued at the weighted average price per unit of the inventory held. In other words, add up the total physical amount of inventory held for the item and add up the total value of the inventory and divide the value by the physical amount. This price per unit is used when items are issued to production.
- **Last-In First-Out (LIFO):** Material is issued at the most recent prices paid for the inventory held.

In the UK and other countries that adopted the international accounting standards, LIFO isn't permitted for corporate financial reporting purposes. In the US, the US GAAP sets out the rules for corporate financial reporting and allows the use of LIFO. Internal reporting isn't regulated, and so LIFO can be used in the UK, so long as it isn't the method applied for external reports.

In the rest of this section, we show you how to record inventory values under each method using the same set of data (though, typically, a business uses one method only).

Here's the data that we use for each of the three techniques:

- On 1 August, the stores held 30 units valued at £267.
- Further stock was received as follows: 3 August, 20 units at £180; 21 August, 20 units at £184.
- Issues were made to production as follows: 9 August, 16 units; 16 August, 24 units; 26 August, 12 units.

Completing an inventory record

The following approach applies to exam candidates and to anyone faced with dealing with a collection of invoices, delivery notes, purchase orders, goods received notes and stores requisitions at work:

1. **Put all the transactions in date order and enter the dates into the date column of the stores record card.**
2. **Enter the quantities received and issued (and where they've been provided, any cost values).** *Note*: No calculations are needed at this stage.

From this point on, you need to know which of the three issue valuation methods (which we cover in each of the following three sections) you're going to use (for Steps 1 and 2, they're all identical).

For now, your record card looks like Table 3-3.

Table 3-3 The First Steps to Completing an Inventory Record

Date	*Receipts*			*Issues*			*Balance*		
Aug	Qty	£ p	£	Qty	£ p	£	Qty	£ p	£
1							30		267.00
3	20		180.00						
9				16					
16				24					
21	20		184.00						
26				12					

Note how after each transaction the balance is ruled-off. This technique helps to show you and whoever's reading that you know precisely how many units are held at the end of the day, and how the stock has been broken down.

In a paper-based exam, we recommend writing the valuation method on the top of the record card as a constant reminder of the method you should be using. In a computer-based exam, write it on your workings papers.

Finding out about First-In First-Out

First-In-First-Out (FIFO) means using the earliest prices of inventory received to value the first inventory issued. So, with the example data that we introduce earlier in this section, because the inventory at the end of 3 August is made up of (first-in) 30 units that cost £267, or £8.90 each, the next 30 units issued will be issued at £8.90 each. When these units have been issued, the price changes to £9 (the unit cost of the 20 units bought costing £180). The 'Balance' section is made up of three columns. The first shows the total number of units and the third the total value, but you don't have a total value for the middle column showing the 'per unit' (£ p); see Table 3-4. Here we've inserted an X: as inventory is issued based on the value of the earliest cost (first-in values), a total value for cost per unit (£ p) for the balance serves no useful purpose.

Following on from Steps 1 and 2 in the preceding section, we now have Step 3 using FIFO.

3. **Use FIFO with the entries on the Inventory Record Card for 3–26 August.**

   - 3 August: 20 units are received into the store; the total value of £180 has already been entered in the receipts column. In the balance column the 30 in the balance on 1 August are brought forward, and the 20 received are added. This gives a total of 50 units and a total value of £447. The cost per unit of each receipt is not totalled and we have put a letter X in that column. The date is ruled-off.
   - 9 August: 16 units are issued, all priced at £8.90, and are deducted from the balance to leave 64 in inventory at £8.90 plus the 20 at £9. The new balances are stated and the date ruled-off.
   - 16 August: 24 units are issued, and so 14 are priced at £8.90 and 10 at £9, which leaves a balance of 10 units at £9.

     The total units as provided are shown in Table 3-4 and the total value of the issue is calculated, but (as in the balance on 3 and 9 August) no total is given in the (£ p) per unit column.

   - 21 August: Another receipt, and so you add the new inventory to the balance.
   - 26 August: 12 units are issued, and so you follow the same procedure as on 16 August.

Table 3-4 Inventory Record Card using FIFO valuation

Date	*Receipts*			*Issues*			*Balance*		
Aug	Qty	£ p	£	Qty	£ p	£	Qty	£ p	£
1							30		267.00
3	20		180.00				30	8.90	267.00
							20	9.00	180.00
							50	X	447.00
9				16	8.90	142.40	14	8.90	124.60
							20	9.00	180.00
							34	X	304.60
16				14	8.90	124.60	10	9.00	90.00
				10	9.00	90.00			
				24		214.60			
21	20		184.00				10	9.00	90.00
							20	9.20	184.00
							30		274.00
26				10	9.00	90.00	18	9.20	165.60
				2	9.20	18.40			
				12		108.40			
Totals	**See Step 3 in text**		**364.00**			**465.40**			

Exam marking schemes usually make a distinction between two different types of error, and so the next (and invariably not asked for) step is very useful. Following on from Step 3 in the preceding section:

4. **Check that the inventory (or stores) record card is arithmetically correct.** Many marking schemes allow one error of analysis but don't allow any arithmetical errors. By cross-checking, you show that you've recognised that the opening inventory, receipts and issues can be used as a check on the closing inventory valuation. We recommend totalling the value of receipts and issues and adding this Inventory Reconciliation table neatly below any inventory record card (as we show in Table 3-5).

Table 3-5 Inventory Reconciliation FIFO

	£ p	
Opening inventory	267.00	
Receipts total	364.00	
Issues total	–465.40	
Closing stock	165.60	It agrees with the closing balance

Making use of Average Cost (AVCO)

Strictly speaking, the heading for this section ought to be 'weighted average cost', because the Average Cost (AVCO) technique used finds and uses the *weighted* average cost of the balance held and issues inventory using this value.

This section picks up from Step 2 in the earlier section 'Completing an inventory record'. We now have step 3 using AVCO. The total value of inventory on any day is divided by the total number of units in inventory to find an average value per unit. This average cost per unit is updated after each receipt.

3. **Use AVCO with the entries on the Inventory Record Card for 3–26 August.** The record card is identical to the FIFO record card at 3 August in the preceding section. You add the average cost per unit in the balance, which typically gives a value that isn't an exact number of pence. In this case, £447 divided by 50 units gives an average cost per unit of £8.94 (see Table 3-6). Exactly how many places are required is specified in exam questions. We use up to four decimal places in this example.

   - 9 August: 16 units are issued at the average price calculated, and so the 16 units at £8.94 are valued at £143.04 and the inventory balance valued as 34 at £8.94: £303.96.
   - 16 August: 24 units are issued, and as on 9 August, the £8.94 price is used. Using FIFO, no attempt is made to total the price per unit.
   - 21 August: 20 units are received and entered on the record card in the same way as on 3 August, giving a value that goes to several decimal places (we use four).
   - 26 August: 8 units are issued. All can be priced at average cost per unit calculated on 21 August, and the same unit cost applied to the closing balance.

The totals are added for receipts and sales, and the cross-check carried out (see Table 3-7).

Table 3-6 Inventory Record Card Using AVCO Valuation

Date	*Receipts*			*Issues*			*Balance*		
Aug	Qty	£ p	£	Qty	£ p	£	Qty	£ p	£
1							30		267.00
3	20		180.00				30	8.90	267.00
							20	9.00	180.00
							50	8.94	447.00
9				16	8.94	143.04	34	8.94	303.96

(continued)

Table 3-6 *(continued)*

Date	*Receipts*		*Issues*			*Balance*		
16			24	8.94	214.56	10	8.94	89.40
21	20	184.00				10	8.94	89.40
						20	9.20	184.00
						30	9.1133	273.40
26			12	9.1133	109.36	18	9.1133	164.04
Total		**364.00**			**430.51**			

Table 3-7 Inventory Reconciliation AVCO

	£ p	
Opening inventory	267.00	
Receipts total	364.00	
Issues total	–466.96	
Closing inventory	164.04	It agrees

Learning about Last-In First-Out

This section continues on from Step 2 in the earlier section 'Completing an inventory record'.

3. **Use LIFO for the entries on the Inventory Record Card for 3–26 August.**

   The most recent prices of inventory received are used to value the inventory issued. The record card is identical to the earlier FIFO record card at 3 August (see 'Finding out about First-In First-Out'), and then proceeds as follows (see Table 3-8):

   - 9 August: 16 units are issued at the last price received. As the total receipt on 3 August was more than 16, all are issued at £9.00 each and the inventory balance valued as 4 at £9, plus 30 at £8.90.
   - 16 August: 24 units are issued. So both the unit prices in the inventory balance are needed: 4 at £9 and 20 at £8.90. As with FIFO, no attempt is made to total the price per unit.

- 21 August: 20 units are received and entered on the record card in the same way as for FIFO.
- 26 August: 12 units are issued. All can be priced at the latest receipt price of £9.20 per unit and the balance adjusted.

The totals are added for receipts and sales, and the cross-check carried out (see Table 3-9).

Table 3-8 Inventory Record Card Using LIFO Valuation

Date	*Receipts*			*Issues*			*Balance*		
Aug	Qty	£ p	£	Qty	£ p	£	Qty	£ p	£
1							30		267.00
3	20		180.00				30 20 50	8.90 9.00 X	267.00 180.00 447.00
9				16	9.00	144.00	30 4 34	8.90 9.00 X	267.00 36.00 303.00
16				4 20 24	9.00 8.90 X	36.00 178.00 214.00	10	8.90	89.00
21	20		184.00				10 20 30	8.90 9.20	89.00 184.00 273.00
26				12	9.20	110.40	10 8 18	8.90 9.20	89.00 73.60 162.60
Totals	**See Step 4**		**364.00**			**468.40**			

Table 3-9 Inventory Reconciliation LIFO

	£ p	
Opening inventory	267.00	
Receipts total	364.00	
Issues total	–468.40	
Closing inventory	162.60	It agrees

The best way to master the valuation of issues tasks is to practise: find three or four exam-style questions and work through them. The date sequence becomes particularly important when you're flicking between orders, invoices and requisitions. But using a disciplined series of steps (as we describe in the preceding sections) helps you to feel competent in this area.

Here's a question that can help you to check your own understanding. As with a lot of exam questions, although different to the example with different numbers, it does test the same knowledge and understanding. Table 3-10 contains all the necessary figures.

Table 3-10 Information to Use in the Introductory Fishing Pack Practice

Date	*Receipts*			*Issues*			*Balance*		
July	Qty	£ p	£	Qty	£ p	£	Qty	£ p	£
1							50	9.00	450.00
2	20	10.75	215.00				70		665.00
4				30	9.00	270.00	40		395.00
5				20	9.50	190.00	20		205.00

Introductory Fishing Packs are sold to children interested in fishing and are popular products with holidaymakers. The packs are sold to local holiday parks and shops where they're sold on to end-customers.

Ashley has recently taken over from the previous accounting technician who kept the inventory records. He hands the Introductory Fishing Pack record to you because he can't understand why the balance value of 20 packs is different from the issue value of 20 packs.

Your task is as follows:

- Write a memo to Ashley that addresses the difference.
- Explain how the issues on 4 July were valued.
- Using the same method of valuation used on 4 July, recalculate the value of issues on 5 July and the value of the balance on 5 July.
- Briefly outline how a future new member of staff can be trained to complete inventory record cards.

Examining the Treatment of Labour Costs within the Accounting System

Labour costs need to be measured and recorded accurately. Labour is often a major direct cost of products manufactured. The earlier section 'Distinguishing Direct from Indirect Manufacturing Costs' outlines how to separate one from the other. This section deals with how labour costs are allocated as direct and indirect. Just as the choice of valuation method for materials issued is a company policy decision, the same labour costs are treated differently from one business to another based on company policy. One example where differences exist is the treatment of the extra wages over and above the normal hourly rate a worker receives for work carried out in overtime.

In this section, we describe identifying which labour costs are direct and which are indirect, and preparing the cost-accounting entries (often as journals. *Journals* are the books a business uses to record the initial records of a transaction. Entering a transaction is called a journal).

In the real-world of work, the data provided is in the form of original documents such as job cards and timesheets. In the exam, however, the labour cost information is usually provided in a simpler format, sometimes as a completed card produced with errors that requires correction. Plus, at work you're told how to treat overtime; in an exam you have to read the question carefully because it depends on company policy.

Working with overtime premium

The point at issue is the overtime premium: the *extra wages,* paid over the normal rate, to staff working overtime. For example, someone may work a basic 37-hour week and get paid £8 per hour, but earn time and a half (£12 per hour) for any hours worked over the 37 hour basic. The overtime premium in this case would be the extra £4: the extra over the basic hourly rate.

Last month a company's direct employees worked the hours shown in Table 3-11 to produce its cream of mushroom soup range.

Table 3-11	Record of Hours Worked on Mushroom Soup
Hours worked during normal time	420
Hours worked in the evenings and Saturdays	60
Hours worked on Sundays	40
Total hours worked	520

Here's the rest of the necessary information:

- Direct employees in this department are paid at a basic rate of £7 per hour.
- All work in the evenings and Saturdays is paid at time and a half.
- All work on Sundays is paid at double time.
- The overtime premium is included as part of the direct labour cost.

Your task is to calculate the total cost of direct labour used to produce the cream of mushroom soup range last month. Check out Table 3-12 for the completed table.

Memorise the clear layout to use for this type of question, particularly the column headings. Doing so enables you to answer any question on this topic. This is a cost-accounting approach rather than a payroll approach. As a cost or management accountant you need to look at costs in terms of what caused the labour cost. Payroll staff are interested in the gross wages of the employees; they want the total labour cost values. Management accountants want the breakdown of the labour cost so that the costs are charged to the correct codes within the accounting system.

Table 3-12 Labour Cost Calculation (Using a Management Accounting Approach)

	Hours	*Rate per hour*	*Total*
Total hours worked	520	£7.00	£3,640.00
Saturday/evening premium	60	£3.50	£210.00
Sunday premium	40	£7.00	£280.00
			£4,130.00

If the original data had said: the overtime premium is treated as an indirect labour cost and charged to the ingredients mixing overhead control account, the alternative question would be: make the appropriate entries in the wages control account to show where the labour cost should be charged. The Wages Control Account is shown in Table 3-13.

The layout in Table 3-12 allows you to answer the question easily.

Look at the Wages Control Account (Table 3-13). The entry of £4,130 as the charge for 'Ingredients Mixing – Work-in-Progress' and 0 for 'Ingredients Mixing – Production overhead' is correct because the question said: 'The overtime premium is included as part of the direct labour cost.' The entries would have been £3,640 as the charge for 'Ingredients Mixing – Work-in-Progress' and £490 for 'Ingredients Mixing – Production overhead' if the question said: 'The overtime premium is treated as an indirect labour cost and charged to the ingredients mixing overhead control account.'

Table 3-13 Wages Control Account

	£		£
Wages expense	4,130	Ingredients mixing – Work-in-Progress	4,130
		Ingredients mixing – Production overhead control	0
	4,130		4,130

Read the question carefully, because different businesses treat overheads in different ways. Look out for the following two possibilities:

- The overtime premium is included as part of the direct labour cost.
- The overtime premium is treated as an indirect labour cost or charged to the overhead control account.

Analysing timesheets

Management accounting staff are often involved in gross wages calculation work alongside the payroll staff. Invariably the total gross pay of each individual member of staff is the purpose of such work from the payroll point of view, whereas the amount of labour cost to charge the various production departments and the split between direct and indirect is the primary concern of the management accountant.

Here's a timesheet exercise that's an example for someone working in the assembly department of a manufacturing company. Remember that in an exam, you're often given a scenario for a working situation where you have to follow company policy regarding the treatment of overhead premium payments.

Referring to the weekly Mattalot Manufacturing Company timesheet in Figure 3-1, your task is to complete the columns headed 'Basic Wages', 'Overtime Premium' and 'Total Wages'.

Complete the analysis of total wages for the week, showing the breakdown of the total wage into its direct and indirect cost elements. (Overtime premium is classified as an indirect labour cost.)

The basic working week is eight hours per day from Monday to Friday inclusive. Any hours in excess of eight per day are paid at the basic hourly rate plus an overtime premium of 50 per cent of basic pay. Any hours worked on Saturday and Sunday are paid an overtime premium of 100 per cent of basic pay.

Here's the recommended sequence for this exercise:

1. **Go down the timesheet filling in the values in the basic wage, overtime and total wages columns on a day-by-day basis.** Basic wages are the total hours worked (irrespective of the type of task) multiplied by the hourly rate. For example, on Wednesday, 8 hours × £10 per hour = £80.

2. **Enter the total for each of the three columns at the bottom of Figure 3-1.**

   At this stage you've done nothing more than a payroll clerk; the following analysis is what provides the difference.

3. **Calculate the direct wage cost, following company policy.** In this case it's the total from the 'Basic Wages' column less the cost of the three hours of work on indirect tasks.

4. **Calculate the total indirect wage cost, made up of work on indirect tasks and overtime premium.** Add the cost of the three hours worked on indirect tasks to the total from the 'Overtime Premium' column.

   These two values enter the accounting system. They're credited to the Wages Control Account and debited (in this case) to Assembly Work-in-Progress (direct) and Assembly Production Overhead (indirect).

EMPLOYEE NUMBER: 1010	DATE week ending 15 May 2013
EMPLOYEE NAME: JESSICA WILLS	COST CENTRE: ASSEMBLY
Basic hourly rate for all hours worked:	£10.00

Day	Hours Worked			Basic Wages	Overtime Premium	Total Wages
	Direct Tasks	Indirect Tasks	Comments			
Monday	8					
Tuesday	10					
Wednesday	7	1	Staff Meeting 10am–11am			
Thursday	9					
Friday	6	2	Training 3pm–5pm			
Saturday	6					
Sunday	3					
Total	49	3				

Analysis of Total Wages for Week	£
DIRECT WAGES	
INDIRECT WAGES	
TOTAL WAGES	

Figure 3-1: Mattalot Manufacturing Company's weekly timesheet.

5. **Total the two wage cost values.** They need to equal the total in the total wages column.

Figure 3-2 shows you the correctly completed timesheet (but don't peek before you're finished!).

Always read exam questions carefully, and then answer the task in exactly the way the question asks. Typically, AAT Costs and Revenues exams state that you're to enter nil or zero values where no value applies. Because it's a computer-marked exam, this comment gives a clue that you may well receive a mark for recognising that no value applies. Notice that we enter '0.00' in Figure 3-2 wherever no value exists. This approach is very good discipline for real-world work too, because it shows that the table is complete and that those boxes haven't simply been ignored.

Day	Hours Worked			Basic Wages	Overtime Premium	Total Wages
	Direct Tasks	Indirect Tasks	Comments			
Monday	8			80.00	0.00	80.00
Tuesday	10			100.00	10.00	110.00
Wednesday	7	1	Staff Meeting 10am–11am	80.00	0.00	80.00
Thursday	9			90.00	5.00	95.00
Friday	6	2	Training 3pm–5pm	80.00	0.00	80.00
Saturday	6			60.00	60.00	120.00
Sunday	3			30.00	30.00	60.00
Total	49	3		520.00	105.00	625.00

Analysis of Total Wages for Week		£
DIRECT WAGES	£520.00 – (3 hrs × £10)	490.00
INDIRECT WAGES	£105.00 – (3 hrs × £10)	135.00
TOTAL WAGES		625.00

Figure 3-2: Completed timesheet for Mattalot Manufacturing Company exercise.

There's always an exception . . .

On very rare occasions, management accountancy lecturers don't agree with the examiners who set and mark the exams their students sit. If you're studying for the AAT Costs and Revenues exam, you have one of those rare instances. The examiner for this course has accepted answers to timesheet-based questions exactly in the way that we outline them, but he expresses a preference for a slightly different interpretation to overtime premium in a limited number of situations.

Look at Figure 3-2 and Jessica Wills's row for Sunday. We show 3 hours at the basic rate (£30) and 3 hours of overtime premium (100 per cent × £3 = £30). The examiner's point is that work that hasn't been contracted can be treated as being entirely overtime premium payment. If he'd answered this question, we believe that he'd have treated the Sunday as Basic Wages £0 and Overtime Premium £60, which would mean that subsequent values following from this differ from our answer.

To date both approaches have been treated as equally valid for Cost and Revenues computer-based assessments, but future candidates may want to check their AAT magazine to see if the examiner continues to accept both options. Future exam questions may include a clue in the form of 'hours contracted are between Monday and Saturday, and any work done on Sundays would be over and above those on the worker's contract'. This aspect is worth looking for as well as the approach to overtime premium we use in this section.

Two Other Ways to Classify Costs

A management accountant needs to understand many classifications of costs. We end this chapter by looking at two more: one of these is conversion costs, and the other looks at division of costs between those that are costs incurred in creating products and those that are attributable to the accounting period rather than the products themselves (product costs and period costs).

Assessing conversion costs

Conversion costs are the costs of converting raw materials into products that are bought by customers. Virtually all businesses survive because they can sell what they produce for more than it costs them. The action of increasing the value of the product from its raw to its finished state is a conversion process, and it incurs conversion costs.

In this section, we look at the conversion process of transforming raw materials into finished goods. We're no longer concerned with 'belonging' (in the sense that we describe in the earlier 'Distinguishing Direct from Indirect Manufacturing Costs' section); instead, we're looking at the transformation, what management accountants call conversion costs.

Conversion costs 'convert' raw materials into finished goods. To determine conversion costs, you add direct labour costs and overhead (check out the earlier sections 'Costing direct materials and direct labour' and 'Understanding indirect costs: Production overhead', respectively).

The distinction between raw materials and conversion costs is important to understand, because direct materials are usually added at the beginning of production whereas conversion costs are added during production.

For example, hamburgers start as the minced beef patty, a bread roll, some sauce and some salad. The beef patty raw material is grilled, the roll cut in half and the salad chopped up. The cooked patty is put into the roll, the salad added with a squirt or two of sauce. The grilling and chopping and assembly all make up the conversion process. When looking at conversion cost, the cost of paying the cook and the kitchen overheads such as fuel are added together. We consider this aspect in Chapter 7 in the context of long production runs and the valuation of part-finished stock.

Telling the difference between product and period costs

Accountants split all costs into two categories – product costs and period costs. This is used both for the financial reporting requirements of financial accounting, and also because this can help management decision-making. In Chapter 10, we discuss alternative approaches, but at this point we stick with the financial-reporting definition of product cost as being made up of all the direct costs and the production overhead.

Think hard before classifying certain costs as product or period. Classification depends on the purpose of the cost:

- **Product cost:** Needed for manufacturing. It doesn't have to be direct, but when you look at the inventory of finished goods you must be able to say that the firm incurred those costs to get the product to its present condition and location.
- **Period cost:** Everything else, not falling under product costs.

For example, you classify depreciation on a factory is a product cost, but depreciation on the headquarters' office building is a period cost. Similarly, the wages paid to employees working in the factory are part of product cost (whether they're direct or indirect labour), but the cost of employees working in a sales office is a period cost.

Identifying product costs

Product costs include all the costs of making products:

- Direct materials
- Direct labour
- Overhead

Check out 'Costing direct materials and direct labour' earlier in this chapter for details of the first two items and 'Understanding indirect costs: Production overhead' for the third point. You classify product costs as inventory, an asset on the balance sheet, until you sell the product. (Flip to the earlier section 'Distinguishing Direct from Indirect Manufacturing Costs' for more on the listed costs.)

Whitek Ltd spends £10,000 on direct materials, £3,000 on direct labour and £6,000 on overhead to make 100 gadgets during the year. Total product costs in this scenario equal £19,000 (see Table 3-14). You classify the costs of making these gadgets as Finished Goods Inventory on the Balance Sheet (Statement of Financial Position) until you sell them.

Picking period costs

All costs that don't fall under product costs (see the preceding section) are considered *period costs.* This category includes selling and administrative expenses. Subtract these costs from revenues on the Income Statement when you get the benefit from them.

For example, suppose that you pay your salespeople £10 in commission for every whatchamacallit they sell. If they sell 30 whatchamacallits, they have to subtract £300 in sales commission expense on the period's Income Statement.

Table 3-14 illustrates the separation of product and period costs.

Table 3-14 Whitek Ltd Product Costs and Period Costs

Product Costs	£	Period Costs	£
Direct materials	10,000	Sales commissions	300
Direct labour	3,000	Administrative overheads	2,000
Production overhead	6,000	Delivery costs	1,000
Total product costs	**19,000**	**Total period costs**	**3,300**

Splitting up overlapping costs

You need to allocate overlapping costs between the product and period categories. For example, suppose that Scrumdiddlyumptious by Sofi (from the earlier section 'Distinguishing Direct from Indirect Manufacturing Costs') dedicates one-third of the building's total area to baking and two-thirds of it to selling.

If the monthly rent is £3,000, you classify one-third of that amount (£1,000) as a product cost (overhead), because this floor space is used to make products. This product-cost part of the rent is recorded as part of the Finished Goods Inventory on the Balance Sheet (Statement of Financial Position).

Two-thirds of the rent (£2,000) goes down as a period cost (selling expense) because this floor space is used to sell products. Like all period costs, these costs get recorded as expenses on the Income Statement. You treat all occupancy costs (such as rent, heat and maintenance) in this way for any business that manufactures and sells goods on the same premises.

Chapter 4

Allocating, Apportioning and Absorbing Overhead

In This Chapter

- Understanding the importance of budgeting overhead costs
- Using direct labour to apply overhead
- Assigning overhead with activity-based costing

In Ancient Greek mythology, Zeus sentenced Atlas to support all the celestial spheres on his shoulders, an event that many accountants consider the ultimate allocation of overhead! Loads of managers probably feel a lot like Atlas, because they too have to bear unreasonably disproportionate shares of overhead.

Overhead costs include all the costs of doing business that don't fit neatly into *direct materials* and *direct labour* – the materials and labour you can directly trace to a product (read more about identifying direct and indirect/overhead costs in Chapter 3). That said, you can't ignore overhead just because allocating it is difficult. You'd simply underestimate costs of products and processes, which spells disaster if you then underprice based on those figures and lose money.

As factories and processes automate (and robots replace people), the direct labour needed to produce goods manually tends to decrease, and the overhead necessary to operate, maintain and repair the machines tends to increase. Accordingly, as the overall importance of overhead increases, managers and accountants need to pay careful attention to how they allocate overhead to the different products their companies make.

In this chapter, we explain how and why you need to allocate the cost of overhead to individual products. We describe a traditional system for allocating overhead, based on direct labour, as well as a more innovative allocation system known as activity-based costing. For both systems, we lead you through what to do when you allocate too much or too little overhead to products, and give you a chance to try out the techniques for yourself.

Introducing Budgeting Overhead Costs

Managers need the help of management accountants when setting prices. Traditional approaches to pricing require detailed information about the cost of products so that the prices charged are sufficient to generate the necessary profits.

To find the full absorption cost of a product – in other words, the cost of producing the product – managers need the direct and indirect production costs. By definition, the direct costs are ones that belong to the product, but the production overheads are indirect. They have to be budgeted because you can't very well go up to someone at the end of the year and say, 'oh, you know the cakes that you bought from me in March, well at the end of the year our overhead added up to £350,000, so I'd like £0.10 now for each of the cakes you bought.' It just wouldn't work.

Overhead costs in products have to be budgeted costs based on a budgeted total overhead cost and a budgeted total number of units to be produced. Records have to be kept and a reconciliation carried out of actual overhead incurred and the overhead absorbed (as we discuss in the later section 'Reporting on overhead and overhead absorbed: Monthly management accounts'). Management accountants have to use the best information at their disposal to produce budgeted overhead costs for products, and in this chapter we show you how.

Charging Production Overheads into Products: Traditional Approach

Overhead costs are the indirect costs of making goods. They include the following:

- Indirect materials
- Indirect labour
- All other fixed and variable costs

A repair workshop in a garage is an example of a production department where indirect production costs *(production overheads)* need to be built into the price paid by the customer.

When a garage offers to repair your car for £85 per hour plus parts, it doesn't mean that the mechanics are paid £85. £85 is its way of building in a charge for overhead, the garage's profit and the mechanics' wages. You see only the hourly charge, but behind the scenes this amount is broken down and a significant part is expected to pay for the indirect costs the garage incurs, particularly the indirect costs of running the repair workshop.

A lot of the costs are related to the equipment the workshop needs. Diagnostic tools and computers, lifting equipment, and so on all cost the garage, but these costs aren't specific to the repair of your car. The management accountant budgets all the indirect costs of running the repair workshop, budgets the number of hours that will be worked repairing cars and can then calculate the budgeted overhead rate per hour worked. This rate is sometimes referred to as the budgeted overhead *absorption* rate, and sometimes the budgeted overhead *recovery* rate. Both terms mean exactly the same thing. The overhead is being absorbed into the job being done (or product being made) and as such the company is collecting a contribution towards (or recovering) the total production overhead for the department.

Table 4-1 uses a product manufacturer to show how the overhead costs, plus costs of direct materials and direct labour, flow into the cost of the finished products.

Table 4-1 Role of Overhead Costs in Overall Product Cost

		£	£
Direct materials	2.5 kilograms	20.00 per kilogram	50.00
Direct labour	4 hours	10.00 per hour	40.00
Prime cost			90.00
Overhead absorbed	4 hours	8.00 per hour	32.00
Full absorption cost			122.00

When measuring the cost of products, you need to determine exactly how much direct labour/materials and overhead go into each item you make. You can often measure exactly how much of the direct costs go into each product. For example, a pencil may contain 300 grams of wood and 100 grams of graphite, and so you apply the costs of those specific amounts of materials to that individual pencil. Similarly, if each worker takes an average of one hour to assemble a gadget, the cost of direct labour equals the cost of paying that worker for one hour.

Allocating overhead, however, is another story. Overhead is indirect, and so understanding how it benefits individual products is difficult. For example, how much electricity cost do you need to apply to each widget on your assembly line?

One way to allocate overhead costs is to use direct labour hours as a guide: the more direct labour hours that go into a product, the more overhead that goes with it. This approach makes sense because direct labour hours seem to cause overhead to increase. The more hours worked, the more money you need to pay for electricity, maintenance and other overhead costs. The following sections give you the lowdown on the direct labour hour method of allocating overhead.

Instead of allocating overhead based on direct labour hours worked, management accountants can choose to use direct labour costs, units produced or even machine hours. In some service industries, entirely different recovery rates are used. For example, a bus company may recover overhead using a rate per mile travelled.

Calculating overhead allocation

Isted Pottery manufactures . . . well, pottery. The manufacturing department has four cost centres: two where the pottery passes through, moulding and glazing, and two that service those 'production' cost centres, maintenance and canteen.

We suggest that you picture the company's set-up: it's probably relatively small and located on an industrial estate. The whole of the pottery's manufacturing department takes up 5,000 square metres of floor space. It's divided up; try to visualise the workspace. Perhaps you can see a rectangular unit where 3,000 square metres are used for moulding the clay – probably leading from the goods received where clay is delivered. Plus the department has work areas and potters wheels and an area where the moulded clay can be held before being transferred to be glazed.

Here, 1,000 square metres of floor space is taken up with the appropriate work benches and kilns where pots are fired. To one side are two other rooms, one 500 square metres for the four maintenance staff to use to store their equipment and carry out some repairs, and the other a small canteen area also 500 square metres in floor size.

This sort of detail is important, because some of the overhead costs for the whole of the manufacturing department need to be divided up between the four cost centres, and the amount of floor space each has provides a possible basis for doing so.

Table 4-2 shows some other factors that you can choose to use as bases for dividing up overhead costs.

Table 4-2 The Basis to Use to Divide Up Overhead Costs: Isted Pottery Example

Basis	*Moulding*	*Glazing*	*Maintenance*	*Canteen*
Floor space (sq m)	3,000	1,000	500	500
Power costs	£1,200	£3,290	£250	£300
Indirect staff costs	£1,100	£2,010	£3,800	£2,000
Machine depreciation	£1,710	£6,600	–	–
Number of employees	26	8	4	*none*

Often you're not given the total floor space, and so on. One of the purposes of an AAT test or exam may be to see whether you understand that you need it.

This particular question is comparatively easy, because the money value of the expenses used in each department is given for most of the costs.

Table 4-3 shows a list of budgeted expenditure for the whole of the manufacturing department (all four cost centres).

Table 4-3 Budgeted Production Overheads for Isted Pottery

Budgeted Overhead	*Amount (£)*
Indirect glazing materials	1,140
Rent and other property overheads	15,000
Power costs	5,040
Indirect staff costs	8,910
Machine depreciation	8,310
Total budgeted overhead	**38,400**

Allocating and apportioning overhead

At this stage you can start to look at dividing up these *total cost* values into the amounts to charge each cost centre. Two terms are used: allocation and apportionment.

Allocated costs

Allocated costs require no further calculations. They're costs that the accounting system can divide up for you. For example, when you produce labour cost calculations, you often add the cost centre and expenditure codes so that they're posted appropriately.

Isted Pottery has budgeted to spend a total of £8,910 on indirect labour costs (some on training, some on overtime premiums and some on cleaning). This budgeted total has already been broken down as Table 4-4 shows, and so the total cost has been *allocated* across the four cost centres. We add the total, just to show that they do indeed add up.

Table 4-4 Isted Pottery's Budget for Indirect Labour (in Pounds)

	Moulding	*Glazing*	*Maintenance*	*Canteen*	*Total*
Indirect staff costs	1,100	2,010	3,800	2,000	8,910

This example contains quite a lot of allocated overhead (from Table 4-3):

- Indirect materials are used in the glazing department, and so we allocate all £1,140 to glazing.
- Power costs have been specified on a cost centre basis.
- Machine depreciation has also been stated.

Apportioned costs

Apportioned costs are those costs you have to divide up yourself:

1. **Look for a suitable basis for apportioning a cost.** In this case you need to apportion rent and other property costs. As five possible bases are given (see Table 4-2), you need to decide which is likely to give the closest measure of how much each cost centre will incur in such property-related costs (see Table 4-5).

Table 4-5 Selecting the Basis to Apportion the Rent and other Property Overheads

Basis	*When the Basis is Appropriate for Apportion Overheads*
Floor space (sq m)	Often a good measure, because often the total **rent** charge has been set using the square metres of the whole industrial unit or factory
Machine value	Probably better for dividing up **depreciation or machine insurance** rather than rent
Number of employees	Similarly unsuitable for dividing up rent, but can be used for **staffing related overhead**
So we choose floor space to apportion rent and other property overheads	

2. **Work out the overhead to apportion to each department.** You can do so in several ways, but this approach is quick and an excellent use of the limited time available in an AAT exam:

   1. **Find the total of the basis, in this case the total of the floor space: 3,000 + 1,000 + 500 + 500 = 5,000 square metres.**
   2. **Divide the total *rent and other property overheads* cost of £15,000 by the 5,000 square metres to give the charge per square metre: £3.**
   3. **Press the '×' button twice on a normal (non-scientific) calculator to create a constant in the calculator memory.**
   4. **Type in the square metres in each department and = to find the rent cost to apportion: in this case, 3000 = gives £9,000, 1000 = gives £3,000 and 500 = gives £1,500.**
   5. **Enter the amounts in the overhead analysis table shown in Table 4-6.**

3. **Add up the columns for each cost centre.** Cross check your arithmetic; see whether the sum of the totals is equal to the £38,400 in the total column.

   We haven't got onto the canteen row yet (check out the next section).

The canteen and the maintenance costs need to be added up and re-apportioned to the moulding and glazing departments.

Table 4-6 Overhead Analysis (in Pounds)

Batch Number	*Moulding*	*Glazing*	*Maintenance*	*Canteen*	*Total*
Indirect glazing materials					1,140
Rent and other property overhead					15,000
Power costs					5,040
Indirect staff costs					8,910
Machine depreciation					8,310
					38,400
Canteen				( )	
Maintenance			( )		

The production centre overhead costs are used relatively easily. But trying to find out how much to charge based on the cost centres that service the production cost centres would be extremely difficult. Therefore, you re-apportion their totals in much the same way as the total rent cost was apportioned initially (see the next section).

Re-apportioning production service centre overhead

Re-apportionment can be carried out using a direct approach or a step-down approach. Direct means that service cost centres are charged to the production cost centres directly. So, for example, Isted Pottery can take the total cost of the canteen and, using a suitable basis, divide up the cost between moulding and glazing. Then in a similar way they can adopt the same approach with the maintenance total cost.

We use the step-down approach, however, in which you identify whether one service cost centre services the other and re-apportion that one first. This enables you to charge the canteen costs which are attributable to maintenance staff using the canteen, to the maintenance department. Using the step-down method should give a more accurate overhead absorption rate for each production department.

1. **Re-apportion the canteen costs.**

You know that the canteen column total is £3,800. On the assumption that all the employees use the canteen, divide that value by the total number of employees (38). So the canteen costs £100 per employee, and using the 'press the × button twice' approach (as outlined in Step 3 of the previous Practice section), you apportion £2,600 to moulding, £800 to glazing and £400 to maintenance, and minus £3,800 to canteen.

2. **Ensure that you're clear precisely how much has to be re-apportioned when re-apportioning maintenance costs.**

   In the initial analysis (see the earlier Table 4-6), you found that the total overhead costs for maintenance are £5,550. Since then, you've apportioned £400 of the canteen costs as well in Step 1, totalling £5,950. The £5,550 is the total you should have entered in the maintenance column below the machine depreciation row in Table 4-6. Go back and check if you got a different total. If you need to see a complete table, turn to Table 4-7.

3. **Re-apportion the total of £5,950.**

   The maintenance department records of previous months show that the maintenance staff typically carries out 80 per cent of their work in the glazing department and 20 per cent of their work in the moulding department. So on the basis that 80 per cent of the work of the maintenance work is for the benefit of glazing, you re-apportion 80 per cent of the £5,950 to the the glazing department (£4,760), and because 20 per cent of the work benefits moulding, you re-apportion £1,190 to the moulding department (as we show in Table 4-7).

4. **Total the production cost centre columns and check that the sum of these adds up to the overall total.**

   The cross check to £38,400 is okay (see Table 4-7).

Table 4-7 Overhead Analysis Completed (in Pounds)

	Moulding	*Glazing*	*Maintenance*	*Canteen*	*Total*
Indirect glazing materials		1,140			1,140
Rent and other property overhead	9,000	3,000	1,500	1,500	15,000
Power costs	1,200	3,290	£250	300	5,040
Indirect staff costs	1,100	£2,010	3,800	2,000	8,910
Machine depreciation	1,710	6,600	–	–	8,310
	13,010	16,040	5,550	3,800	38,400
Canteen	2,600	800	400	(3,800)	0
Maintenance	1,190	4,760	(5,950)		0
	16,800	21,600			38,400

5. **Calculate the overhead absorption rate.**

   Knowing the budgeted overhead on a cost centre basis is useful, but to be able to find how much overhead to charge to each product requires the calculation of an overhead absorption rate. Generally, you use one of two methods of absorbing overhead in the unit standards: *machine hours* and *direct labour hours.* These two are the most popular ones used by the examiner if you're sitting an AAT exam. They aren't the only ones, though, and certain questions set in service industries require alternatives.

   You may have gleaned clues when you drew a mental picture of the Isted Pottery. The labour-intensive moulding department uses far more labour hours than machine hours, whereas all the kilns suggest that more machine hours than labour hours are used for glazing. Now you're given the facts:

   - Budgeted labour hours for moulding are 4,000.
   - Budgeted machine hours for glazing are 6,000.

   You calculate the overhead absorption rates by dividing the total budgeted overhead cost for that cost centre by the budgeted number of hours, expressed in terms of labour or machine hours:

   - Moulding: £16,800 divided by 4,000 labour hours = £4.20 per labour hour.
   - Glazing: £21,600 divided by 6,000 machine hours = £3.60 per machine hour.

This stage is as far as AAT exam questions have gone in the past, but this chapter makes several references to the purpose of the overhead absorption rate calculation so it makes sense to see this being used. Future AAT exam questions, and certainly CIMA and ACCA exams, are highly likely to test the use of overhead calculations in job cost calculations.

Absorbing overhead as part of product costs

Isted Pottery has received an order for a range of pottery items from Amber Ceramics. You're given the following information:

- **Materials:** £35
- **Direct labour:**

  Moulding: 8 hours at £7.50 per hour

  Glazing: 4 hours at £8 per hour
- **Machine hours in glazing:** 5 hours

Table 4-8 shows the calculations involved.

Table 4-8 Job Cost Calculation for Amber Ceramics Order

			£
Materials			35.00
Direct labour	Moulding	8 hours × £7.50	60.00
Direct labour	Glazing	4 hours × £8.00	32.00
Overhead	Moulding	8 hours × £4.20	33.60
Overhead	Glazing	5 hours × £3.60	18.00
Total cost			**178.60**

The various overheads absorbed are added to the direct costs of materials and labour. They're described as being absorbed because the order absorbs the overhead absorption rate per hour on the basis of the number of hours used to make the order. Here, 8 labour hours are needed in moulding and so the £4.20 per labour hour is multiplied by the 8 hours. Similarly the £3.60 per machine hour is multiplied by the 5 hours of machine time needed in glazing to find how much is absorbed there.

Here's an opportunity for you to put this technique into practice.

Dawsons Ltd Production comprises three departments:

- Cutting
- Stitching
- Maintenance

The budgeted fixed production overheads for May are as shown in Table 4-9.

Table 4-9 Dawsons Ltd's Budgeted Fixed Production Overheads

	£
Machine insurance	600
Rent and other property overhead	4,200
Power costs	1,250
Cutting:	
Stitching	450
Maintenance	200
Indirect staff costs:	
Cutting	1,270
Stitching	1,900
Maintenance	1,530
Total budgeted fixed production overheads	**11,400**

The information in Table 4-10 is also relevant.

Table 4-10 Dawsons Ltd's Other Information

Department	*Floor Space Occupied (Square Metres)*	*Net Book Value of Fixed Assets (£000)*
Cutting	1,500	35
Stitching	3,250	10
Maintenance	250	5

Allocate and apportion overhead between departments using the most appropriate method. Then re-apportion total maintenance overhead to the cutting and stitching departments. The maintenance records show that 90 per cent of the time is spent in the cutting department and 10 per cent in the stitching department.

Complete the missing information in Table 4-11, showing the allocation and apportionment of fixed overhead between the three departments.

The cutting department is capital intensive and absorbs overhead on a machine hour basis; the stitching department is labour intensive and absorbs overhead on a direct labour hour basis (see Table 4-12).

Table 4-11 Dawsons Ltd's Fixed Overhead Information

Fixed Overhead for May	*Basis*	*Total (£)*	*Cutting (£)*	*Stitching (£)*	*Maintenance (£)*
Machine insurance		600			
Rent and other property overhead		4,200			
Power costs		1,900			
Staff costs		4,700			
Maintenance					( )
		11,400			

Table 4-12 Dawsons Ltd's Cutting and Stitching Departments

Budgeted	*Cutting Department*	*Stitching Department*
Machine hours	200 hours	
Direct labour hours		10,800 hours

Find the overhead absorption rate for each department.

Dealing with overhead as work is carried out

The system of costing finished goods requires you to apply all direct materials, direct labour and overhead costs to products made. Overhead costs in this case are the ones absorbed rather than actually incurred. This approach allows you to charge overhead every time an hour of direct labour is worked, instead of waiting until the end of the accounting period.

At Isted Pottery, the order for Amber Ceramics has the accounting entries in Table 4-13 in relation to the overhead absorbed.

Table 4-13 Isted Pottery's Accounting Journal Entries

Date	*Account (or Code)*	*Debit (£)*	*Credit (£)*
10 May 2013	Moulding work-in-progress	33.60	
10 May 2013	Moulding production overhead		33.60
Narrative: The absorption of £33.60 of production overhead into product cost in the moulding department			
10 May 2013	Glazing work-in-progress	18.00	
10 May 2013	Glazing production overhead		18.00
Narrative: The absorption of £18.00 of production overhead into product cost in the glazing department			

If you use debits and credits to compute product costs, don't panic. Debits go to the left and credits go to the right. All costs are debits and go to the left. Any reductions of costs are credits and go to the right. Essentially, the Production Overhead account is charging the Work-in-Progress account for the overhead used to produce the order for Amber Ceramics.

The Production Overhead Control Account is debited (or charged with) all the overhead incurred and then charges the Work-in-Progress account.

As you start recording overhead costs in your accounting system, you don't need the budgeted costs or the budgeted hours. You do need the budgeted overhead absorption rates (OARs) because you use them in the accounting system.

In exams, the data provided needs to spell out clearly which costs are budgeted and which are actual costs.

In the earlier section 'Re-apportioning production service centre overhead', we state the following overhead absorption rates for the Isted Pottery example:

- Moulding: £16,800 divided by 4,000 labour hours = £4.20 per labour hour.
- Glazing: £21,600 divided by 6,000 machine hours = £3.60 per machine hour.

Well, that was all done before the month started.

Reporting on overhead and overhead absorbed: Monthly management accounts

Isted Pottery is now at the end of the month and you're trying to record the appropriate transactions in the accounts.

- In the moulding department, the payroll clerks report that 4,200 direct labour hours have been worked.
- The works manager says that 5,600 machine hours have been worked in the glazing department.
- The accounting system records the production overhead charged (debited) to each of the departments as follows:
  - Production Overhead Control Account for moulding department: £17,200.
  - Production Overhead Control Account for glazing department: £20,850.

You need to answer two questions:

- **Question 1:** How much production overhead has each department *absorbed* into production?
- **Question 2:** How much production overhead is left *(under-absorbed)* or is the overhead absorbed more than the amount incurred *(over-absorbed)*?

In answer to Question 1, various overheads are absorbed on the basis of the *actual* hours worked:

- **In the moulding department:** 4,200 direct labour hours were worked. You use the overhead absorption rate calculated before the accounting period started: £4.20 per direct labour hour.

  You absorb: 4,200 hours × £4.20 per hour = £17,640
- **In the glazing department:** 5,600 machine hours were worked. You use the overhead absorption rate calculated before the accounting period started: £3.60 per machine hour.

  You absorb: 5,600 hours × £3.60 per hour = £20,160

Table 4-14 shows the T-account transactions.

Table 4-14 Isted Pottery's T-account Transactions

Production Overhead Control Account: Moulding Department			
		WIP Moulding	***£17,640***

Work-in-Progress Account: Moulding Department			
Prod. Ohd Control Moulding	***£17,640***		

Production Overhead Control Account: Glazing Department			
		WIP Glazing	***£20,160***

Work-in-Progress Account: Glazing Department			
Prod. Ohd Control Glazing	***£20,160***		

Under- and over-absorbed production overhead

You now have two amounts in your Production Overhead Control Accounts:

- **Absorbed overhead:** That you've just entered.
- **Actual overhead:** That was incurred (the £17,200 and £20,850 we show in the preceding section that came from the accounting system), for example, rent and insurance costs.

Always write them in this order, so that the difference is easy to recognise:

- You've *over-absorbed* the overhead if absorbed less actual gives a positive answer (that is, more absorbed than actual).
- You've *under-absorbed* the overhead if absorbed less actual gives a negative answer (that is, more actual than absorbed).

Table 4-15 contains a comparison of the two Isted Pottery departments.

Table 4-15 Looking at the Two Isted Pottery Departments

Department	*Moulding*	*Glazing*
Overhead absorbed	£17,640	£20,160
Actual overhead incurred	£17,200	£20,850
(Under-)/over-absorbed amount	£440	(£690)
	Over-absorbed	Under-absorbed

You record the T-account transactions as shown in Table 4-16.

Table 4-16 Recording Isted Pottery's Under-/Over-Absorbed Overhead

Production Overhead Control Account: Moulding Department			
U/O Absorbed Moulding	£440		

Under-/Over-Absorbed Overhead Account: Moulding Department			
		Prod. Ohd Control Moulding	***£440***

Production Overhead Control Account: Glazing Department			
		U/O Absorbed Glazing	***£690***

Under-/Over-Absorbed Overhead Account: Glazing Department			
Prod. Ohd Control Glazing	£690		

Affect on profit for the period

The £440 over-absorbed by the moulding department has been credited to the Under-/Over-Absorbed Overhead Account for moulding as an entry for the accounting period. This approach keeps the difference separate from the production of moulded clay and can help management control. The amount under-/over-absorbed is highlighted and easily recognised by management who can then decide what actions to take.

The £440 will eventually be debited in the Under-/Over-Absorbed Overhead Account and credited to the Profit and Loss account *effectively increasing the profit for the period by £440.*

The £690 under-absorbed by the glazing department has been debited to the Under-/Over-Absorbed Account for glazing as an entry for the accounting period, which keeps the difference separate from the glazing of clay products and can help in control by showing the value on its own within any accounts presented to the management.

The £690 will eventually be credited in the Under-/Over-Absorbed Overhead Account and debited to the Profit and Loss account *effectively decreasing the profit for the period by £690.*

Taking Advantage of Activity-Based Costing for Overhead Allocation

Activity-based costing (ABC) emphasises the need to obtain a better understanding of the behaviour of overhead costs. It ascertains what causes overhead costs and how they relate to products. ABC recognises that in the long run most costs aren't fixed and seeks to understand the forces that cause overhead costs to change over time.

ABC assumes that:

- Activities cause costs
- Products (or services) create demands for activities

A link is made between activities and products by assigning costs of activities to products based on an individual product's consumption or demand for each activity.

The design of ABC systems involves four stages, which we describe in the next four sections:

1. **Identifying the major activities that take place in an organisation.**
2. **Creating a cost pool/cost centre for each activity.**
3. **Determining the cost driver of each major activity.**
4. **Assigning the cost of activities to products according to the product's demand for activities.**

Identifying the major activities in the organisation

The major activities may include:

- **Machine-related activities:** For example, machining cost centres.
- **Direct-labour related activities:** For example, assembly departments.
- **Various support activities:** For example, ordering, receiving, materials handling, parts administration, production scheduling, packing and dispatching.

Creating a cost pool for each activity

For example, the total cost of all set-ups can constitute one cost pool for all set-up-related costs.

Determining the cost driver for each major activity

Cost driver describes the events or forces that significantly determine the cost of the activities. For example, the production scheduling cost may be generated by the number of set-ups (see Table 4-17). Thus set-ups would represent the cost driver for production scheduling.

Table 4-17 Summary of Common Cost Drivers for Overhead Cost Pools

Overhead Cost Pool	*Common Cost Drivers*
Production scheduling/set-up costs	Number of production runs/set-ups
Receiving department	Number of receiving orders
Purchasing department	Number of purchase orders
Dispatch department	Number of dispatch orders

For costs that are purely variable with output in the short term, ABC systems use volume-related cost drivers, such as direct labour hours or machine hours.

Assigning the cost of activities to products according to the product's demand for activities

The number of transactions it generates for the cost driver measures a product's demand for the activities.

We recommend three steps to find the overhead to charge each unit:

1. **Find the *charge out rate* per batch.**

   Table 4-18 demonstrates how to do so. In this case, you add up all the costs related to setting up the machines needed for all the production runs that are budgeted for the accounting period. You add up all the set-ups that will be needed in the period. The charge out rate is the cost per set-up. The charge out rate for the other cost pools are calculated in the same way (total overhead cost pool divided by the total budgeted number of times the cost driver will be used in the period – see Table 4-17 for three other examples). In the Rusbridge Limited example (see the next section), Table 4-21 shows the charge out rates for each of the cost types.

2. **Find the *total overhead* per product.**

   Once you have the charge out rate for each of the cost pools, take each separately, multiplying the charge out rate by the number of cost drivers a particular product will require. This will be the total number to be produced in the period. In the Rusbridge Limited example, this is shown in Table 4-22. For example, production of 100 Dees requires 100 direct labour hours – at £1 per direct labour hour, this adds £100 of short-term variable cost, and two production runs at £700; a total of £1,400 for set-up costs. Once each cost type has been calculated, you can add them up to find the total overhead per product; for example £2,900 in the case of the Dees.

3. **Find the *total overhead per unit* of the product.**

   This is shown in Table 4-23. Divide the total overhead cost per product by the products being produced to find the overhead cost for each unit of the product.

Charge out rate per batch

Here's how to find the charge out rate for set-ups.

Total Cost Pool for set-up related costs	£100,000
Number of set-ups in period	100
Batch size	20
Total Pool ÷ No of transactions for the cost driver	**CHARGE OUT RATE**
£100,000 ÷ 100	£1,000 per set-up

Total overhead per product

Adamant You then multiply the number of set-ups required for a product by the charge-out rate to find the total set-up overhead for the product:

Number of set-ups × Charge out rate = Total set-up overhead for the product

Total overhead per unit

You add together the total of each overhead for the product and divide by the number of units in a batch to find the overhead cost per unit:

$$\frac{\text{Combined total of all overhead cost totals}}{\text{Number of units per batch}} = \text{Overhead cost per unit}$$

The cost objective is often identified as the product (or services) that are being provided, but it can be any identifiable cost object (for example, types of customers, geographical region or distribution channel).

Working Through an Example: Rusbridge Limited

The unit costs of Product Dee and Product Bee are troubling the production manager Debbie Rusbridge. The present unit costs are shown in Table 4-18. Note the other following details:

- **Product Dee:**

  Production: 100 units

  Labour: 1 hour
- **Product Bee:**

  Production: 1,000 units

  Labour: 3 hours

Table 4-18 Unit Costs of the Two Products using the Traditional Approach

	Product Dee (£)	*Product Bee (£)*
Materials	15.00	8.00
Labour (£17/hr)	17.00	51.00
Overhead (OAR £5/hr)	5.00	15.00
Total	**£37.00**	**£74.00**

Debbie Rusbridge has heard that you've been studying ABC techniques. The accounts staff have gone to great lengths to find the details for you (see Tables 4-19 and 4-23). The overhead totals £15,500.

Table 4-19 Cost Breakdown

Cost	*Cost Driver*	*Amount (£)*
Short-term variable costs	Direct labour hours	3,100
Set-up costs	Number of production runs	4,900
Materials handling	Number of parts	4,200
Quality control inspection	Number of inspections	3,300
Total		**15,500**

Table 4-20 Consumption of Activities

Product	*Units*	*Number of Production Runs*	*Number of Parts Per Unit*	*Number of Inspections*
Dee	100	2	4	4
Bee	1000	5	8	7
Total		**7**		**11**

Your task, if you choose to accept it, is to re-calculate the unit costs of the Dee and the Bee using an ABC approach. We provide the answers in Table 4-24 (but don't peek).

Table 4-21 Charge Out Rates

Cost	*Cost Driver*	*Amount (£)*		*Dee*	*Bee*	*Total*	*Charge Out Rate (£)*
Short-term variable costs	Direct labour hours	3,100	Units × hours per unit	100	3000	3100	£1.00 per direct labour hour
Set-up costs	Number of production runs	4,900		2	5	7	£700.00 per production run
Materials handling	Number of parts	4,200	Units × parts per unit	400	8000	8400	£0.50 per part
Quality control inspection	Number of inspections	3,300		4	7	11	£300.00 per inspection
Total		**15,500**					

Table 4-22 Total Overhead per Product

Cost	*Dee (£)*	*Bee (£)*
Short-term variable costs	100	3,000
Set-up costs	1,400	3,500
Materials handling	200	4,000
Quality control inspection	1,200	2,100
Total	**2,900**	**12,600**

Table 4-23 Total Overhead Per Unit of the Product

Cost	*Dee*	*Bee*
Total overhead	£2,900	£12,600
Products	100	1000
Overhead per unit	£29.00	£12.60

Table 4-24 Unit Costs of Dee and Bee Using an ABC Approach

	Product Dee		*Product Bee*	
		£		£
Materials		15.00		8.00
Labour (£17/hr)	1 hour	17.00	3 hours	51.00
Overhead		29.00		12.60
Unit costs		**61.00**		**71.60**

Chapter 5

Costing Products Flowing Through a Business

In This Chapter

- Understanding how inventory flows through a business
- Tracking cost of production to product sold
- Calculating the number of units sold

Two essential truths apply to commercial businesses if they're to earn money:

- Manufacturers have to make products for less money than they can sell them for.
- Retailers have to buy products for less money than they can sell them for.

Therefore, measuring the cost of products manufactured or purchased is critically important to understanding a business's profitability.

This concept explains why the item Cost of Goods Sold usually appears as the first and largest expense on a manufacturer's or retailer's income statement. How well a company can make or buy goods and then sell them at a profit is fundamentally important to the company's profitability and success. This fact applies to businesses across the spectrum, from mass-market retailers to elite, high-end retailers to manufacturers.

In this chapter, we show you how goods and their costs flow through a business. You can then use the same method to understand how to calculate Cost of Goods Produced and Cost of Goods Sold. We also explain how to prepare the Cost of Goods Produced statement. All this information gives you a critical understanding of your business.

Tracking the Flow of Products

Retailers purchase products from other companies and then sell these products in shops or online to their customers. Products flow through a retailer in the following order:

1. **Supplier supplies the purchased products to the retailer.**
2. **Retailer displays the products so that customers can see them.**
3. **Customers buy the products and take them home.**

Product costs flow through a retailer's books just as the products themselves flow through the retailer's operations. When the retailer purchases products, it owes the cost of these products to the supplier. When the retailer sells the products to its customers, it records sales and the cost of goods sold. *Cost of Goods Sold* then appears as an item on the income statement as an expense.

Manufacturers go through the same basic process as retailers, but with a few more-involved steps which are necessary to make the products physically.

Here are the main stages for manufacturers making goods:

1. **They purchase raw materials.**
2. **They pay for labour and overhead to work on these raw materials (after entering production, raw materials become Work-in-Progress (WIP) inventory, which we discuss later in the 'Charging (debit) production costs to work-in-progress' section).**
3. **They complete manufacture of the goods, and so the Work-in-Progress inventory becomes Finished Goods.**
4. **They sell the goods to customers.**

Just as the goods flow through a manufacturer's operations, the cost of those goods flows through to the manufacturer's books.

Following the Phases of Production and Sale

In this section, we lead you through the different stages of these processes, using the example of The Apple Pie Company bakery, which makes and sells truly scrumptious apple pies.

Accounting for direct costs and production overhead

Direct materials are the physical materials needed to make products. They're 'direct' in the sense that you can trace direct materials easily to individual products. For example, suppose that your factory produces apple pies and each apple pie requires 1 kilogram of apples, 140 grams of sugar and 350 grams of flour. Each of the three main ingredients is a direct material.

The terms *direct materials* and *raw materials* aren't exactly interchangeable. As we explain in Chapter 3, direct materials are the cost of raw materials that can be easily traced directly to the actual products made. Raw materials, therefore, may include direct materials and indirect materials, the cost of materials that you can't easily trace directly to individual products. Indirect materials are included in Production Overhead.

To help see the difference, consider this example. When bakers make apple pies they often have hot pans. To warn the washing-up staff that a pan is hot, they often sprinkle the handles with flour. Flour is also used when rolling out the pastry to prevent it sticking. In these instances the flour is an essential production cost, but isn't part of the apple pie recipe and so is treated as a production overhead (*indirect* material). It may be exactly the same grade of flour as that used to make the pastry. The flour that can be traced to the apple pie directly is called *direct* material and is charged to Work-in-Progress. Although the flour used to help rolling out the pastry and to warn the washing-up staff, and the flour that's part of the recipe has all come from the same bag, it's classified as direct or indirect according to how it is used.

When considering if an item is direct or indirect, think 'What are we using the flour for?' If the item goes into a product, it's direct material; if it's used to enable production to go ahead without being directly attributable to a specific product, it's indirect material. It isn't the product that determines if a material is direct or indirect, but how it is used. Direct materials are charged to Work-in-Progress.

The company and its supplier usually negotiate and set the price of buying materials. However, the overall cost of materials may also include charges for shipping the materials to your place of business (often referred to as *carriage-in*) and any costs of storing and maintaining the materials.

Some of the transactions in the accounts appear as shown in Figure 5-1 (it's common accounting practice to provide a narrative after entries).

Accounts Payable Control Account (Suppliers)			
		Inventory	£97.50

Inventory (Flour)			
Accounts Payable Control	£97.50		

The purchase of the flour from the supplier for £97.50 on credit terms.

Inventory (Flour)			
		WIP (Bakery)	£9.10

WIP Account (Bakery)			
Inventory (Flour)	£9.10		

The issue of 7 kg of flour from the stores to enable the bakers to make 20 apple pies.

Inventory (Flour)			
		Production Overhead (Bakery)	£1.30

Production Overhead Control Account (Bakery)			
Inventory (Flour)	£1.30		

The issue of flour to the bakery for the general use within the department.

Figure 5-1: Example of a Direct Material Cost as individual transactions.

We display the inventory T-account three times to indicate each transaction, but within all accounting systems each transaction would be entered into a single account, as per Figure 5-2.

Inventory (Flour)			
Accounts Payable Control	£97.50		
		WIP Bakery	£9.10
		Production overhead Bakery	£1.30

Figure 5-2: Example of a Direct Material Cost in a single account.

Charging (debit) production costs to work-in-progress

Work-in-Progress inventory involves materials that have gone into production but haven't yet been finished. The production of apple pies has direct labour costs – the time taken to make the apple pies and other direct materials – and also has the Production Overhead absorbed. This account starts with the flour from the previous example and has four added entries; apples, sugar, direct labour and Production Overhead (see Figure 5-3).

Work-in-Progress Account (Bakery)			
Inventory (Flour)	£9.10		
Inventory (Apples)	£25.00		
Inventory (Sugar)	£5.90		
Direct Labour (4 hours)	£40.00		
Production overhead (absorbed) (4 labour hours)	£20.00		
	£100.00		

Figure 5-3: Example of a Work-in-Progress Account.

Crediting work-in-progress when products become finished goods

Finished goods are completed products that are ready for sale. The cost of finished goods inventory, known as *Cost of Goods Produced,* includes all the costs associated with the products: direct materials, direct labour and production overhead.

The accounting entry for finished goods is to credit WIP and debit finished goods inventory. If we assume that all apple pies have now been produced, the transaction appears as shown in Figure 5-4.

Work-in-Progress Control Account (Bakery)			
		Inventory	£100.00

Inventory (Finished Goods – Apple Pies)		
WIP Bakery	£100.00	

The transfer of 20 completed apple pies to the finished goods store.

Figure 5-4: Transfer of apple pies to the finished goods store.

The finished goods remain in the store until they're sold (or deteriorate and become unsellable). Thankfully apple pies have a few days of shelf life. A sales transaction occurs at the point of an apple pie being sold as well as a transfer from the Finished Goods to Cost of Sales. The two transactions happen together, but they are different.

Chalking up the inventory and charging Cost of Goods Sold

Think of the costing transaction as the apple pie leaving the finished goods store to become the cost of the sale (see Figure 5-5).

Inventory (Finished Goods – Apple Pies)			
		Cost of Goods Sold	£5.00

Cost of Goods Sold			
Inventory Apple Pies	£5.00		

Figure 5-5: Sale of one apple pie.

The sale of one apple pie at a production cost of £5.00 (£100/20 pies).

In a similar way, you can see the sales transaction as the customer paying for the apple pie (no doubt nobly intending to share it with the family, but probably scoffing it all on the way home!): see Figure 5-6.

Sales			
		Accounts Receivable	£15.00

Accounts Receivable Control Account (Customers)			
Sales	£15.00		

Figure 5-6: Credit sale of one apple pie.

Creating the income statement

The accounting system generates a very simple statement based on the Sales and Cost of Sales accounts (see Table 5-1).

Table 5-1 Income Statement for The Apple Pie Company, January 2013.

	£
Sales Revenue	15.00
Cost of Sales	(5.00)
Gross Profit	10.00

Although this statement is a useful summary for financial reporting, management reports may need to show more information, such as the inventory levels (see Figure 5-7).

				£
Sales Revenue				15.00
	Opening Inventory (Raw Material flour)	0.00		
	Material Purchases (flour)	97.50		
	Closing Inventory (Raw Material flour)	(88.40)		
	Raw Material (flour used)		9.10	
	Apple used		25.00	
	Sugar used		5.90	
	Total Direct Materials		40.00	
	Direct Labour		40.00	
	Production Overhead		20.00	
	Total Cost of Production		100.00	
	Opening Inventory (Finished goods – apple pies)	0.00		
	Closing Inventory (Finished goods – apple pies)	(95.00)		
	Increase in inventory (Finished goods – apple pies)		(95.00)	
Cost of Sales				(5.00)
Gross Profit				10.00

Figure 5-7: Detailed Income Statement as part of the Management Accounts for The Apple Pie Company, January 2013.

Just-in-time

Many companies use a system called *just-in-time,* which is designed to minimise inventory levels of direct materials, WIP inventory and finished goods. Just-in-time requires the manufacturer to time purchasing and production to meet customer demand. When a customer orders goods, the just-in-time manufacturer immediately orders and takes delivery of direct materials, puts them into the production process and despatches them to the customer. When a business uses just-in-time *purchasing* there's no need for a raw material inventory account because deliveries are made straight into production for conversion into finished goods. When a business uses just-in-time *production,* goods are only produced when they're ordered. As soon as they're produced the goods are sold, so no inventory of finished goods is held and a finished goods account isn't needed.

Cracking Cost of Goods Sold

When a retailer or manufacturer sells goods, the goods become an expense called *Cost of Goods Sold,* which includes all the direct materials, direct labour and overhead associated with the items sold during the year. Cost of Goods Sold is usually the largest expense on a manufacturer's or retailer's income statement.

Don't confuse Cost of Goods Sold with Cost of Goods Produced:

- **Cost of Goods Sold:** Measured as the cost of goods that were actually sold during the period, regardless of when they were completed. It goes onto the income statement.
- **Cost of Goods Produced:** Measured as the cost of goods that were actually completed during a period, regardless of whether they were sold.

The difference between the two values is the change in the value of the finished goods inventory between the start and the end of the accounting period. So, for The Apple Pie Company example in the preceding section, the Cost of Goods Produced is £100, but because £95 worth of the stock hasn't yet been sold and remains in the closing inventory, the Cost of Goods Sold is £5.

Computing Units Sold

Although some purchased direct materials are put into production, some are stored for future use. As a result, the amount of materials purchased is likely to be different from the amount of materials put into production.

Table 5-2 helps to explain this relationship and shows how to work out the total number of units sold.

Table 5-2 Calculating Units Sold

		Units
Opening inventory		
Plus inputs (for example, purchases)	+	
Sub-total	=	
Less closing inventory	–	
Equals outputs (for example, units sold)	=	

In this case:

- **Opening** means the inventory on the first day of the time period.
- **Inputs** refers to purchases or transfers from other parts of the company.
- **Closing inventory** is the amount held at the end of the last day of the time period.
- **Outputs** indicates the units that completed the production process: the stuff that's ready to be sold to customers (or if it needs further work, then it's ready for the next stage of production).

You can apply Table 5-2 to the quantity of units in inventory and put into production, and also to the costs of those same units.

You can also rearrange this illustration for other situations, such as when a number of orders is received and you have to calculate the amount of raw material that needs to be purchased to meet those orders.

Racing to accurate bar sales

One of the authors (Sandy) used to carry out inventory control work that included the bars and snack outlets at the Goodwood race circuit, and the table in Figure 5-9 is valuable for controlling bar sales. By valuing the outputs (or sales) from the table and then comparing this value with the actual cash collected in the till, you can judge how well each bar manager has performed in terms of inventory and cash control. A well-managed bar is one where the value of the inventory sold matches the money taken.

A corner shop starts the year with 10 jars of coffee, and during the year buys another 200 jars. At the end of the year, the shop counts 7 jars of coffee in stock. How many jars did it sell?

Beginning + Inputs – Ending = Outputs

10 jars + 200 jars purchased – 7 jars = 203 jars sold

Think of material storage in the same way. A factory keeps materials on hand so that they're ready to be put into production (or be sold to customers).

Chapter 6

Job Costing: Pricing Individual Orders

In This Chapter

- Organising the documentation for a job order cost system
- Accounting in a job order cost system

If you're looking to buy a teddy bear, you're likely to pop into your local supermarket or toy shop where you can choose from a few different colours and sizes to find the bear you like. Supermarket teddy bears are usually manufactured on assembly lines, often in batches of thousands of identical bears. To measure the cost of these products being made, companies use process costing, which we cover in Chapter 7.

If you're a discriminating bear aficionado, however, you may want to have your teddy bear made to order. This way, you can choose size, fur colour, eye colour, paw pads and even tattoos (a heavy-metal bear anyone?). You can also select from a wide selection of clothing or even have outfits made to order. When craftspeople sew and assemble these custom bears, they use a system called job order costing to track the exact cost of each bear.

Managers can use information about product cost to set and adjust prices and decide how to best use limited production capacity. In this chapter, we explain how companies accumulate costs in a job order costing system and how they apply overhead to the individual products made.

Keeping Records in a Job Costing System

A manufacturer who makes unique goods – or batches of goods – to order usually uses a job costing system to determine how much each job costs to make. Such goods may include custom teddy bears, made-to-order suits or aircraft, private catering functions or specially baked cakes; the individual units or batches are called *jobs*.

In *job order costing*, an information system traces the exact value of raw materials put into the process and the value of direct labour and overhead used to transform those raw materials into finished goods. This information system ensures that the company accounts for all direct materials, direct labour and overhead costs and accumulates the cost of each job. The following sections walk you through the record-keeping documents and process.

Getting the paperwork in order

Job order costing uses a few specific forms to keep track of the resources that go into an individual job: a job order cost sheet, materials requisition forms and time sheets.

Job order cost sheet

To keep track of jobs, companies typically use a form called a *job order cost sheet.* As Figure 6-1 shows, the job order cost sheet accumulates all the direct materials, direct labour and overhead costs applied to that job. This form is usually kept with the job itself, so that any additional costs incurred can be documented quickly.

Job. No.__________
Item__________
Customer__________
Quantity__________
Date requested__________

Date	Direct Materials	Direct Labour	Overhead
Totals			
Total cost			
Cost per unit			

Figure 6-1: A blank job order cost sheet.

Don't let references to 'sheets' and 'forms' confuse you into thinking that companies keep these records on paper. Some do, but most businesses store their records electronically.

Materials requisitions

When factory personnel need raw materials, they complete a *materials requisition.* This form, illustrated in Figure 6-2, starts the manufacturing process so that the factory can begin to work on the raw materials needed to make the goods. In this case, stores personnel issue ten cases of plastic pellets, stock number AA45, to the Assembly Department. These cases cost £300 each, totalling £3,000.

Date *16 July, 2013*
Job No. *1245*
Deliver goods to Department: *Assembly*

Quantity	Description	Stock No.	Cost per Unit	Total Cost
10 cases	*Plastic Pellets*	*AA45*	*£300*	*£3,000*

Requested by *Steven Kevins*
Approved by *Alysha MacRae*
Received by *Scott King*

Figure 6-2: The materials requisition authorises stores personnel to issue raw materials.

After they put the goods into production, the manufacturing employees copy the cost of the materials listed on the materials requisition slip to the job order cost sheet. They keep the two forms together, usually with the job itself.

Time sheets

As employees work, they complete time sheets to indicate how much time they spend working on each job, as shown in Figure 6-3. This time sheet indicates that Jon Garfunkel worked on Job 1245 for two hours. This direct labour adds £40 to the cost of this job.

Allocating overhead

Along with direct materials and direct labour, employees add the cost of overhead to the job order cost sheet. As we note in Chapter 4, the process for allocating overhead under activity-based costing has four steps:

1. **Add up total overhead.**

Date *17 July, 2013*				
Employee name *Jon Garfunkel*				
Department: *Assembly*				
Job No. *1245*				
Start	Stop	Hours	Hourly Rate	Total Cost
9:00 a.m.	*11:00 a.m.*	*2.0*	*£20*	*£40*
Employee *Jon Garfunkel*				
Approved by *Mary Pat Kinzler*				

Figure 6-3: Employees use a time sheet to keep track of the jobs they work on.

At the beginning of the period, add up projections of indirect materials, indirect labour and all product costs not included in direct materials and direct labour. For the purposes of Job 1245, assume that the company incurs £10,000 worth of overhead overall.

2. **Identify one or more cost drivers.**

   Find measures that drive your overhead. Many companies assume that direct labour drives all overhead. Here, assume that the company uses a single overhead cost pool, with direct labour hours as the cost driver.

3. **Compute the overhead absorption rate for each cost pool.**

   To compute the overhead absorption rates, divide total overhead in each cost centre by its cost driver. In this case, note that employees in the company are projected to work 5,000 direct labour hours this year.

   $$\frac{\pounds 10{,}000}{5{,}000 \text{ hours}} = \pounds 2 \text{ per direct labour hour}$$

4. **Apply overhead.**

   Multiply the cost pool's overhead absorption rate by each job's cost driver. So far, employees worked two hours on Job 1245. Therefore, this job would absorb £4 worth of overhead (2.0 hours at £2 per hour).

Completing the job cost calculation

The materials-requisition, time-sheet and overhead-absorption information all go on the job order cost sheet. So to determine the total cost of the completed job, employees simply add up the figures on the sheet. Figure 6-4 tallies the cost of Job 1245.

Job. No *1245*			
Item *Speciality Gadgets*			
Customer *SenyoCo*			
Quantity *1,000 units*			
Date requested *1 August, 2013*			
Date	Direct Materials	Direct Labour	Overhead
16 July	*£3,000.00*		
17 July		*£40.00*	*£4.00*
Totals	*£3,000.00*	*£40.00*	*£4.00*
Total cost			*£3,044.00*
Cost per unit			*£3.044*

Figure 6-4: Enter information from materials requisition slips and time sheets onto the job order cost sheet.

Understanding the Accounting for Job Costing

Recording journal entries and posting them to general ledger accounts in a cost accounting system isn't difficult. Almost all accounts in cost accounting are assets or expenses, and so debits increase most balances and credits decrease balances. (A few exceptions do exist, which we elaborate on later in this section.) Accordingly, a *T-account* – illustrated in Table 6-1 – lists increases in the debit column to the left and decreases in the credit column to the right.

Table 6-1 Debits (To The Left) Increase and Credits (To The Right) Decrease

Debits	*Credits*
Increase costs	Decrease costs
Add costs coming from other accounts	Subtract costs going to other accounts

Accountants use journal entries to record any changes to these T-accounts. Journal entries record transactions – namely, transfers between different accounts. Therefore, each journal entry affects at least two accounts, and total debits (increases to the left) must equal total credits (decreases to the right). For example, to purchase £1,000 worth of raw materials, debit the account Raw materials inventory (an increase to the left) and credit the account Cash (a decrease in cash to the right), as shown in Table 6-2.

Table 6-2 Journal Entries Record Transactions Between Different Accounts

Date	*Accounts*	*Debit*	*Credit*
20 July 2013	Raw materials inventory	1,000	
	Cash		1,000

Assume that the company starts with £10,000 worth of cash. As shown in Figure 6-5, you post this journal entry to the accounts, debiting the Raw materials inventory control account for £1,000 (increasing to the left) and crediting the Cash account for £1,000 (decreasing to the right). This reduces Cash by £1,000 while increasing Raw materials inventory control by £1,000.

Raw materials inventory

Debit	Credit
Cash 1,000	

Cash

Debit	Credit
Opening balance 10,000	Raw materials 1,000
	Closing balance 9,000
10,000	10,000

Figure 6-5: How the journal entry in Table 6-2 affects the accounts.

As taught in financial accounting courses, the debit–credit system in fact features two different kinds of accounts – *debit accounts* and *credit accounts*. So far in this section, you use debits (to the left side) to increase debit accounts and use credits (to the right side) to decrease debit accounts. Credit accounts, however, which include Liabilities, Shareholders' equity and Revenue accounts, work in the opposite direction. To increase these accounts, credit them (to the right side). To decrease them, you debit them (to the left side).

This book primarily deals with debit accounts, in which debits increase to the left and credits decrease to the right. Here we use only two credit accounts: Accounts payable (moneys owed to suppliers) and Wages payable (moneys owed to employees). To increase one of these credit accounts, credit it to the right. To decrease it, debit to the left.

The following sections take you through an example of accounting for the job order costing system. Here's the premise: fictional National Snow Globe Ltd manufactures custom souvenir snow globes for tourist gift shops. The company makes snow globes in large batches. Each globe features a unique three-dimensional image inside, a custom logo and one of four different grades of snow.

Purchasing raw materials

On 3 January, National Snow Globe purchases £50,000 worth of raw materials on account. As illustrated in Figure 6-6, you debit the Raw materials inventory for £50,000 and credit Accounts payable for £50,000.

Figure 6-6: Journal entries to record purchase of materials.

Date	Accounts	Debit	Credit
3 Jan., 2013	***Raw materials inventory***	***50,000***	
	Accounts payable		***50,000***

Raw materials inventory	
Accounts payable 50,000	

Accounts payable	
	Raw materials 50,000

The debit to Raw materials inventory (a debit account) increases that account's balance; the credit to Accounts payable (a credit account) increases that account's balance.

Paying for direct labour

On 31 January, National Snow Globe records payroll for direct labour amounting to £20,000. Over this time period, employees work 2,000 hours. As shown in Figure 6-7, you debit Direct labour for £20,000 and credit Wages payable for the same amount.

Figure 6-7: Journal entries to record direct labour cost.

Date	Accounts	Debit	Credit
31 Jan., 2013	***Direct labour***	***20,000***	
	Wages payable		***20,000***

Direct labour	
Wages payable 20,000	

Wages payable	
	Direct labour 20,000

The debit to Direct labour (a debit account) increases that account's balance; the credit to Wages payable (a credit account) increases that account's balance.

Paying for overhead

Overhead costs are all product costs not included in direct materials and direct labour. Typically they encompass indirect materials, indirect labour, business rates on the factory, depreciation of factory equipment, factory maintenance and the cost of factory supervision.

On 31 January, National Snow Globe pays £30,000 for overhead. As shown in Figure 6-8, you debit Overhead for £30,000 and credit Cash for this amount.

Figure 6-8: Journal entries to record payment for overhead.

Date	Accounts	Debit	Credit
31 Jan., 2013	***Overhead***	***30,000***	
	Cash		***30,000***

Overhead	
Cash 30,000	

Cash	
	Overhead 30,000

Requisitioning raw materials

The Work-in-progress account accumulates all direct materials, direct labour and overhead costs that a company puts into production.

On 14 January, National Snow Globe receives an order from the Hannah MacGregor Theme Park for 5,000 snow globes. The factory manager numbers this job BRM-10.

On 15 January, Supervisor Jane Smiley sends the raw materials store a materials requisition slip for job BRM-10, requesting £4,000 worth of raw materials to put into production. Logistics personnel deliver the goods to Jane's department. Jane then notes receipt of the goods on the job order cost sheet. (Check out Figure 6-1 and Figure 6-2 earlier in the chapter for a sample job order cost sheet and materials requisition slip, respectively.) Figure 6-9 illustrates the journal entry. You debit the Work-in-progress account and credit Raw materials for £4,000.

Figure 6-9: Journal entries to record requisition of materials for job BRM-10.

Date	Accounts	Debit	Credit
15 Jan., 2013	***Work-in-progress inventory***	***4,000***	
	Raw materials inventory		***4,000***

Work-in-progress inventory		Raw materials inventory	
Raw materials 4,000		***Opening balance 50,000***	***WIP 4,000***

A previous transaction means that the company already had £50,000 in its Raw materials inventory account. After this transfer shifts £4,000 from Raw materials inventory into Work-in-progress, the company has a remaining balance in Raw materials inventory of £46,000.

Using direct labour

Amanda Carpa, an employee in Jane Smiley's department, spends six hours working on job BRM-10. Jane notes the cost of Amanda's hours on the job order cost sheet. At the end of the day, she completes a time sheet. (Figure 6-3 earlier in the chapter illustrates a sample time sheet.) The company pays Amanda £10 per hour, and so the total direct labour cost for six hours equals £60 (6 hours × £10 per hour). The journal entry in Figure 6-10 debits the Work-in-progress account and credits Direct labour for £60.

Figure 6-10: Journal entries to apply direct labour to job BRM-10.

Date	Accounts	Debit	Credit
15 Jan., 2013	***Work-in-progress inventory***	***60***	
	Direct labour		***60***

Work-in-progress inventory		Direct labour	
Raw materials 4,000		*Wages payable 20,000*	***WIP 60***
Direct labour 60			

Applying overhead

To apply overhead in this example, you work through the following four steps:

1. **Add up total overhead.**

   National Snow Globe estimates that overhead would amount to £30,000 for the month.

2. **Identify one or more cost drivers.**

   The company evaluates its overhead, identifying two appropriate cost drivers. It records £10,000 in the Utilities cost pool. Managers determine that the appropriate cost driver for this cost pool is to be direct labour hours; as we note in the earlier section 'Paying for direct labour,' the activity level for this pool is 2,000 hours.

   The company also records £20,000 in a cost pool called Set-ups. Management determines that the appropriate cost driver for this cost pool is to be the number of set-ups, estimating that it would have a total of 50 set-ups during the month.

3. **Compute the overhead charge-out rate for each cost pool.**

   Divide the estimated overhead in each cost pool by its cost driver activity level, as shown in Table 6-3. For example, in the Utilities cost pool, the company expects to incur £10,000 worth of overhead. The company also expects to have employees work 2,000 direct labour hours. Therefore, the overhead charge-out rate comes to £5 per hour. Each direct labour hour also comes with £5 worth of overhead. Similarly, the overhead cost pool for set-ups comes to £20,000, and the company plans to do 50 set-ups. Therefore, the company assigns £400 worth of overhead for each set-up.

Table 6-3 Computing Overhead Absorption Rates for National Snow Globe

Activity Cost Pool	*Estimated Overhead*	*Estimated Cost Driver Activity Level*	*Overhead Application Rate*
Utilities	£10,000	2,000 hours	£5 per hour
Set-ups	20,000 hours	50 set-ups	£400 per set-up

4. **Apply overhead.**

   To figure out the overhead assigned to job BRM-10, measure the activity level of each cost driver and then multiply it by its respective overhead absorption rate, as shown in Table 6-4.

   Six hours of direct labour are expended to make job BRM-10 and the overhead absorption rate for Utilities is £5 per hour, and so you assign £30 in overhead cost to BRM-10. The job entails one set-up (at an overhead absorption rate of £400 per set-up), and so you assign another £400 worth of overhead to this job. Therefore, BRM-10 gets assigned a total of £430 worth of overhead.

Table 6-4 Allocating Overhead for National Snow Globe

Activity Cost Pool	*Activity Level*	*Overhead Absorption Rate*	*Cost Assigned*
Utilities	6 hours	£5 per hour	£30
Set-ups	1 set-up	£400 per set-up	£400
Total overhead			£430

As soon as the company's management accountants are able to estimate overhead assigned to the job, they add this cost to the job's job order cost sheet (see Figure 6-1 earlier in the chapter for a blank example).

The journal entry to allocate overhead debits (increases) Work-in-progress and credits (decreases) Overhead (see Figure 6-11). This entry effectively moves the overhead cost of the products out of the overhead pools and into the cost of the goods that the company makes.

Date	Accounts	Debit	Credit
31 Jan., 2013	*Work-in-progress inventory*	*430*	
	Overhead		*430*

Work-in-process inventory

Raw materials 4,000	
Direct labour 60	
Overhead 430	

Overhead

Cash 30,000	*WIP 430*

Figure 6-11: Journal entry to allocate overhead.

After the firm finishes manufacturing the goods, you add all the costs of making BRM-10 as shown in Figure 6-12. Remember to include direct labour, direct materials and overhead costs, so that the total cost of job BRM-10 sums to £4,490.

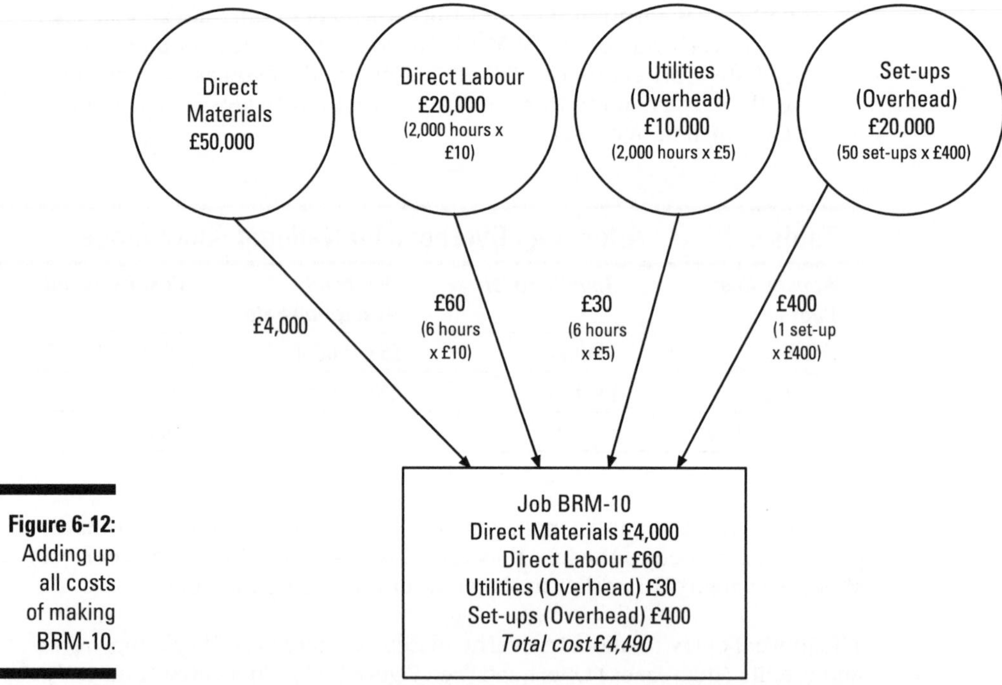

Figure 6-12: Adding up all costs of making BRM-10.

To record that the company has finished making the goods, you transfer this cost from the Work-in-progress inventory to Finished goods inventory by debiting (increasing) Finished goods inventory and crediting (decreasing) Work-in-progress inventory.

Note how transactions in the books reflect what happens in the factory. As the goods are moved off the assembly line and into the finished goods warehouse, the management accountants take their cost out of the account Work-in-progress inventory and into the account Finished goods inventory. See Figure 6-13 for the journal entry to record this transfer.

Date	Accounts	Debit	Credit
31 Jan., 2013	*Finished goods inventory*	*4,490*	
	Work-in-progress inventory		*4,490*

Work-in-progress inventory	
Raw materials 4,000	
Direct labour 60	
Overhead 430	*Finished goods 4,490*

Finished goods inventory	
WIP 4,490	

Figure 6-13: Journal entry to transfer goods from Work-in-progress inventory to Finished goods inventory.

Figure 6-14 provides a job order cost sheet for BRM-10. It illustrates how the company keeps track of direct materials, direct labour and overhead costs throughout the production process.

Job. No. *BRM -10*

Item *Singing Legend Snow Globes*

Customer *Hannah MacGregor Theme Park*

Quantity *5,000 units*

Date requested *1 January, 2013*

Date	Direct Materials	Direct Labour	Overhead
15 January	*£4,000.00*		
15 January		*£60.00*	*£430.00*
Totals	*4,000.00*	*60.00*	*430.00*
Total cost			*£4,490.00*
Cost per unit			*£0.898*

Figure 6-14: Job order cost sheet for job BRM-10.

When the products are sold, the cost of the products is moved from Finished goods inventory to Cost of goods sold. Figure 6-15 illustrates the journal entry used to reflect this shift; it debits (increases) Cost of goods sold and credits (decreases) Finished goods inventory.

Date	Accounts	Debit	Credit
15 February	*Cost of goods sold*	*4,490*	
	Finished goods inventory		*4,490*

Finished goods inventory	
WIP 4,490	
	Cost of goods sold 4,490

Cost of goods sold	
Finished goods 4,490	

Figure 6-15: Journal entry to record the sale of inventory.

Chapter 7

Process Costing: Tracking What's Produced and How Much it Costs

In This Chapter

- Distinguishing process costing from job order costing
- Making accounting entries for process costing
- Looking at revealing process-costing examples

People give Henry Ford credit for inventing the assembly line, which enabled him to produce thousands of identical Model T cars ('in any colour, as long as it's black') starting in 1907. Mass-producing cars dramatically reduced their cost and price, making them affordable for many families.

But standardised production goes back much farther than Henry Ford. At the end of the 1700s, Eli Whitney started to manufacture standardised parts to make guns, reducing costs and simplifying production. Workers no longer needed to spend time custom-fitting every part to work in each unit. If any part of one of Whitney's muskets broke, an equivalent part could easily replace it.

Today, the principles behind Whitney's standardised production and Ford's assembly line work hand-in-hand, allowing manufacturers to mass-produce quality goods quickly and at low cost. In modern mass production, continuous production output and work-in-progress (WIP) is monitored with a system called *process costing,* which keeps track of units produced and the costs involved to produce them. In this chapter, we explain how companies accumulate costs in a process costing system and how they apply overhead to individual products made. We also provide you with several illustrative examples to show how the system works in practice.

Comparing Process Costing and Job Costing

Some manufacturers make unique products, such as aircraft, made-to-order suits or custom teddy bears. Others produce large numbers of similar or identical items, such as soft drinks, sheets of paper and boxes of cereal: this is called *mass production*. To mass-produce products at a minimal cost, assembly lines move materials and partially finished goods from one section or department to the next until they get completed, becoming finished goods.

Process costing handles the same types of manufacturing costs as job order costing, which we explain in Chapter 6. Both systems deal with tracking how manufacturing costs such as direct materials, direct labour and overhead flow through WIP to Finished Goods and finally, when the goods are sold, to Cost of Goods Sold.

But whereas job order costing accumulates costs by job, using job cost sheets that stay with the inventory as it flows through the production process, process costing accumulates costs by department.

Process costing gives each department its own separate WIP account for accumulating costs and tallies costs at the end of each accounting period (in comparison, job costing uses only a single WIP account for all unfinished jobs and tallies the cost of a job when it's finished). Although job order costing measures the cost of each individual job, process costing measures the cost of work actually done on WIP during a period.

Unlike job order costing, which sends costs directly to individual jobs, process costing uses a two-step method:

1. **Sends direct materials, direct labour and overhead costs to departments.**
2. **Sends department costs to the units produced.**

Figure 7-1 illustrates the flow of this process.

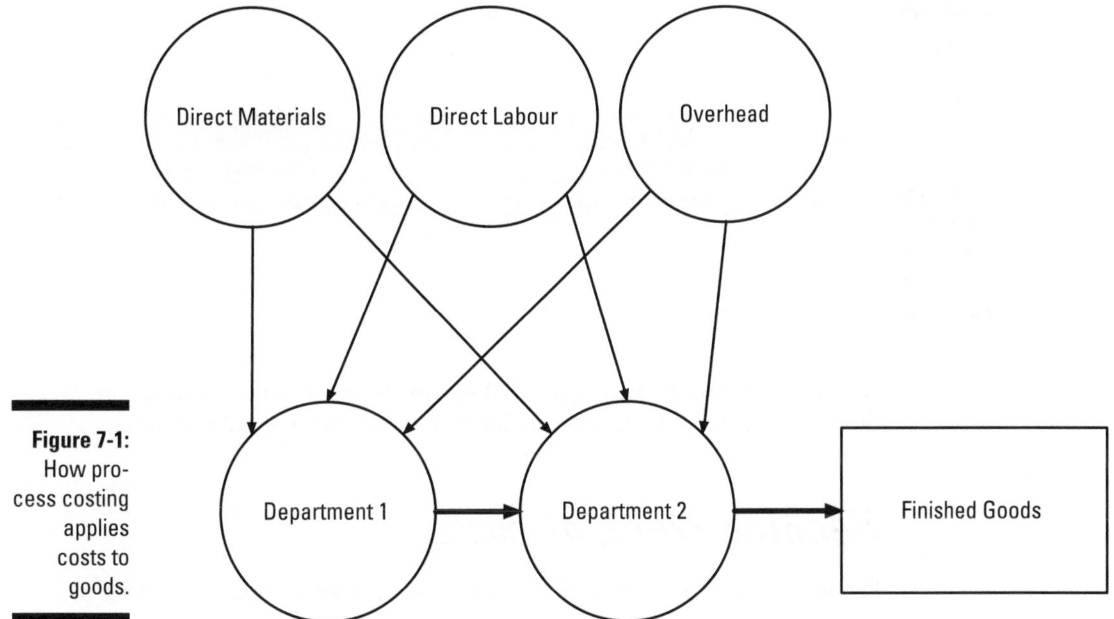

Figure 7-1: How process costing applies costs to goods.

Maintaining Process-Costing Books

To help you understand process costing, in this section we review a few basics – namely, how to use debits and credits, how to keep track of the costs of goods that you make and sell, and how goods and their costs move through a typical production line. We are then able to introduce you to the two important parts of process costing in the later section 'Meeting the two key aspects of process costing'.

Debiting and crediting

When costing goods, almost all accounts are either assets or expenses, so that in most cases, debits increase balances and credits decrease balances. Accordingly, when using T-accounts, increases go in the debit column on the left, while decreases go in the credit column on the right, as shown in Figure 7-2. (Note that liabilities, such as Accounts Payable and Wages Payable, go in the opposite direction. Debits decrease these accounts and credits increase them.)

Figure 7-2: Debits (to the left) increase balances and credits (to the right) decrease balances.

Debits	Credits
Increase costs	Decrease costs
Add costs coming from other accounts	Subtract costs going to other accounts

When you're costing goods, journal entries transfer balances between different accounts. Chapter 6 explains this process in greater detail.

Keeping track of costs

Products have three different kinds of costs (as we explain in Chapter 3):

- **Direct materials:** The cost of materials that you can trace easily to manufactured products. For example, if you're making peanut butter sandwiches, direct materials include 80 grams of peanut butter and two slices of bread per sandwich.
- **Direct labour:** The cost of paying employees to make your products. Direct labour for making peanut butter sandwiches includes the cost of paying employees for the five minutes they take on average to prepare a single sandwich.
- **Overhead:** All other costs necessary to make your products. For peanut butter sandwiches, overhead includes the costs of running the kitchen, including utilities and cleaning.

Accountants need to first accumulate costs and then assign them to individual departments. The roadmap in Figure 7-3 shows how debits and credits steer through the accounts.

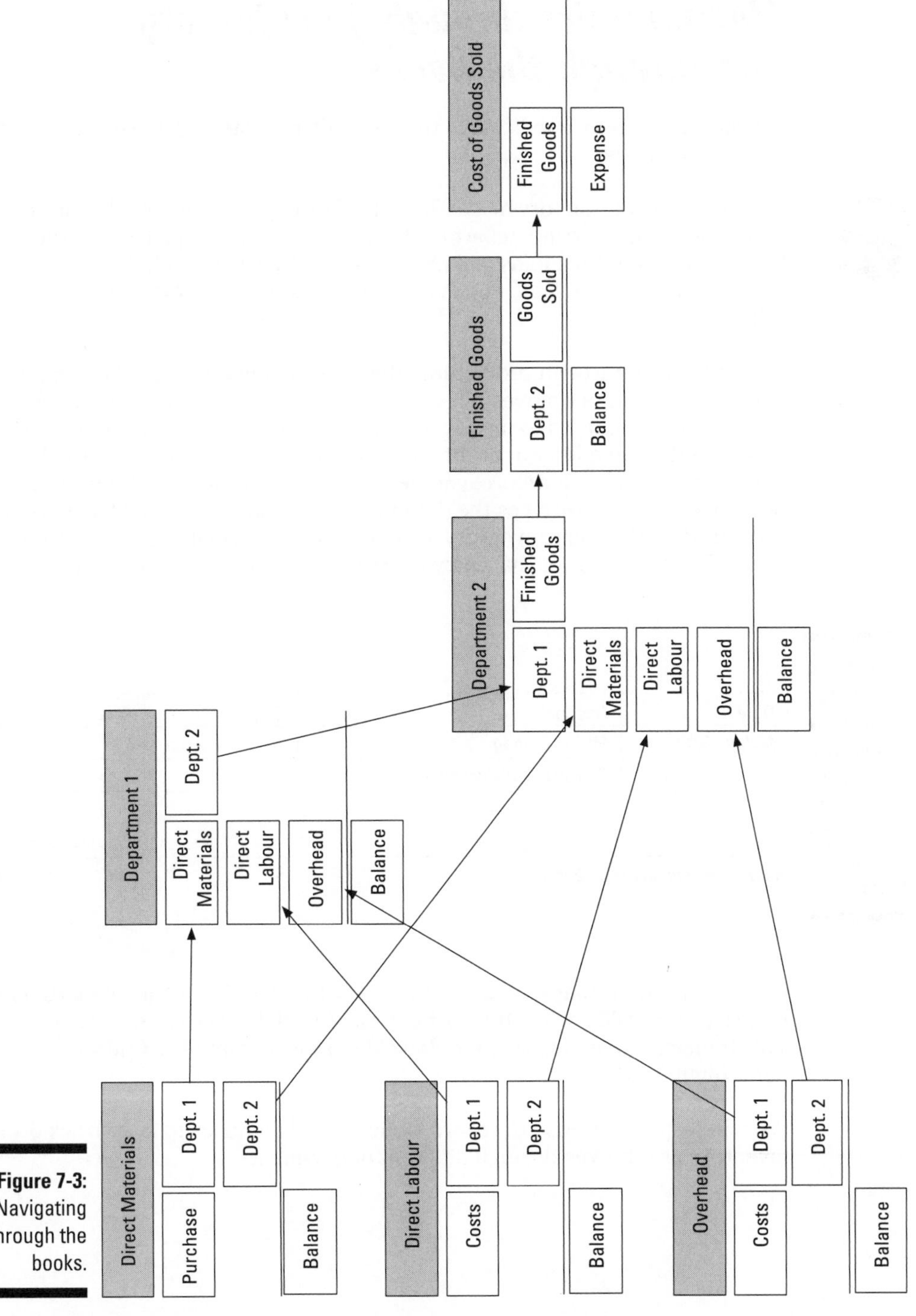

Figure 7-3: Navigating through the books.

Moving units through your factory – and through the books

In mass production, goods move through different factory departments until they're completed.

Suppose that your factory makes T-shirts. One department cuts the fabric and then sends it to a second department, which sews the cut pieces together. A third department then folds and packages the T-shirts into plastic bags. Then you can call the completed goods *finished goods* because they're ready for sale.

As goods move through production, their costs move through the company's books. As the factory moves direct materials into the Cutting department, you use journal entries to move the cost of those direct materials out of the Raw Materials inventory account and into the Cutting department's WIP inventory account. Therefore, you debit/increase the account WIP Cutting department, which receives the direct materials, and you credit/decrease the account Raw Materials inventory account, where the materials came from. Figure 7-4 shows the journal entry to transfer materials costing £2,000.

Figure 7-4: Transferring materials from Raw Materials inventory into the Cutting department.

Date	Accounts	Debit	Credit
10 Jan., 2013	*WIP – Cutting*	*2,000*	
	Raw materials inventory		*2,000*

WIP – Cutting	
Raw materials inventory 2,000	

Raw materials inventory	
	WIP - Cutting 2,000

Here, the account that represents the cost of WIP in the Cutting department increases by £2,000, while the cost of Raw Materials decreases by £2,000. This transfer moves £2,000 out of Raw Materials and into the Cutting department's WIP.

From here, you continue to record similar journal entries to keep track of inventory as it moves through different departments.

Meeting the two key aspects of process costing

Process costing often involves some waste as part of the process to produce the goods. Process costing looks at waste and calls the expected waste *normal loss*.

Process costing applies to continuous production. At the end of the accounting period some part-finished products will be left. These are called *work-in-progress (WIP) closing inventory*, and become the *opening inventory* in the next accounting period.

Understanding the significance of normal loss is important, because the value of products made is calculated based on the net cost of the inputs. In other words, the cost of all the inputs less the scrap value of the normal loss.

Understanding the significance of WIP is also important; this is valued based on the degree to which each of the inputs have been used to produce the part-finished goods.

Normal loss

Process costing deals with inputs and outputs.

In a clothing factory, cotton cloth is an input and shirts or blouses are an output. The process of cutting is continuous, and includes a certain amount of waste. As the cotton cloth is cut, small off-cuts are lost because not all the cloth is needed for the shirts. The off-cuts are waste.

In fact, a certain amount of waste is expected: this is the *normal loss.* For example, when apple pies are being produced, normal loss exists in the process where the apples are peeled and cored before going into the pastry to make the pies.

Normal loss is typically a proportion of the input material.

Work-in-progress (WIP)

Usually, production is continuous where process costing is used, and so typically part-finished products exist at the end of each accounting period. These products need to be valued. To do so you need to look at each of the inputs separately and identify the extent to which any WIP is complete.

You're accounting for a busy sandwich factory where beef joints are being roasted continually. You find that four beef joints have been cooking for an hour and yet still need more time before they can be sliced ready for the sandwiches. Here, all the beef has been input into the process, but labour time is only 25 per cent complete, because only 25 per cent of the total time is made up of the preparation prior to cooking, whereas 75 per cent takes place after the beef has been cooked when it's sliced ready for the next process.

Demonstrating Process Costing in Action

Following a collection of examples can help you better understand the flow of the process-costing system.

We use the Saxby Soup Factory for this demonstration, in which all material inputs and outputs are measured in tonnes rather than litres. We look at the boiling process that follows the chopping process, which in turn is followed by the packaging process where the soup is put into containers to be dispatched to customers.

Nine examples follow. The first five are progressively more complex as you work through them. The first shows the way to work through the process: what to do first, then the next action, through to producing a completed Process Account. Examples 6 to 9 show the valuation of Work-in-Progress (WIP) in the Process Account and how a Cost of Production Report can be used to calculate the value.

Introducing the Process Account

Examples 1 to 5 in the following sections involve no loss or normal loss (see the earlier section 'Meeting the two key aspects of process costing'). They're examples of the various ways the AAT Cost and Revenues and the ACCA F2 exam typically test process costing when no WIP applies at the beginning or the end of the period.

Example 1 – No loss: Asparagus Soup

Data: The inputs to the Boiling department are 400 tonnes of asparagus at a cost of £180 per tonne, all of which are from the Chopping department (no additional material is added) and 160 labour hours where direct labour costs £12.50 per hour and overhead is absorbed at £5 per direct labour hour (see Figure 7-5). Output for the period is 400 tonnes, with no closing WIP inventory at the end of the accounting period.

You enter the physical inputs and outputs first to identify whether any process losses have been incurred. In this case, there are none: 400 tonnes in = 400 tonnes out.

Figure 7-5: Boiling department Process Account: Asparagus Soup – the physical units.

Inputs	Tonnes		£	Outputs	Tonnes		
Chopping	400			Packaging	400		
Materials	0			Work-in-Progress			
Labour (160 hrs @ £12.50)							
Overhead (160 hrs @ £5)							
Total	400			Total	400		

Next you add the values. The input column is just a case of taking the physical units that go into the boiling process. This is taken from the data paragraph for Example 1 – No loss: Asparagus Soup. The per-unit value of the soup being transferred to packaging is calculated using the following formula:

$$\frac{\text{Total input cost less scrap value of normal loss}}{\text{Total expected output}} = \text{Cost per unit transferred}$$

There is no normal loss (in fact no loss at all) as the expected output is exactly the same as the input (400 tonnes).

Formula using the values for Asparagus Soup:

$$\frac{\text{£74,800 input cost} - \text{£0 scrap value of normal loss}}{\text{400 units of expected output}} = \text{£187.00 per unit}$$

See Figure 7-6.

Figure 7-6: Boiling department Process Account: Asparagus Soup – showing the values.

Inputs	*Tonnes*	*Per unit*	*£*	*Outputs*	*Tonnes*	*Per unit*	*£*
Chopping	*400*	*£180.00*	*72,000*	*Packaging*	*400*	*£187.00*	*74,800*
Materials	*0*		*0*	*Work-in-Progress*			*0*
Labour (160 hrs @ £12.50)			*2,000*	*Normal Loss*			
Overhead (160 hrs @ £5)			*800*				*0*
Total	*400*		*74,800*	*Total*	*400*		*74,800*

Example 2 – Normal loss, no scrap value: Beetroot Soup

Normal loss has to be identified to be able to identify the expected output. Once you know the expected output you can calculate the cost per unit produced.

Data: Here, the inputs to the Boiling department are 400 tonnes at a cost of £182 per tonne from the Chopping department (no additional material is added) and 160 labour hours where direct labour costs £12.50 per hour and overhead is absorbed at £5 per direct labour hour (see Figure 7-7). The normal loss in production is 10 per cent of the input and, because it's due to evaporation, it has no scrap value. Output for the period is 360 tonnes, with no closing WIP inventory at the end of the accounting period.

You enter the physical inputs and outputs first to identify whether any process losses apply. In this example, the number is 40 tonnes: 400 tonnes in = 360 tonnes out. This is exactly the same as the normal loss expectation of 10 per cent of the input material (10 per cent × 400 tonnes = 40 tonnes).

Figure 7-7: Boiling department Process Account: Beetroot Soup – the physical units.

Inputs	*Tonnes*	*Per unit*	*£*	*Outputs*	*Tonnes*	*Per unit*	*£*
Chopping	*400*			*Packaging*	*360*		
Materials	*0*			*Work-in-Progress*			
Labour (160 hrs @ £12.50)				*Normal Loss*	*40*		
Overhead (160 hrs @ £5)							
Total	*400*			*Total*	*400*		

You then add the values. The input column is just a case of taking the physical units that go into the boiling process. This is taken from the data paragraph (for Example 2 – Normal loss, no scrap value: Beetroot Soup). The per-unit value of the soup being transferred to packaging is calculated using the following formula:

Total input cost less scrap value of normal loss / Total expected output	=	Cost per unit transferred

Normal loss is 10 per cent of the input. This means that the expected output is 90 per cent of the input (400 × 90% = 360 tonnes).

Formula using the values for Beetroot Soup:

£75,600 input cost – £0 scrap value of normal loss / 360 units of expected output	=	£210.00 per unit

See Figure 7-8.

Inputs	*Tonnes*	*Per unit*	*£*	*Outputs*	*Tonnes*	*Per unit*	*£*
Chopping	*400*	*£182.00*	*72,800*	*Packaging*	*360*	*£210.00*	*75,600*
Materials	*0*		*0*	*Work-in-Progress*			*0*
Labour (160 hrs @£12.50)			*2,000*	*Normal Loss*	*40*	*0*	*00*
Overhead (160 hrs @£5)			*800*				
Total	*400*		*75,600*	*Total*	*400*		*75,600*

Figure 7-8: Boiling department Process Account: Beetroot Soup – showing the values.

Example 3 – Normal loss with scrap value: Carrot Soup

The cost per unit produced has to be calculated *after* deducting the scrap value of normal loss from the input costs. You divide the net input cost by the expected output to find the cost per unit produced.

Data: Here, the inputs to the Boiling department are 400 tonnes at a cost of £182.20 per tonne from the Chopping department (no additional material is added) and 160 labour hours where direct labour costs £12.50 per hour and overhead is absorbed at £5 per direct labour hour (see Figure 7-9). The normal loss in production is 10 per cent of the input and has a scrap value of £20 per tonne. Output for the period is 360 tonnes, with no closing WIP inventory at the end of the accounting period.

You enter the physical inputs and outputs first to identify whether any process losses apply. Here the amount is 40 tonnes: 400 tonnes in = 360 tonnes out, which is exactly the same as the normal loss expectation of 10 per cent of the input material (10 per cent × 400 tonnes = 40 tonnes).

Figure 7-9: Boiling department Process Account: Carrot Soup – the physical units.

Inputs	Tonnes		£	Outputs	Tonnes		
Chopping	400			Packaging	360		
Materials	0			Work-in-Progress			
Labour (160 hrs @ £12.50)				Normal Loss	40		
Overhead (160 hrs @ £5)							
Total	400			Total	400		

The per-unit value of the soup being transferred to packaging is calculated using the following formula:

Total input cost less scrap value of normal loss / Total expected output	=	Cost per unit transferred

There is 10 per cent normal loss so the expected output is 90 per cent the input (400 tonnes × 90% = 360 tonnes).

Formula using the values for Carrot Soup:

£75,680 input cost – £800 scrap value of normal loss / 360 units of expected output	=	£208.00 per unit

See Figure 7-10.

Figure 7-10: Boiling department Process Account: Carrot Soup – showing the values.

Inputs	Tonnes	Per unit	£	Outputs	Tonnes	Per unit	£
Chopping	400	£182.20	72,880	Packaging	360	£208.00	74,880
Materials	0		0	Work-in-Progress			0
Labour (160 hrs @ £12.50)			2,000	Normal Loss	40	£20.00	800
Overhead (160 hrs @ £5)			800				0
Total	400		75,680	Total	400		75,600

Example 4 – Normal loss with scrap value and an abnormal loss: Duck Soup

Having worked through the first three examples, we now add a discrepancy for you. The sequence is important as the examples become more complex. Completing the physical units before adding the values highlights whether the inputs and outputs agree or not. This is the first example when they do not agree; in this case the total loss (wastage) is more than the normal loss expected.

Here the inputs to the Boiling department are 400 tonnes at a cost of £184 per tonne from the Chopping department (no additional material is added) and 160 labour hours where direct labour costs £12.50 per hour and overhead is absorbed at £5 per direct labour hour (see Figure 7-11). The normal loss in production is 10 per cent of the input and has a scrap value of £20 per tonne. Output for the period is 340 tonnes, with no closing WIP inventory at the end of the accounting period.

You enter the physical inputs and outputs first to identify whether any abnormal process losses or gains apply. Here, that's 60 tonnes of losses: 400 tonnes in less 340 tonnes out, which is 20 tonnes more than the normal loss expectation of 10 per cent of the input material (10 per cent × 400 tonnes = 40 tonnes). Therefore, the abnormal loss is 20 tonnes.

Figure 7-11: Boiling department Process Account: Duck Soup – the physical units.

Inputs	*Tonnes*		*£*	*Outputs*	*Tonnes*		
Chopping	*400*			*Packaging*	*340*		
Materials	*0*			*Work-in-Progress*			
Labour (160 hrs @£12.50)				*Normal Loss*	*40*		
Overhead (160 hrs @£5)				*Sub total*	*380*		
Total	*400*			*Total*			

Note that the two columns in Figure 7-11 don't agree. Having more inputs than outputs means that the wastage rate is higher than the expected 10 per cent. The loss over and above the normal loss (the abnormal loss of 20 tonnes) is valued at the same cost as the output transferred to the packaging department. Ultimately, this abnormal loss is added to the normal loss to increase the scrap sales. The difference in value is charged (debited) to the costing income statement, reducing the profit.

The per-unit value of the soup being transferred to packaging is calculated using the following formula (see Figure 7-12):

$$\frac{\text{Total input cost less scrap value of normal loss}}{\text{Total expected output}} = \text{Cost per unit transferred}$$

There's 10 per cent normal loss, so the expected output is 90 per cent the input (400 tonnes × 90% = 360 tonnes).

Formula using the values for Duck Soup:

$$\frac{\text{£76,400 input cost} - \text{£800 scrap value of normal loss}}{\text{360 units of expected output}} = \text{£210.00 per unit}$$

Inputs	Tonnes	Per Unit	£	Outputs	Tonnes	Per unit	£
Chopping	400	£184.00	73,600	Packaging	340	£210.00	71,400
Materials	0		0	Work-in-Progress			0
Labour (160 hrs @£12.50)			2,000	Normal Loss	40	£20.00	800
				Sub total	380		
Overhead (160 hrs @£5)			800	Abnormal Loss	20	£210.00	4,200
Total	400		76,400	Total	400		76,400

Figure 7-12: Boiling department: Process Account: Duck Soup – showing the values.

Example 5 – Normal loss with scrap value and an abnormal gain: Egg Soup

This Egg Soup example demonstrates the same technique as Example 4 (Duck Soup). This time, the physical unit inputs add up to a lower total than the outputs. This has been caused by the process not having as much wastage as expected. The difference between the actual wastage and normal loss in this case is called *abnormal gain.*

Here the inputs to the Boiling department are 400 tonnes at a cost of £184 per tonne from the Chopping department (no additional material is added) and 160 labour hours where direct labour costs £12.50 per hour and overhead is absorbed at £5 per direct labour hour (see Figure 7-13). The normal loss in production is 10 per cent of the input and has a scrap value of £20 per tonne. Output for the period is 380 tonnes, with no closing WIP inventory at the end of the accounting period.

You enter the physical inputs and outputs first to identify whether any abnormal process losses or gains apply. Here, the amount is 20 tonnes: 400 tonnes in but 380 tonnes out, which is less loss than the normal loss expectation of 10 per cent of the input material (10 per cent × 400 tonnes = 40 tonnes). The result is an abnormal gain of 20 tonnes.

Inputs	Tonnes		£	Outputs	Tonnes		
Chopping	400			Packaging	380		
Materials	0			Work-in-Progress			
Labour (160 hrs @ £12.50)				Normal Loss	40		
Overhead (160 hrs @ £5)							
Sub total	400			Sub total	420		
Total				Total			

Figure 7-13: Boiling department Process Account: Egg Soup – the physical units.

The two columns in Figure 7-13 don't agree. Having more outputs than inputs means that the wastage rate is lower than the expected 10 per cent. The loss is less than the normal loss (the abnormal gain of 20 tonnes) and is valued at the same cost as the output transferred to the packaging department. Ultimately, this abnormal gain is deducted from the normal loss to decrease the scrap sales. The difference in value is credited to the costing income statement, increasing the profit.

The per-unit value of the soup being transferred to packaging is calculated using the following formula (see Figure 7-14):

$$\frac{\text{Total input cost less scrap value of normal loss}}{\text{Total expected output}} = \text{Cost per unit transferred}$$

There's 10 per cent normal loss so the expected output is 90 per cent the input (400 tonnes × 90% = 360 tonnes).

Formula using the values for Egg Soup:

$$\frac{\text{£76,400 input cost} - \text{£800 scrap value of normal loss}}{\text{360 units of expected output}} = \text{£210.00 per unit}$$

Inputs	Tonnes	Per Unit	£	Outputs	Tonnes	Per Unit	£
Chopping	400	£184.00	73,600	Packaging	380	£210.00	79,800
Materials	0		0	Work-in-Progress			0
Labour (160 hrs @ £12.50)			2,000	Normal Loss	40	£20.00	800
Overhead (160 hrs @ £5)			800				
Sub total	400			Sub total	420		
Abnormal loss	20	£210.00	4,200				
Total	420		80,600	Total	420		80,600

Figure 7-14: Boiling department Process Account: Egg Soup – showing the values.

Valuing the WIP: The Cost of Production Report as a workings table

The five examples in the preceding section involve calculating the cost per unit that will be transferred to the next process. These look at varying degrees of normal loss, ranging from no loss to losses that are more or less than expected. The next four examples require a Cost of Production Report.

The following examples have no losses. Instead you use the Cost of Production Report to calculate the cost per unit of completed production and to value the closing WIP inventory. (For explanations of valuing WIP, flip to the earlier section 'Meeting the two key aspects of process costing'). Work-in-progress in process costing is highly likely; some people might even say inevitable. Continuous production means that some inputs are continually being added and outputs are rolling off the production line all the time. So it's likely that at any given point in time there will be part-finished products. At the end of an accounting period this is called the *closing WIP inventory.*

Work-in-progress means products where the work has started but is part-finished. As a result, the costs incurred during the accounting period are sufficient to complete both the products that have now been transferred to the next process, and the products that are part-finished and need further work to be completed. In the calculation of the cost per unit of finished products, management accountants first convert the number of units of closing WIP to the equivalent number of finished products, and then add these to the completed units before dividing the total into the costs.

Examples 6 to 9 demonstrate how this process is done, because most WIP is incomplete in different proportions from one input to another. The roast beef example from the earlier section 'Meeting the two key aspects of process costing' is typical. The beef has been prepared, and so material inputs are 100 per cent but the labour time is only 25 per cent complete.

To help with the calculations you use a *Cost of Production Report* (see Figure 7-15). Just as you have to complete Process Accounts (check out the earlier section 'Introducing the Process Account') in a specific order, the same applies to Cost of Production Reports.

In this section, we use the following abbreviations:

- **C WIP** means closing work-in-progress
- **EU** means equivalent units
- **CPU** means cost per unit

	Total	Previous Period	Additional Materials	Direct Labour	Overhead
Cost					
Units					
Completed					
C WiP					
Total EU					
CPU					
Evaluation					
Completed					
C WiP					
Total					

Figure 7-15: Format of the Cost of Production Report.

Example 6 – Closing WIP with all inputs equally part-used: Fish Soup

Most firms using process costing have several processes: for example, in the soup business, chopping ingredients followed by boiling and then packaging. This example assumes that we're looking at the first process; in other words, there hasn't been a process before it. This is to enable all the inputs in the WIP to be at the same stage of completion.

Here the inputs are additional material with a total value of £69,920 and 182.4 labour hours, where direct labour costs £12.50 per hour (total £2,280), and overhead is absorbed at £6.25 per direct labour hour (total £1,140), with no losses in production. Output for the period is 360 tonnes, with 40 tonnes of closing WIP. The WIP is 50 per cent complete in terms of the material input, labour time and overhead.

You enter the data as follows:

1. **Cost:** On an input by input basis, and then add up to find the total.
2. **Units (Completed):** On the 'Completed' row, write the number of units that will be transferred to the next process (or to finished goods where no more processes are needed). In the fish soup example, 360 tonnes of processed fish are transferred to the next process. We entered 360 in each column because every tonne is 100 per cent complete, such as 100 per cent of the material needed to make 360 tonnes of process fish, 100 per cent of the labour needed and 100 per cent of the overhead needed: 100 per cent of 360 is 360.
3. **Units (WIP):** C WIP (closing work-in-progress) as completed, but find the equivalent units produced: for example, in additional materials 40 units × 50 per cent complete = 20.
4. **Total EU:** Add up each input column. This gives the equivalent number of units (EU) produced. For example, the material input has enabled 360 completed units to be made and the equivalent of 20 more units that are still WIP. So, as far as material is concerned, there's 380 EU of production (the total column doesn't serve a purpose at this stage).
5. **Cost per unit (CPU):** Divide the cost per input by the total equivalent units, then add them up to find a total cost per unit.
6. **Evaluation:** Multiply the cost per unit of each input by the number of units completed and then do the same for the equivalent units of closing WIP.
7. **Total:** Add across to find the totals, and add down to find the totals; the bottom row should agree with the top row for cost.

The sequence is very important, and so we lay out the order of filling in the worksheet (see Figure 7-16) before showing a completed one (in Figure 7-17). Each step number corresponds with the section on the report where that number is shown.

Because you've completed the Cost of Production Report, the entries into the Process Account become a copying exercise (see Figure 7-18).

	Total	Previous Process	Additional Materials	Direct Labour	Overhead
Cost			1	1	1
Units					
Completed			2	2	2
C WiP			3	3	3
Total EU			4	4	4
CPU	Total (5)		5	5	5
Evaluation					
Completed	7		6	6	6
C WiP	7		6	6	6
Total			7	7	7

Figure 7-16: Cost of Production Report showing the 7 steps in the appropriate sections.

	Total	Previous Process	Additional Materials	Direct Labour	Overhead
Cost	£73,340		£69,920	£2,280	£1,140
Units					
Completed			360	360	360
C WiP	40		20	20	20
Total EU			380	380	380
CPU	£193		£184	£6	£3
Evaluation					
Completed	£69,480		£66,240	£2,160	£1,080
C WiP	£3,860		£3,680	£120	£60
Total	**£73,340**		**£69,920**	**£2,280**	**£1,140**

Figure 7-17: Cost of Production Report for Fish Soup.

Inputs	*Tonnes*	*Per unit*	*£*	*Outputs*	*Tonnes*	*Per unit*	*£*
Chopping	*0*			*Packaging*	*360*	*£193.00*	*69,480*
Materials			*69,920*	*Work-in-Progress*	*40*		*3,860*
Labour (182.4 hrs @ £12.50)			*2,280*	*Normal Loss*	*0*		
Overhead (182.4 hrs @ £6.25)			*1,140*				
Total			*73,340*	*Total*			*73,340*

Figure 7-18: Boiling department Process Account: Fish Soup.

Example 7 – Closing Work-in-Progress with inputs part-used in different proportions: Gazpacho Soup

Here, the inputs are from the chopping process, with a total value of £72,000 and 207.2 labour hours, where direct labour costs £12.50 per hour (total £2,590), and overhead is absorbed at £6.25 per direct labour hour (total £1,295), with no losses in production (see Figures 7-19 and 7-20). Output for the period is 360 tonnes, with 40 tonnes closing WIP at the end of the accounting period. The WIP is 100 per cent complete in terms of the material input, and 25 per cent complete in terms of labour time and overhead.

	Total	Previous Process	Additional Materials	Direct Labour	Overhead
Cost	£75,885	£72,000		£2,590	£1,295
Units					
Completed		360		360	360
C WiP	40	40		10	10
Total EU		400		370	370
CPU	£190.50	£180.00		£7.00	£3.50
Evaluation					
Completed	£68,580	£64,800		£2,520	£1,260
C WiP	£7,305	£7,200		£70	£35
Total	£75,885	£72,000		£2,590	£1,295

Figure 7-19: Cost of Production Report for Gazpacho Soup.

Inputs	*Tonnes*	*Per unit*	*£*	*Outputs*	*Tonnes*	*Per unit*	*£*
Chopping			*72,000*	*Packaging*	*360*	*£190.50*	*68,580*
Materials	*0*			*Work-in-Progress*	*40*		*7,305*
Labour (207.2 hrs @ £12.50)			*2,590*	*Normal Loss*	*0*		
Overhead (207.24 hrs @ £6.25)			*1,295*				
Total			*75,885*	*Total*			*75,885*

Figure 7-20: Boiling department Process Account: Gazpacho Soup.

Both the AAT Cost and Revenues and ACCA F2 exams test equivalent units in examples with no losses. Typically, the questions are along the lines of this Gazpacho Soup example. Sometimes they ask for only one input cost per unit of output.

Example 8 – Closing WIP to find labour cost per unit of output: Hare Soup

This example assumes that this is the second process, the boiling. (The chopping is the first process.)

Here, only the direct labour costs are of interest: £67,200 is incurred, with no losses in production (see Figure 7-21). Output for the period is 5,200 tonnes, with 2,000 tonnes of closing WIP at the end of the accounting period. The WIP is 100 per cent complete in terms of the material input, and 40 per cent complete in terms of labour time and overhead.

Your task is to find the direct labour cost per tonne of hare soup transferred to packaging.

	Direct Labour
Cost	£67,200
Units	
Completed	5,200
C WiP	800
Total EU	6,000
CPU	£11.20

Figure 7-21: Cost of Production Report for Hare Soup (Direct Labour section).

Example 9 – Opening WIP with inputs part used in different proportions: Italian Soup

This example assumes that this is the second process, the boiling. The first process is chopping and has been done. We start the period with opening WIP from the previous period, and this amount is added to find the total cost (called the *average cost inventory valuation* method). Only CIMA C01, P1 and P2 test this method in process costing questions. No closing WIP is involved.

The opening WIP is valued as £7,200 direct materials, £70 direct labour and £35 overhead (see Figures 7-22 and 7-23). The inputs are from the chopping process (value of £72,000) and 196 labour hours, where direct labour costs £12.50 per hour (total £2,450), and overhead is absorbed at £6.25 per direct labour hour (total £1,225), with no losses in production. Output for the period is 360 tonnes, with no WIP at the end of the accounting period.

The costs incurred producing the 360 tonnes of Italian Soup are the opening WIP value plus the costs incurred during the period. You add them together and divide by the completed soup to find the cost per unit.

	Total	Previous Process	Additional Materials	Direct Labour	Overhead
Cost					
Opening WiP	£7,305	£7,200		£70	£35
Period cost	£75,675	£72,000		£2,450	£1,225
	£82,980	£79,200		£2,520	£1,260
Units					
Completed		360		360	360
C Wip					
Total EU		360		360	360
CPU	£230.50	£220.00		£7.00	£3.50
Evaluation					
Completed	£82,980	£79,200		£2,520	£1,260
C Wip					
Total	£82,980	£79,200		£2,520	£1,260

Figure 7-22: Cost of Production Report for Italian Soup.

Inputs	*Tonnes*	*Per Unit*	*£*	*Outputs*	*Tonnes*	*Per unit*	*£*
Opening WiP			*7,305*				
Chopping			*72,000*	*Packaging*	*360*	*£230.50*	*82,980*
Materials	*0*			*Work-in-Progress*	*0*		
Labour (196 hrs @ £12.50)			*2,450*	*Normal Loss*	*0*		
Overhead (196 hrs @ £6.25)			*1,226*				
Total			*82,980*	*Total*			*82,980*

Figure 7-23: Boiling Department Process Account – Italian Soup.

In the AAT Cost and Revenue and ACCA F2 exams, the questions either test cost per equivalent unit with opening WIP or with closing WIP, but not both.

Chapter 8

Observing How Variable and Fixed Costs Behave

In This Chapter

- Looking at fixed and variable costs in terms of cost drivers
- Breaking down semi-variable costs
- Predicting costs within your relevant range

Training your dog involves teaching him to react to different stimuli. When you say 'sit!', he sits on his hind legs. When you hold your hand up in the air, he tries to stand. When you whisper 'quiet', he stops barking. That's the plan, anyway. Unfortunately, dogs have trouble learning certain things. No matter how hard you try to train him, he continues to sit and watch you eat, waiting for delicious human food to fall on the floor.

Like pet dogs, costs react to some stimuli but not to others. For example, manufacturing twice as many goods is likely to double your material costs, but no matter how many goods your factory produces, rent remains the same. In this chapter, we explain how to tell the difference between variable costs, which change in response to the number of goods you make, and fixed costs, which aren't affected in the same way. These distinctions help you predict how costs react to different stimuli within your business. We also discuss semi-variable costs, which contain components from both groups, and the importance of keeping your predictions within your cost relevant ranges.

Investigating Cost Behaviour

Businesses incur all sorts of different costs, but for accounting purposes they're split into one of two groups:

- **Variable business costs:** These change in response to certain stimuli. For example, the total quantity of material used to make cakes will increase as the number of cakes made increases, and the postage costs of products sold on eBay increases as the number of units of a product are sold.
- **Fixed business costs:** These don't change directly as production changes. Examples include factory insurance, which is typically based on the value of the equipment, or the road tax cost of sales representatives' cars, which is based on the emissions of the car. Neither cost changes as the number of units produced increases or the number of units sold increases.

Determining whether a cost is variable or fixed requires considering the behaviour of the cost. The following sections explain the nature of variable and fixed costs, and the importance of understanding how certain factors drive variable costs.

Understanding that how much you produce and/or sell affects variable costs

Variable costs change in response to certain stimuli, called *cost drivers.* Get it? Cost drivers drive up the cost. Two key drivers exist: units produced and units sold.

In this chapter, we focus on number of units produced as a cost driver. In businesses where sales staff receive a commission based on the units sold, or where goods have to be posted to customers, the number of units sold (rather than produced) determines the total sales commission or the total postage.

Illustrating total variable costs

You can graphically represent costs by charting total variable cost (on the left axis) against the cost driver (on the bottom axis). In Figure 8-1, you can see how producing 100 caps drives total variable costs of £200.

A change in a cost driver always results in a corresponding change to the total variable cost. For example, increasing the cost driver by 50 per cent causes total variable costs to increase by 50 per cent.

As regards manufacturing your caps: increasing the number of caps produced by 50 per cent (to 150; 100 + [0.5 × 100]) costs 50 per cent more, or £300 (£200 + [0.5 × £200]).

Figure 8-2 shows how a 50 per cent increase in the number of caps made affects total variable costs. Producing 50 more units (a 50 per cent increase) causes total variable costs to increase by £100 (a 50 per cent rise in total variable costs).

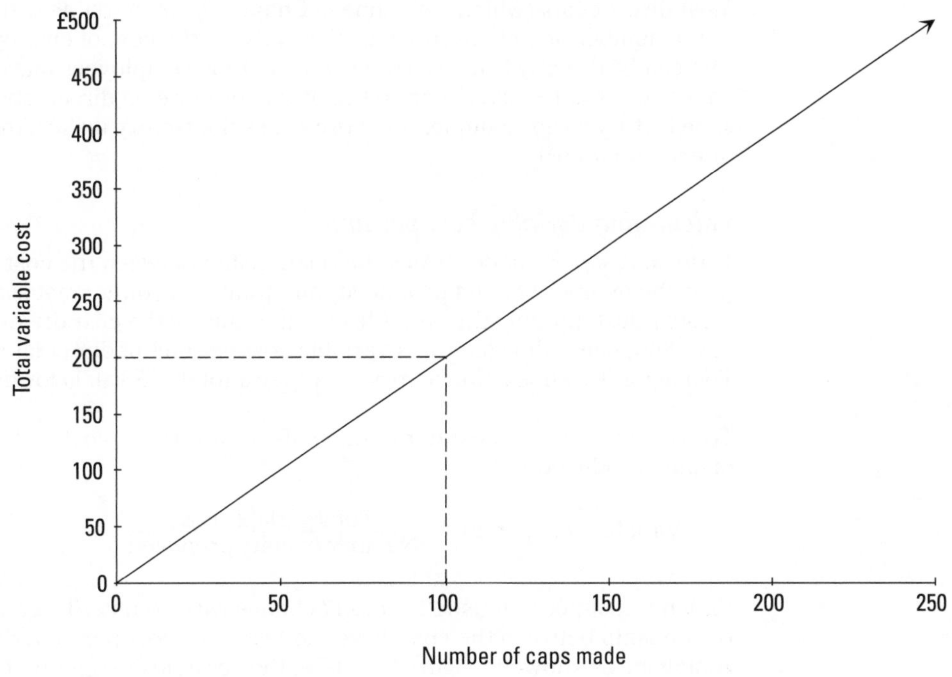

Figure 8-1: Graphing total variable costs.

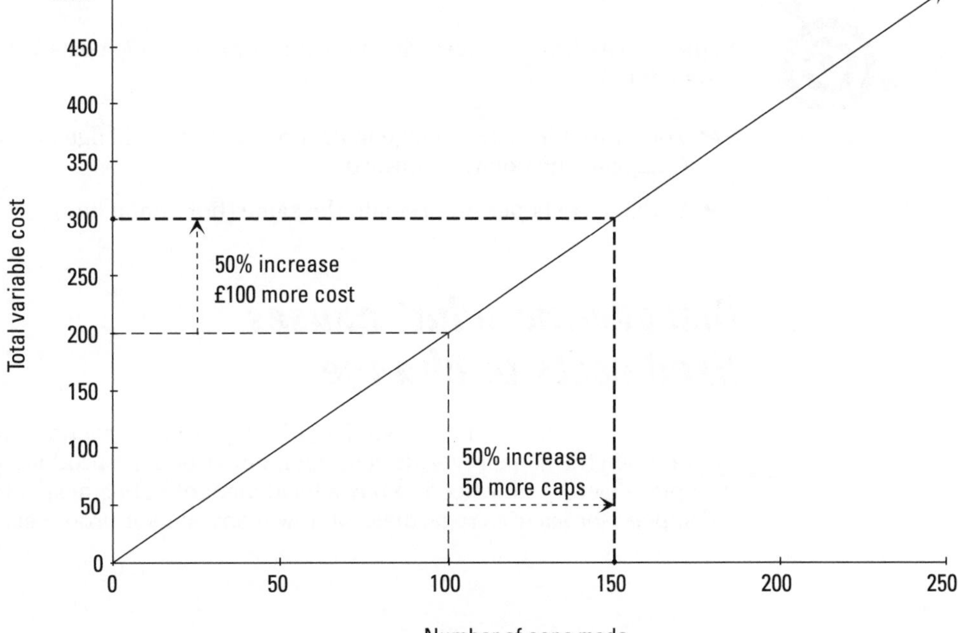

Figure 8-2: Effect on total variable costs of increasing the cost driver by 50 per cent.

Most direct costs (which we define in Chapter 1) are variable with respect to the number of units produced. *Direct labour* (the cost of employee wages that can be directly traced to the products those employees make) is another common variable cost. (Head to Chapter 3 for more on direct labour.) Take a shoe factory as an example: the more shoes the factory makes, the higher the direct labour cost.

Calculating variable cost per unit

Variable cost per unit describes the relationship between the cost driver (say, the number of units produced) and total cost (direct materials or direct labour). Just multiply the variable cost per unit by the cost driver to get total cost. Suppose a shoe factory's variable cost per unit of direct labour is £30. To make 1,000 shoes, the factory must pay a total of £30,000 for direct labour.

To compute variable cost per unit, divide total variable cost by the number of units produced:

$$\text{Variable cost per unit} = \frac{\text{Total variable cost}}{\text{Number of units produced}}$$

Variable cost per unit usually *doesn't* change with volume. To graph the relationship between the cost driver and variable cost per unit, draw a horizontal line as shown in Figure 8-3. Here, the variable cost per unit of direct materials needed to make baseball caps is £2 per unit. Even when the company ratchets up production from 100 caps to 150, the variable cost per unit remains steady at £2.

As the activity level changes, don't confuse total variable costs with variable costs per unit:

- Total variable costs change in proportion to the change in activity level (diagonal line pointing upward).
- Variable costs per unit remain the same (horizontal line).

Discovering what causes fixed costs to change

Unlike total variable costs (the subject of the preceding section), total fixed costs remain the same regardless of the number of units produced. For example, a factory may need to pay a fixed amount of business rates, rent and supervisor salaries regardless of how many units it produces.

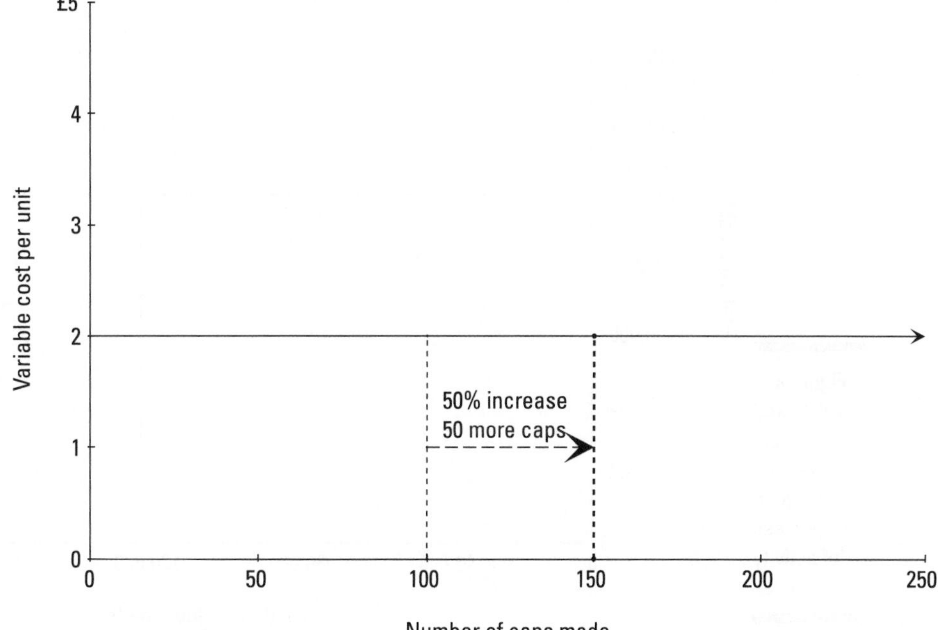

Figure 8-3: Even when volume increases, variable cost per unit remains the same.

You don't connect any cost driver with fixed costs because changes to these costs aren't the result of changes to the units produced. Fixed costs do change of course, all costs do, but they change for other reasons: business rate changes are government decisions, rent changes are landlord decisions, and so on. Some fixed cost changes are outside the management's control, others are discretionary costs. Examples of the latter may be management deciding on training costs or how much to spend on product development, and these costs don't change when the number of units produced changes.

When you graph costs on activity level, you sketch fixed costs as a straight horizontal line as shown in Figure 8-4. Here you can see an entertainment company that produces and sells music videos online. No matter what the activity level – 80,000 or 120,000 downloads – the company must still pay the same amount for salaries and utilities: £100,000.

On the other hand, fixed cost per unit does decrease with volume produced. The more units you make, the lower the fixed cost per unit. Figure 8-5 illustrates this relationship. If your music video download company sells only 20,000 downloads, the fixed costs of one download equal £5 (£100,000 total fixed cost ÷ 20,000 units). However, if the company sells 200,000 units, the fixed cost per unit drops to £0.50 (£100,000 total fixed cost ÷ 200,000 units). If the company sells only one download, the fixed costs for that one download equal £100,000!

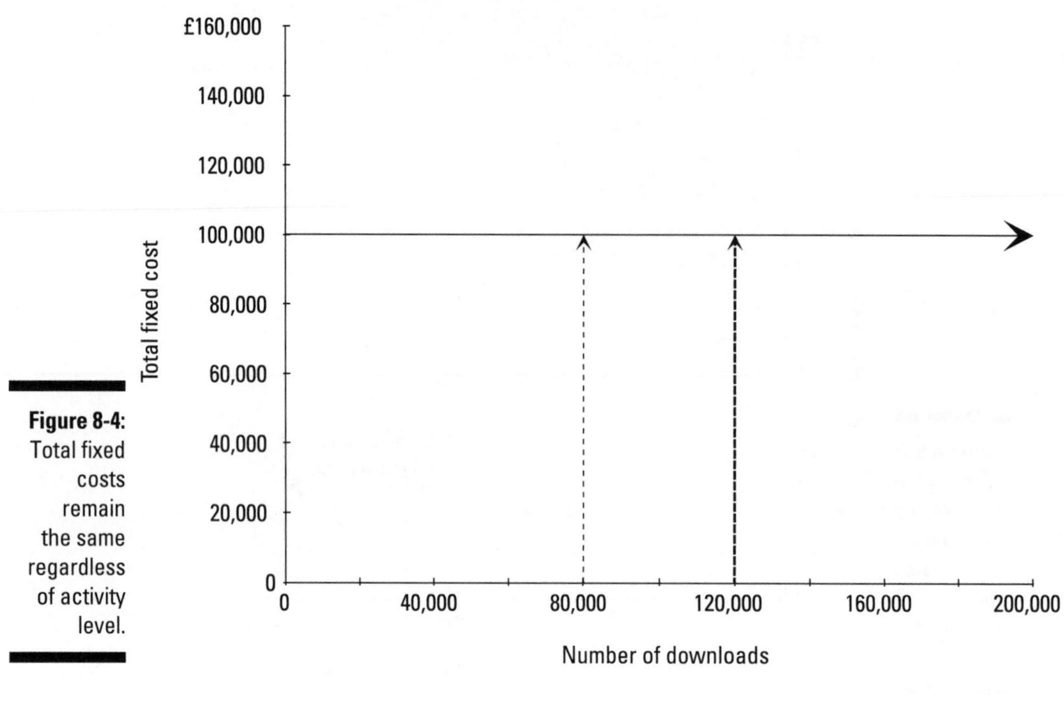

Figure 8-4: Total fixed costs remain the same regardless of activity level.

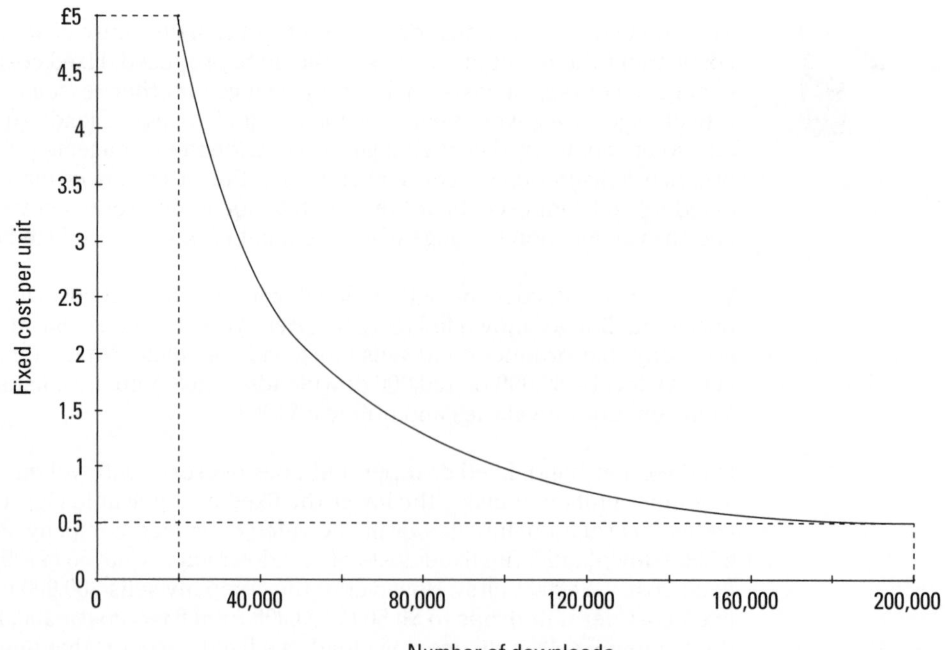

Figure 8-5: Fixed cost per unit decreases with volume.

The more units that are produced, the lower the fixed cost per unit; in effect, the fixed costs are spread more thinly across production. Think of it working in the same way as a sachet of butter being spread more thinly the more pieces of toast it needs to cover!

High fixed costs require significant activity to produce sales to offset those costs. In other words, if your company has to pay £100,000 in fixed costs, it needs to sell enough products to cover this cost.

Separating Semi-variable Costs into Variable and Fixed Components

Factories and other companies have to pay costs that include variable and fixed components, challenging accountants to figure out how much is variable and how much is fixed. These *semi-variable costs* typically change with the level of activity, but not proportionately. Therefore, in order to predict cost behaviour, you need to split semi-variable costs into variable and fixed components with one of four techniques:

- Employing the high–low method
- Analysing accounts
- Using a scattergraph
- Fitting a regression

The following sections break down these techniques, using the example of the fictional Xeon Company, which incurred £120,000 in costs to produce 1,200 units. Notice that even though the data used for each method is the same, each method yields a different answer. Because these methods are designed to estimate and predict future costs, their results typically vary.

When estimating fixed and variable costs with any method, try the eyeball test: that is, glance over your numbers to make sure that they make sense. Does your regression indicate that variable costs come out as negative (for example, the greater the volume, the lower the cost)? If so, your numbers fail the eyeball test. Check everything and try again. Does your high–low test indicate that variable costs come to £0.00000000001 per unit? That's probably not accurate. Try again.

Employing the high–low method

The high–low method tends to be the most time-effective one and is preferred in exams. This approach estimates variable and fixed costs based on the highest and lowest levels of activity during the period. Just follow three steps:

1. **Determine the high and low activity levels based on a table of total costs and activity levels.**

   Look at the production level and total costs to identify the high and low activity levels. Table 8-1 indicates that Xeon Company's highest production level occurred in May, when the company produced 1,300 units at a total cost of £126,000. The lowest production level occurred in January, when the company produced just 800 units costing £93,000.

Table 8-1 Production Level and Total Cost by Time Period

Month	*Production*	*Total Cost (£)*
January	800	93,000
February	1,100	114,000
March	1,200	119,000
April	950	103,000
May	1,300	126,000
June	1,250	124,000
July	1,000	107,000
August	1,050	110,000
September	1,000	105,000
October	900	100,000
November	1,050	110,000
December	1,200	119,500

2. **Use the high and low activity levels to determine the variable cost per unit.**

   To figure out the variable cost per unit, divide the difference between the two total cost values by the difference in the number of units produced. The result is an extra £33,000 to produce the extra 500 units. This gives us a variable cost per unit of £66.

$$\text{Variable cost per unit} = \frac{\text{Total cost}_{\text{high activity}} - \text{Total cost}_{\text{low activity}}}{\text{Units produced}_{\text{high activity}} - \text{Units produced}_{\text{low activity}}}$$

$$= \frac{£126{,}000 - £93{,}000}{1{,}300 - 800} = \frac{£33{,}000}{500} = £66$$

3. **Determine the total fixed cost.**

To compute the total fixed cost, pick the high or the low cost information (either one works); for this example, we pick the high production level – making 1,300 units for £126,000. Plug this information, along with the variable cost per unit from Step 2, into the total cost formula:

$$\text{Total cost} = (\text{Variable cost per unit} \times \text{Units produced}) + \text{Total fixed cost}$$
$$£126{,}000 = (£66 \times 1{,}300) + \text{Total fixed cost}$$
$$£126{,}000 = £85{,}800 + \text{Total fixed cost}$$
$$£40{,}200 = \text{Total fixed cost}$$

Based on your answer, you can determine that making 1,000 units would mean total variable costs of £66,000 (1,000 units × £66 per unit). Total fixed costs equal £40,200. Therefore, total costs would equal £106,200:

$$\text{Total cost} = (\text{Variable cost per unit} \times \text{Units produced}) + \text{Total fixed cost}$$
$$\text{Total cost} = (£66 \times 1{,}000 \text{ units}) + £40{,}200 = £106{,}200$$

The high–low method focuses only on two points: the highest and lowest activity levels. When using this method, don't get confused by activity levels between these two points, even if their costs are out of the bounds of the costs of the highest and lowest activity levels.

Analysing accounts

Call this technique the common sense method. It requires four steps:

1. **Split the total costs into individual types of expenditure.**

   When checking out the trial balance for Xeon Company, you notice the breakdown of costs specified in Table 8-2.

Table 8-2 Xeon Company's Product Costs

Account	*Total (£)*
Direct materials	20,000
Direct labour	45,000
Depreciation	5,000
Fixed utilities	6,000
Variable utilities	5,000
Supervisor salaries	25,000
Other variable overhead	14,000
Total	**120,000**

2. **Use common sense and your knowledge of operations to identify the variable and fixed elements.**

   Go to the earlier section 'Investigating Cost Behaviour' for details on distinguishing variable and fixed costs. As we note there, variable costs change with the cost driver, but fixed costs don't. Table 8-3 shows the categorised Xeon Company costs.

Table 8-3 Classifying Fixed and Variable Costs

Account	*Total (£)*	*Variable or Fixed?*
Direct materials	20,000	Variable
Direct labour	45,000	Variable
Depreciation	5,000	Fixed
Fixed utilities	6,000	Fixed
Variable utilities	5,000	Variable
Supervisor salaries	25,000	Fixed
Other variable overhead	14,000	Variable
Total	**120,000**	

If appropriate, you can classify some accounts as semi-variable and then assign percentages of each that are variable and fixed. For example, an account may be 50 per cent variable and 50 per cent fixed.

3. **Lay out the account to show variable costs and fixed costs separately and add them up.**

   According to the classifications that you set up in Step 2, fully separate and add up the variable and fixed costs as shown in Table 8-4.

Table 8-4 Xeon Company's Fixed and Variable Costs

Account	Total (£)	Fixed Costs	Variable Costs
Direct materials	20,000		20,000
Direct labour	45,000		45,000
Depreciation	5,000	5,000	
Fixed utilities	6,000	6,000	
Variable utilities	5,000		5,000
Supervisor salaries	25,000	25,000	
Other variable overhead	14,000		14,000
Total	**120,000**	**36,000**	**84,000**

4. **Compute variable cost per unit by dividing total variable costs by the number of units produced.**

   $$\text{Variable cost per unit} = \frac{\text{Total variable cost}}{\text{Number of units produced}}$$

   $$\text{Variable cost per unit} = \frac{\pounds 84{,}000}{1{,}200 \text{ units}} = \pounds 70 \text{ per unit}$$

   You can read more about variable cost per unit in the earlier section 'Calculating variable cost per unit'.

After completing the four steps for the Xeon Company example, you know that total fixed costs come to £36,000 (from Table 8-4), and variable costs amount to £70 per unit (from Step 4). Figuring out the total variable costs and adding in fixed costs allows you to predict total cost for another volume of output:

$$\text{Total cost} = (\text{Variable cost per unit} \times \text{Units produced}) + \text{Total fixed cost}$$

Using this formula allows you to determine that making 1,000 units would cost £70,000 (1,000 units × £70 per unit). Total fixed costs always equal £36,000; therefore, total costs equal £106,000:

$$\text{Total cost} = (\text{Variable cost per unit} \times \text{Units produced}) + \text{Total fixed cost}$$

$$\text{Total cost} = (\pounds 70 \times 1{,}000 \text{ units}) + \pounds 36{,}000 = \pounds 106{,}000$$

Figure 8-6 shows how to graph this information. Note that although the total fixed cost line is horizontal, the slope of the total cost line equals variable cost per unit. The graph shows that when producing no units (a situation known as *zero production*), the company incurs only total fixed costs.

Using a scattergraph

A *scattergraph* helps you to visualise the relationship between activity level and total cost. To scattergraph, just follow these three steps (with explanations for creating the scattergraph in Microsoft Excel):

1. **Set up a table that shows production level and total cost by time period.**

   To prepare a scattergraph, you need basic data about the number of units produced and the total costs per time period. Arrange this data by month, week or some other time period, as the earlier Table 8-1 demonstrates.

2. **Create a graph with the number of units produced on the bottom axis (*x*-axis) and total cost on the left axis (*y*-axis), as shown in Figure 8-7.**

   The total cost on the *y*-axis includes fixed and variable costs.

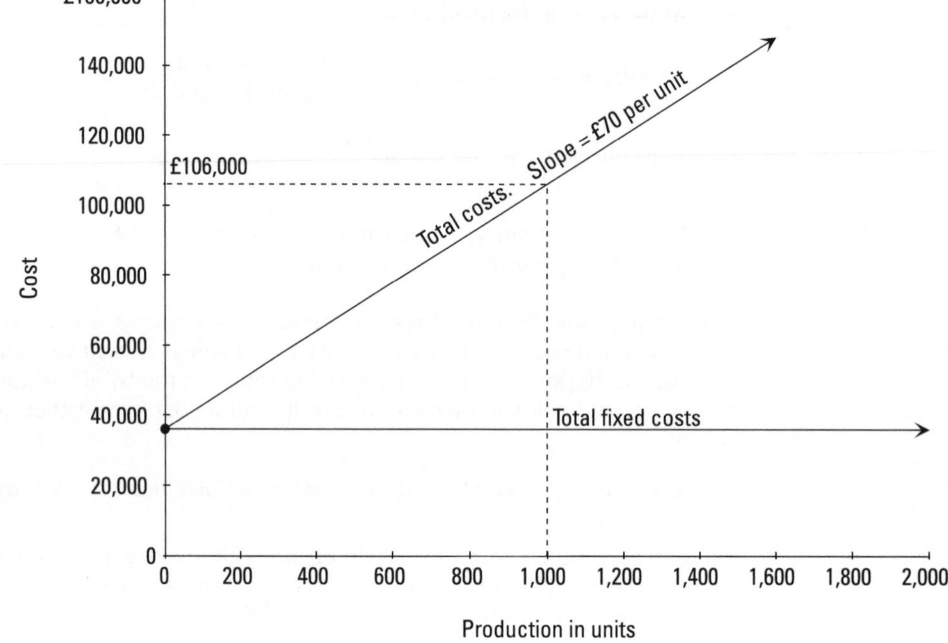

Figure 8-6: How total fixed costs and variable cost per unit interact.

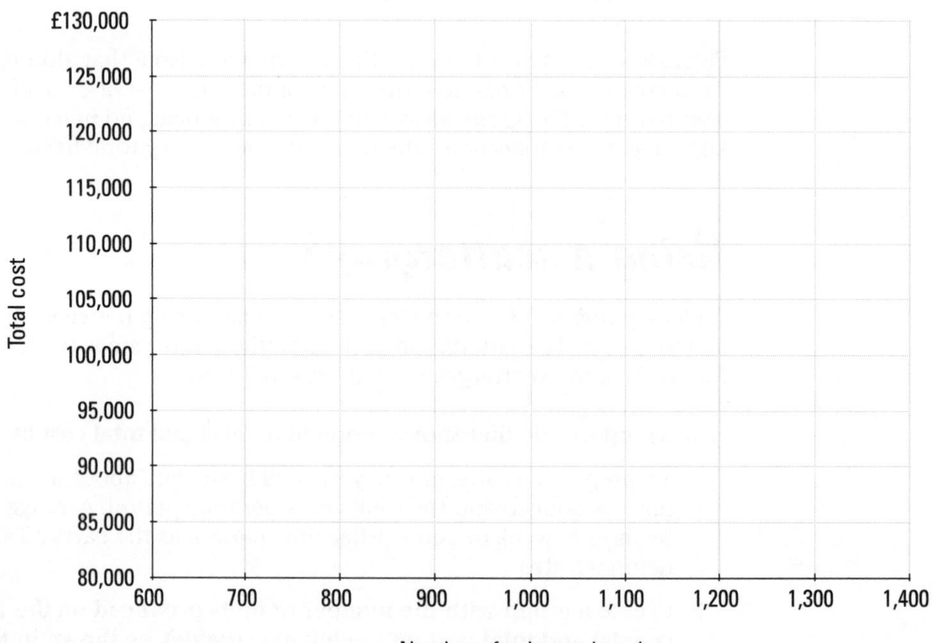

Figure 8-7: Basic graph of total cost per number of units produced.

3. **Plot each data point from the table on this graph.**

   You can do so manually by using graph paper or electronically by using Excel's Chart Wizard:

   A. Enter the data from Step 1 and Table 8-1 into the Excel spreadsheet.

   B. Select only the two columns of data (Production and Total Cost).

   C. Click Scatter in the Insert menu and then Scatter with only Markers.

   A scattergraph appears. Figure 8-8 shows the resulting scattergraph for Xeon Company.

4. **Label the axes appropriately.**

   And you're done!

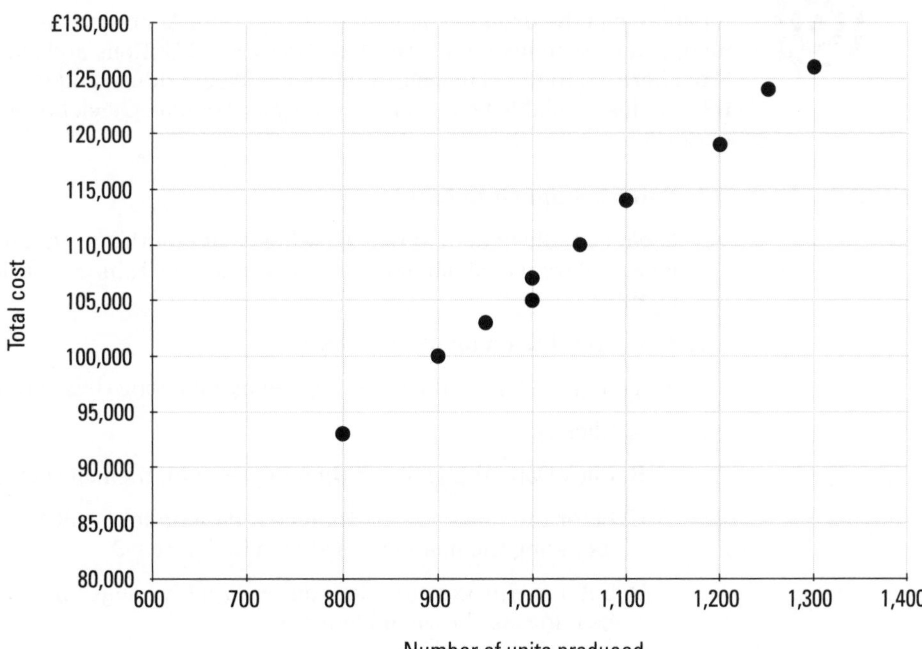

Figure 8-8: Scattergraph of total cost per number of units produced.

If you're trying to predict total costs for a future month, select the anticipated activity level for that month along the *x*-axis. Then use data points from previous months to estimate the total cost.

Fitting a regression

Linear regression allows you to apply basic statistical techniques to estimate cost behaviour. *Regression* means a relationship between two sets of data; *linear* means that the relationship can be drawn as a straight line on a graph. When we looked at Table 8-1 we used the information to identify the variable cost per unit and the fixed cost for the Xeon Company. Once we had these, we could estimate the cost for any level of production. We found that 1,000 units would cost a total of £106,200. We could have found any number of units: they all lie on a line. This is the linear regression line. Don't panic about complex statistical computations! Excel (or a statistical analysis package) can quickly figure out this information for you; the following sections show you how. Also, some scientific calculators have a useful linear regression function.

Before starting, make sure that you've installed the Microsoft Office Excel Analysis ToolPak. To confirm whether you already have it, click Data and look for an item in the dropdown menu that says Data Analysis. If you don't see this item, you need to install the ToolPak. Go to Excel Options and click Add-Ins. From here, go to the Manage box and click Excel Add-ins and then Go. From the Add-Ins Available box, click the Analysis ToolPak check box and then click OK.

1. **Enter the data into Excel.**

   Create a table of data in Excel, listing each month's production activity level and total cost, similar to what appears in Table 8-1 earlier in the chapter.

2. **Run a regression analysis in Excel.**

   Run a regression on the data in Excel by following these steps:

   A. Click Data.

   B. Click Data Analysis and then Regression; then click OK.

   C. Enter the range for the total cost data under Input Y Range, including the heading, as shown in Figure 8-9.

   D. Enter the production data under Input X Range, including the heading, as shown in Figure 8-9.

   E. Click the box for Labels.

   F. Select an output range on your spreadsheet.

   G. Click OK.

When regressing total cost on a cost driver, the total cost data always goes into the Input Y Range and the cost driver data always goes into the Input X Range.

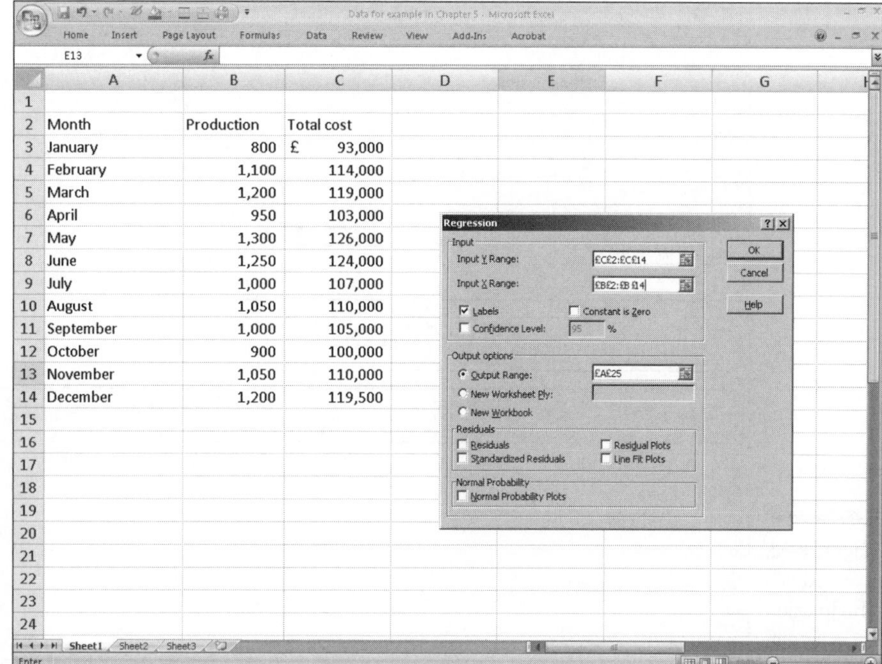

Month	Production	Total cost
January	800	£ 93,000
February	1,100	114,000
March	1,200	119,000
April	950	103,000
May	1,300	126,000
June	1,250	124,000
July	1,000	107,000
August	1,050	110,000
September	1,000	105,000
October	900	100,000
November	1,050	110,000
December	1,200	119,500

Figure 8-9: Input into Excel's Regression menu.

From all the information shown in the output (see Figure 8-10), you really only need two numbers. In the bottom table, look at the column marked Coefficients. The number labelled Intercept (£39,739) is a formula-based estimate of the fixed cost. Look back at the high–low method following Table 8-1. Under high–low we only used the highest and lowest values, and calculated the fixed cost as £40,200. The *Intercept* means the same thing but has used all the values rather than just the ones at the lowest and highest ends of the range.

The number labelled Production (£66.69) gives you a formula-based estimate of the variable cost per unit. This is slightly higher than the high–low variable cost value, because the analysis included every combination of production and total cost (as shown in Table 8-1). Is this a more accurate method of estimating the total fixed cost and the variable cost per unit? Theoretically, yes it is. But the truth of any analytical technique accuracy has to be based on how closely it predicts actual outcomes. Linear regression is less likely to be affected by rogue values than the high–low method as it uses all combinations. If the range of values is fairly narrow this isn't likely to be a problem, and often a sharp eyed management accountant will spot a rogue combination and move onto another pair of values. We hope that no major investment decisions would change if the variable cost is £0.69 higher than £66 and fixed costs are lower by £461 compared to £40,200.

SUMMARY OUTPUT

Regression Statistics	
Multiple R	0.997717425
R Square	0.995440061
Adjusted R Square	0.994984067
Standard Error	708.8961728
Observations	12

ANOVA

	df	SS	MS	F	Significance F
Regression	1	1097037162	1097037162	2183.011765	4.86097E-13
Residual	10	5025337.838	502533.7838		
Total	11	1102062500			

	Coefficients	Standard Error	t Stat	P-value	Lower 95%	Upper 95%	Lower 95.0%	Upper 95.0%
Intercept	39739.86486	1536.187321	25.86915302	1.71298E-10	36317.02623	43162.7035	36317.02623	43162.7035
Production	66.68918919	1.427339877	46.72271144	4.86097E-13	63.50887777	69.86950061	63.50887777	69.86950061

Figure 8-10: Excel's Regression output.

Don't fall into the trap of feeling that the more complicated sums give more useful answers. Good management accountants apply a lot of common sense and think about the ultimate decision-making that follows from the analysis rather than focusing on the analysis for its own sake.

Based on these regression results, you can determine that making 1,000 units would create total variable costs of \$66,690 (1,000 units × \$66.69 per unit). Total fixed costs would equal \$39,739, and so total costs would be \$106,429.

$$\text{Total cost} = (\text{Variable cost per unit} \times \text{Units produced}) + \text{Total fixed cost}$$

$$\text{Total cost} = (\$66{,}690 \times 1{,}000 \text{ units}) + \$39{,}739 = \$106{,}429$$

Checking the accuracy of your estimates

Statistical regression analysis provides useful information to judge the reliability of your estimates. An Adjusted R-square close to 1 (the one in Figure 8-10 is approximately 0.99498) indicates that the model fits the data. Low P-values of the coefficients (here, 1.713×10^{-10} and 4.861×10^{-13}) indicate that the model has high statistical significance. In other words, this model looks pretty accurate.

Sticking to the Relevant Range

When predicting costs, take care to stay within the *relevant range* of cost activity, within which you can expect to make reasonably accurate predictions and estimates based on experience. Outside the relevant range, such as when a factory exceeds its normal capacity or undergoes a shutdown period, the normal patterns of behaviour change. Production may go so high that you have to pay workers overtime (thereby increasing direct labour rates and variable costs) or add a shift (increasing fixed overhead costs), subjects we describe earlier in 'Understanding that how much you produce and/or sell affects variable costs' and 'Discovering what causes fixed costs to change', respectively. Similarly, as production levels fall, your factory may begin to release workers and turn off the heating or air conditioning.

Outside the relevant range, the normal cost patterns change.

As a result, you can only make cost predictions within a certain range of activity. Similarly, bulk discounts may be lost below a critical level causing variable cost per unit to increase (see the earlier section 'Calculating variable cost per unit'). Consider Figure 8-11, which shows how wildly costs and production can change outside the relevant range.

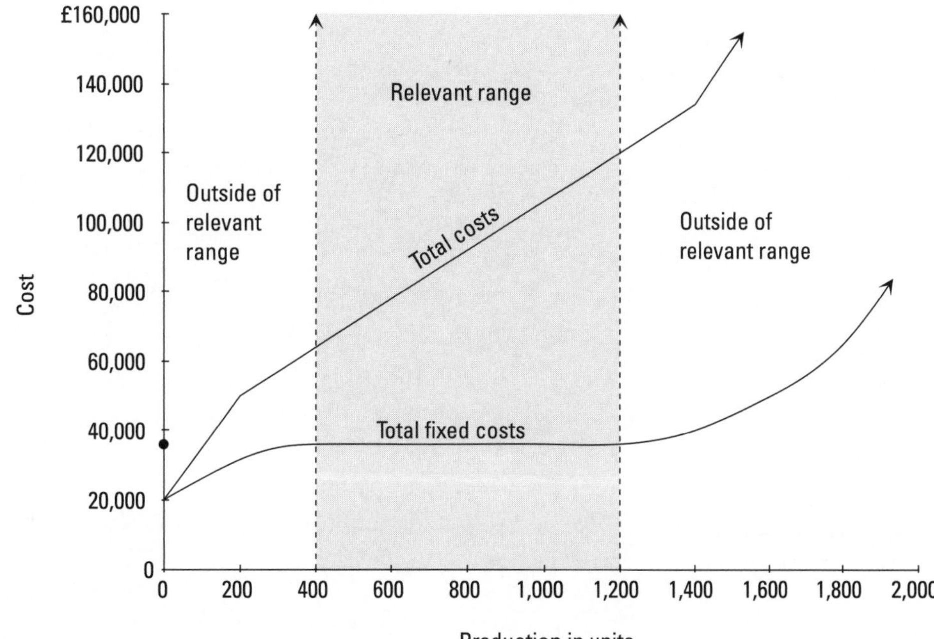

Figure 8-11: What happens outside the bounds of the relevant range.

Part III

Planning and Budgeting

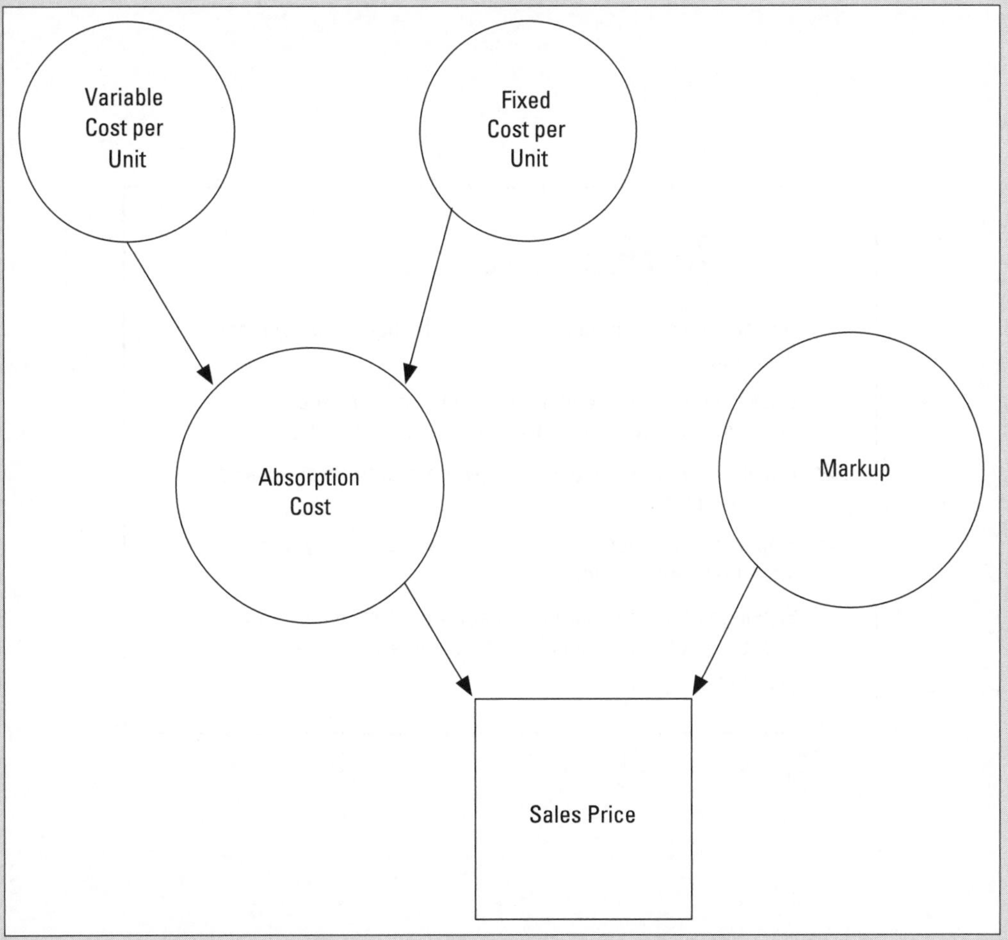

Variable Cost per Unit

Fixed Cost per Unit

Absorption Cost

Markup

Sales Price

Go to www.dummies.com/extras/managementcostaccountinguk for free online bonus content created especially for this book.

In this part . . .

- Use costing techniques (from Part II) to make management decisions.
- Understand contribution margin and how it provides key insights into how specific transactions affect sales.
- Decide whether to invest in long-term assets, using time value of money techniques.
- Employ contribution margin techniques for when you make more than one product.
- Explore setting prices and transfer pricing techniques that encourage different divisions of a company to work together.

Chapter 9

Using Contribution Analysis to Make Better Decisions

In This Chapter

- Introducing contribution
- Using cost-volume-profit analysis to assist decisions
- Analysing your break-even point and target profit
- Calculating the margin of safety
- Exploring operational gearing

Decisions, decisions, decisions – business is full of them: for example, what to sell, in what quantities and at what selling price. Formulas can be invaluable in helping you to make good business decisions. One extremely useful equation that assists with these three particular questions is *contribution*, which measures how a firm's sales affect its net profits.

In this chapter, we show you how to calculate contribution, and how to apply it to different business decisions using graphs and formulas. We describe how to prepare something called a *cost-volume-profit analysis*, which explains how the number of products sold affects profits. We also demonstrate how to prepare a *break-even analysis*, which indicates exactly how many products you need to sell in order to break even and the volume needed to start earning a profit.

In addition, if you set a *target profit* (a goal for this period), we show you how to estimate the number of units you need to sell in order to meet that figure. We also explain how to measure the *margin of safety*, which is how many sales you can afford to lose before your profitability drops to zero, and how to use *operational gearing*, which measures your company's riskiness.

Calculating the Contribution

Consider the following exchange, which occurred in a pub after several pints:

> 'I've got a million-pound idea. Everybody wants a Rolls-Royce, but no one wants to pay for a Rolls-Royce, right?'
>
> 'Yep. They're far too expensive.'
>
> 'Okay, here's my idea: I'm going to sell Rolls-Royces but at a price that people can afford: just £999.95.'
>
> 'But making a Rolls-Royce costs a lot of money. How will you ever earn a profit?'
>
> 'Who cares? At these prices, I can sell so many cars; I'll make it up in volume.'

Surely something's wrong with this logic! The point is that when you have to make a business decision about what to sell, how much of it to sell or how much to charge, you need to understand how your decision is going to affect net profit. For example, if you do sell one Rolls-Royce for £999.95, you need to know how that sale affects your net profit. And if you sell 1,000 Rolls-Royce cars at that price, how does that sales volume affect net profit?

Contribution analysis simplifies these decisions.

Contribution measures how sales affect profits. To compute contribution, you subtract the variable costs of a sale from the value of the sale itself:

Contribution = Sales – Variable costs

For example, if you sell a gadget for £10 and its variable cost is £6, the contribution for the sale is £4 (£10 – £6 = £4) per unit. Selling this gadget increases your profit by £4.

When calculating the contribution, subtract all *variable* costs: the variable manufacturing costs and the variable selling, general and administrative costs. Don't subtract any fixed costs. As we explain in Chapter 2, you compute gross profit by subtracting cost of goods sold from sales. Because cost of goods sold usually includes a mixture of fixed and variable costs, gross profit doesn't have to equal contribution.

You can calculate contribution in three forms, as we discuss in the following three sections:

- **In total:** Check out the next section, 'Looking at the big picture: Total contribution'.
- **Per unit:** Flip to 'Narrowing your focus: Contribution per unit', later in this chapter.
- **As a ratio:** See the later section 'Considering contribution as a proportion of sales: C/S ratio'.

Contribution, in any of its forms, explains how different factors in the company – sales price, sales volume, variable costs and fixed costs –interact. This understanding helps you to make better decisions when planning sales and costs.

This aspect is vital for business and extremely important for all management accounting students. On AAT Cost and Revenue exams, this is task 7, typically the worst-answered task. On AAT Financial Performance exams, this underlies task 8, and those exams where target costing is 9 and the written task 10. It's also required understanding for all the P exams on CIMA and F5 and P5 for ACCA. No pressure then!

Looking at the big picture: Total contribution

Total contribution measures the amount of contribution earned by the company as a whole. You calculate it by using this formula:

Total sales revenue – Total variable costs = Total contribution

To determine overall profitability, find the total contribution and deduct the fixed costs. Net profit equals total contribution minus fixed costs.

You can use total contribution to create something called a *Marginal Costing income statement*, which first subtracts the variable costs and then subtracts fixed costs (see Figure 9-1). Variable costs include variable costs of both production and sales. Likewise, fixed costs include production and selling costs. In this context variable cost and marginal cost mean exactly the same thing.

As a comparison, this document differs from a traditional income statement (produced using absorption costing principles) (as shown in Figure 9-2), where you first subtract Cost of Goods Sold from sales to find Gross Profit and then subtract selling, general and administrative costs. Chapter 4 looks in more detail at absorption costing.

Sales	£1,000
Less: Variable costs	400
Contribution	600
Less: Fixed costs	300
Operating profit	300
Less: Provision for income taxes	100
Net profit	£200

Figure 9-1: Marginal Costing income statement.

Sales	£1,000
Less: Cost of goods sold	600
Gross profit	400
Less: Selling, general and administrative expenses	100
Operating profit	300
Less: Provision for income taxes	100
Net profit	£200

Figure 9-2: Traditional income statement.

The Marginal Costing income statement makes understanding cost behaviour and how sales affect profitability easier. In Figure 9-1, the company generated £1,000 in sales, £400 of which went towards variable costs. This scenario results in £600 of contribution.

These amounts – sales, variable costs and contribution – change in proportion to each other. If sales volume increases by 10 per cent, sales revenue, variable costs and contribution all increase by 10 per cent: £1,100 in sales would increase variable costs to £440 and contribution to £660. On the other hand, fixed costs always remain the same: total fixed costs are £300 regardless of any increase or decrease in sales and contribution.

The Marginal Costing income statement presents the same net profit figure as a traditional income statement, but isn't acceptable for external reporting, where accounting standards lay down the formats that may be used. Managers can use a Marginal Costing income statement internally, however, to better understand their own company's operations.

Narrowing your focus: Contribution per unit

Contribution per unit measures how the sale of one additional unit affects net profit. You calculate it by subtracting variable costs per unit from sales price per unit, as follows:

Selling price – Variable cost per unit = Contribution per unit

Say a company sells a single gadget for £100, and the variable cost of making the gadget is £40. Contribution per unit on this gadget equals £60 (£100 – £40 = £60); therefore, selling the gadget increases net profit by £60.

Increasing the sales price doesn't affect variable costs because the number of units manufactured, not the sales price, is what usually drives variable manufacturing costs. Therefore, if the gadget company raises its sales price to £105, the variable cost of making the gadget remains at £40, and the contribution per unit increases to £65 per unit (£105 – £40 = £65). The £5 increase in sales price goes straight to the bottom line as net profit.

Considering contribution as a proportion of sales: C/S ratio

The term *contribution/sales ratio* (C/S ratio) measures the percentage of sales that would increase net profit. To calculate it, you divide contribution by sales, either in total or per unit:

$$\frac{\text{Total contribution}}{\text{Total sales revenue}} = \text{C/S ratio}$$

or

$$\frac{\text{Contribution per unit}}{\text{Price per unit}} = \text{C/S ratio}$$

Suppose that a gadget selling for £100 per unit brings in £40 per unit of contribution. Its C/S ratio is 40 per cent:

$$\text{C/S ratio} = \frac{40}{100} = 40\%$$

To find out how sales affect net profit, multiply the C/S ratio by the value of sales. In this example, £1,000 in gadget sales increases net profit by £400 (£1,000 × 40 per cent = £400).

The C/S ratio is the same amount whether you use the per unit approach or a total approach, provided that the business has only one product (see Table 9-1).

Table 9-1 Link between the Contribution per Unit and Total Contribution for a Single-P wroduct Business

	Per Unit		*Volume (Number of Units Sold)*		*Total*
Revenue	Price	×	Sales volume	=	Sales Revenue
Variable cost	(Variable cost per unit)	×	Sales volume	=	(Total variable cost)
Contribution	Contribution per unit	×	Sales volume	=	Total contribution
C/S Ratio	Contribution per unit ÷ Price			=	Total contribution ÷ Sales Revenue

Meeting Net Profit Targets with Cost-Volume-Profit Analysis

As we describe in the earlier section 'Calculating the Contribution', contribution indicates how sales affect profitability. When running a business, a decision-maker needs to consider how four different factors affect net profit:

- Sales price
- Sales volume
- Variable cost per unit
- Fixed cost

Cost-volume-profit analysis helps you understand different ways to meet your net profit targets. In this section, we explain cost-volume-profit analysis by using graphical and formula techniques. We pay special attention to computing net profit based on different measures of contribution: total contribution, contribution per unit and the C/S ratio (check out earlier sections 'Looking at the big picture: Total contribution', 'Narrowing your focus: Contribution per unit' and 'Considering contribution as a proportion of sales: C/S ratio', respectively).

In some AAT exams from the period 2005–2010, the C/S ratio is called the profit/volume (PV) ratio. They mean exactly the same thing. Please don't let this discourage you from using old questions for practice; doing so is an excellent way to check that you understand what you've learned. In this section, we look at a graph showing the effect on profit of a change in volume (see later Figure 9-8) and this is called a PV graph.

The graphs that accompany the text that follows (break-even, contribution and PV) provide a helpful way to visualise the relationship among cost, volume and profit. When solving questions about the volume of production and sales, whether at work or in an exam, you'll find that plugging numbers into formulas is much quicker and easier.

Drafting a cost-volume-profit graph

Bosham Basketballs sells basketballs for £15 each. The variable cost per unit of the basketballs is £6. Bosham had total fixed costs of £300 per year.

Figure 9-3 demonstrates how you can describe the relationship visually among cost, volume and profit:

- **Total fixed costs** are represented by a horizontal line, because total fixed costs don't change, whatever the sales volume.
- **Total variable costs** are represented by a diagonal line, starting at the origin (the point in the lower-left corner of the graph where zero sales apply).
- **Total costs** (the sum of total variable costs and total fixed costs) are represented by a diagonal line starting at the £300 mark, because when the company makes and sells zero units, total costs equal the fixed costs of £300. Total costs then increase with volume.
- **Total sales** are represented by a diagonal line starting at the origin and increasing with sales volume.

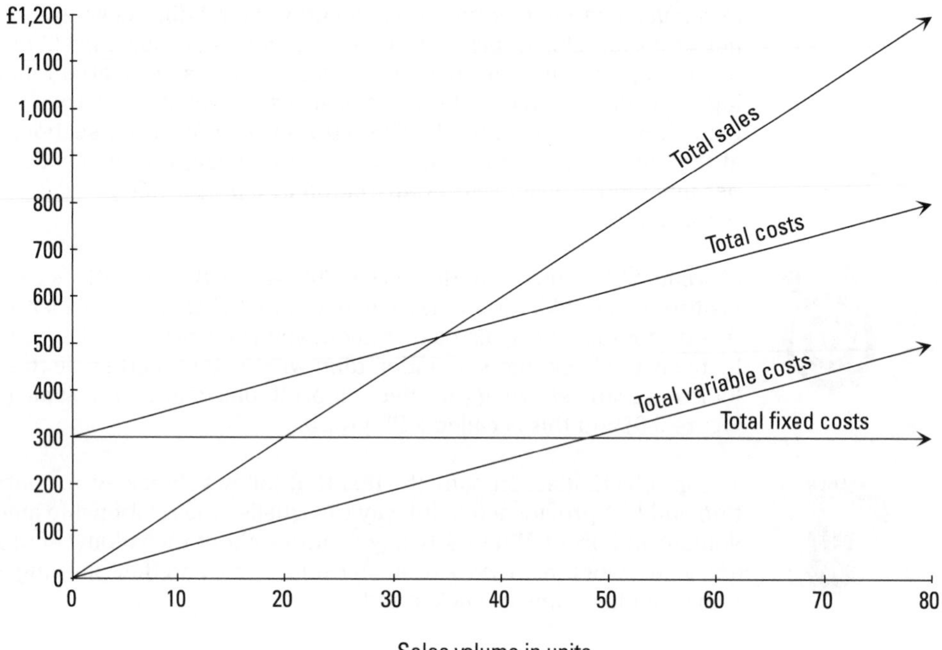

Figure 9-3: Cost-volume-profit graph for Bosham Basketballs.

Figure 9-4 shows when the company will earn a profit or incur a loss. When the sales curve exceeds total costs, the company earns a profit (represented by the shaded right side of the 'X' in Figure 9-4). However, when the total sales value is too low to exceed total costs, the company incurs a loss (the shaded left side of the 'X'). The higher the sales volume – that is, the more sales volume moves to the right of the graph – the higher the company's profit.

Dropping numbers into the chart shows exactly how much income can be earned at different sales levels. Assuming that Bosham has a sales price of £15 per unit, variable cost per unit of £6 and total fixed costs of £300, what happens if Bosham sells 60 basketballs? Total sales come to £900 (60 units × £15). Total variable costs multiply to £360 (60 units × £6). Add these total variable costs to total fixed costs of £300 to get total costs of £660.

Figure 9-5 illustrates these amounts. Total sales (£900) sit on the total sales line and total costs (£660) sit on the total cost line. The difference between these amounts (£240) represents the profit from selling 60 units.

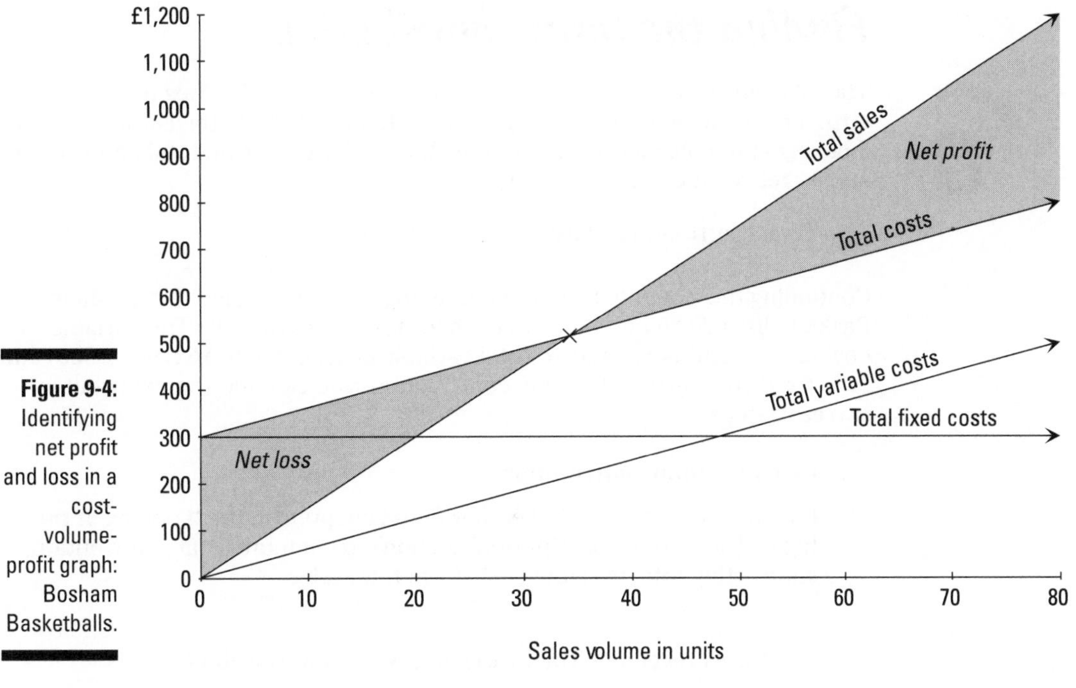

Figure 9-4: Identifying net profit and loss in a cost-volume-profit graph: Bosham Basketballs.

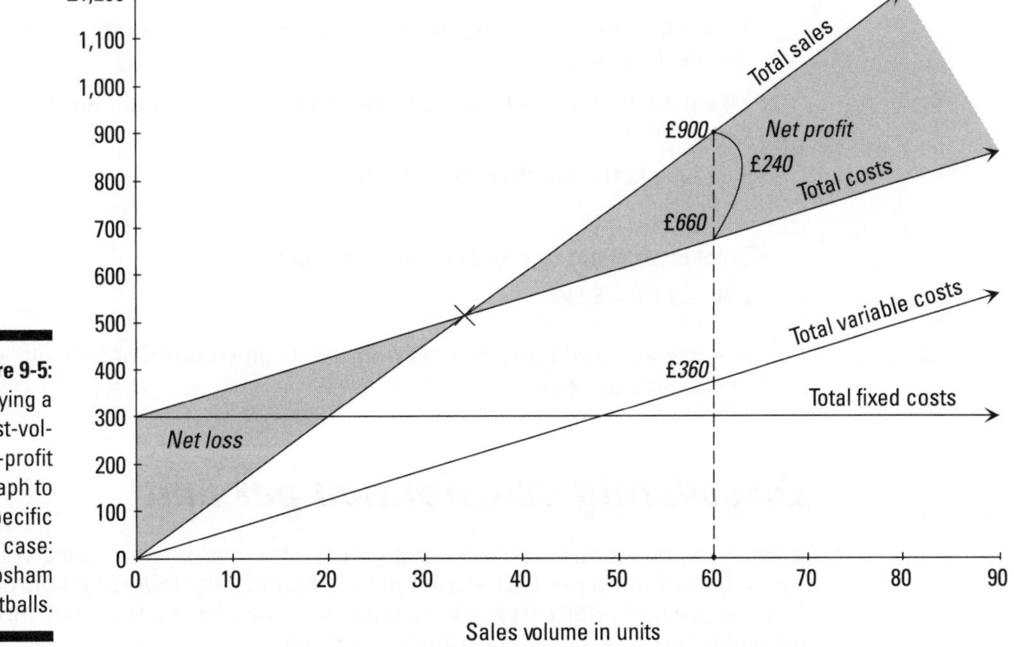

Figure 9-5: Applying a cost-volume-profit graph to a specific case: Bosham Basketballs.

Finding the total contribution

The following formula, based on total contribution margin, uses the same structure as the Marginal Costing income statement (go to the earlier section 'Looking at the big picture: Total contribution' for details on total contribution and its related income statement):

$$\text{Total contribution} - \text{Fixed costs} = \text{Net profit}$$

Continuing the example from the preceding section, assume that Bosham Basketballs sells 60 units for £15 each for total sales of £900. The variable cost of each unit is £6 (and so total variable costs come to £6 × 60 = £360) and total fixed costs are £300. Using contribution, you can find the net profit in two easy steps:

1. **Calculate total contribution.**

   Use the formula provided earlier in the chapter (in the 'Looking at the big picture: Total contribution' section) to compute total contribution, subtracting total variable costs from total sales:

   $$\text{Total sales revenue} - \text{Total variable cost} = \text{total contribution}$$
   $$(60 \times £15) - (60 \times £6) = £540$$

   This total contribution figure indicates that selling 60 units increases net income by £540.

2. **To calculate net profit, subtract the fixed costs from the total contribution.**

   Just plug in the numbers from Step 1:

   $$\text{Total contribution} - \text{Fixed costs} = \text{Net profit}$$
   $$£540 - £300 = £240$$

   Subtracting fixed costs of £300 from total contribution of £540 gives you net income of £240.

Discovering contribution per unit

If you know the contribution per unit (which we cover in 'Narrowing your focus: Contribution per unit' earlier in the chapter), the following approach lets you use that information to calculate net profit. Here's the basic formula for finding net profit with contribution per unit:

$$(\text{Sales volume} \times \text{Contribution per unit}) - \text{Fixed costs} = \text{Net profit}$$

Say Bosham Basketballs (from the example in the earlier section 'Drafting a cost-volume-profit graph') wants to use this formula. It can simply plug in the numbers – 60 units sold for £15 each, variable cost of £6 per unit, fixed costs of £300 – and solve. First find the contribution per unit:

$$\text{Selling price} - \text{Variable cost per unit} = \text{Contribution per unit}$$
$$£15 - £6 = £9$$

Next, plug the contribution per unit into the above formula to calculate the net profit.

$$(\text{Sales volume} \times \text{Contribution per unit}) - \text{Fixed costs} = \text{Net Profit}$$
$$(60 \times £9) - 300 = £240$$

Using the C/S ratio

If you want to estimate profit but don't know the total contribution and can't find out the contribution per unit, you can use the C/S ratio to compute net profit.

As we note in the earlier section 'Considering contribution as a proportion of sales: C/S ratio', you can calculate the C/S ratio by dividing total contribution by total sales. So if your contribution is £540 and your sales £900, your contribution margin ratio is 60 per cent:

$$\frac{\text{Total contribution}}{\text{Total sales revenue}} = \frac{\text{Contribution per unit}}{\text{Price per unit}} = \text{C/S ratio}$$
$$= \frac{540}{900} = 60\%$$

Therefore, 60 pence of every sales pound directly increases profit. After you know the C/S ratio, you're ready for the net profit formula:

$$(\text{Sales revenue} \times \text{C/S ratio}) - \text{Fixed costs} = \text{Net profit}$$

To calculate net profit for the earlier Bosham Basketballs example, you enter the C/S ratio of 60 per cent into the formula:

$$(\text{Sales revenue} \times \text{C/S ratio}) - \text{Fixed costs} = \text{Net Profit}$$
$$(£900 \times 60\%) - 300 = £240$$

Multi-product businesses

Most companies have several products. For example, restaurants, pubs and chemists can't determine a meaningful break-even point in the number of units they sell. A restaurant may break even when 500 steak and chips dinners are sold, but it sells a lot more. In these situations, you can't produce a useful break-even volume, but the break-even sales revenue is very useful. People commonly say: 'How much must have gone through the till to break even?' In other words, at what level of sales have we covered the total fixed cost?

For example, assume that a restaurant has a menu where the contribution/sales margin is 60 per cent. The weekly fixed costs are £1,200 and the break-even sales revenue needed is £2,000 (irrespective of the sales mix). As soon as weekly sales go over £2,000, the restaurant makes a profit. It makes 60 per cent of every sale over £2,000.

The C/S ratio basis for calculating the break-even sales revenue has a wider use in real businesses than the sales volume-based approach to breaking even.

Bringing up Break-Even Analysis

A fundamental question facing all retailers is: 'how much do we need to sell in order to break even?' The *break-even point* (BE) is the amount of sales needed to earn a zero profit – enough sales so that you don't incur a loss, but insufficient sales to earn a profit. In this section, we look at a couple of different ways – graphs and formulas – to help you analyse where your break-even point falls.

Drawing a graph to find the break-even point

In a cost-volume-profit graph, the break-even point is the sales volume where the total sales line intersects with the total cost line. This sales volume is the point at which total sales equals total costs.

Suppose that, as with the basketball example earlier in this chapter (in 'Drafting a cost-volume-profit graph'), a company sells its products for £15 each, with variable costs of £6 per unit and total fixed costs of £300. The graph in Figure 9-6 indicates that the company's break-even point occurs when the company sells 34 units. You identify this point by looking at the x-axis below the point where the total cost and total revenue lines cross. You can also see the break-even sales revenue by looking at the y-axis level with the same point: £510 of sales is needed to break even.

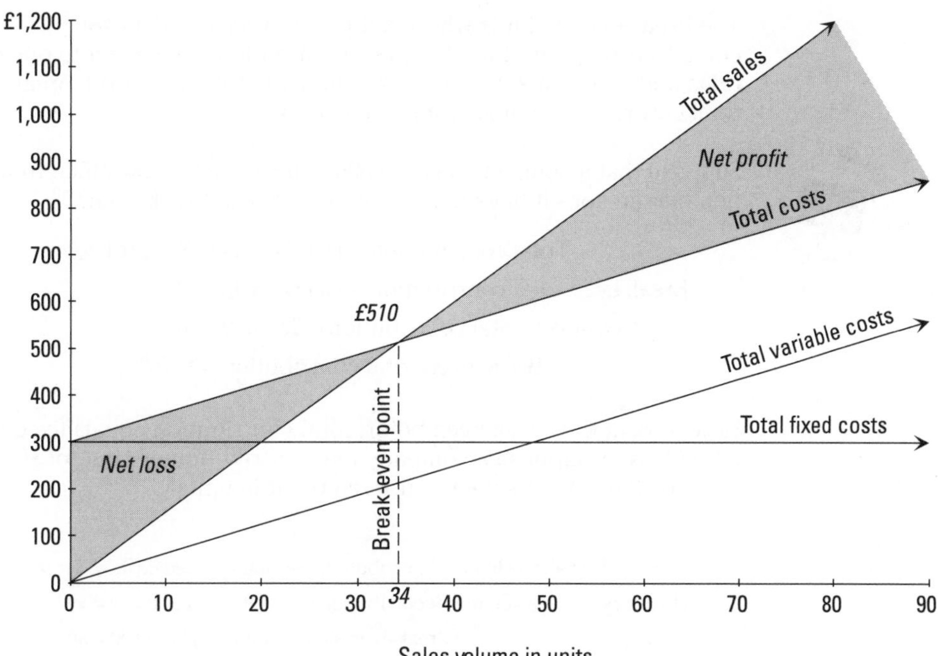

Figure 9-6: Graphing the break-even point.

For many products (such as basketballs) you can only sell whole units. Therefore, if you sell whole units, the break-even point must always be a whole number. This fact means that if break-even analysis results in some fractional volume of sales (such as 33.33333 units), you always need to round *up* (in this case, to 34 units), even if the fraction is closer to the lower whole number than the higher number. Even if your break-even point equals 33.0001, round it up to 34. If you round down (to 33 units), the actual sales volume would be below the break-even point, and at this volume level, your company reports a net loss.

Employing the formula approach

When you need to solve actual problems, drawing graphs isn't always practical. In that case, you want to rely on the three formulas that use contribution to find net profit (explained in 'Meeting Net Profit Targets with Cost-Volume-Profit Analysis' earlier in the chapter):

- Total contribution – Fixed Costs = Net Profit
- (Sales volume × Contribution per unit) – Fixed Costs = Net Profit
- (Sales revenue × C/S ratio) – Fixed Costs = Net Profit

The break-even point is where net profit is zero, and so you just set net profit equal to zero, plug whatever given information you have into one of the equations and solve for sales or sales volume. Better still, at the break-even point, total contribution equals total fixed costs.

Suppose that a company has £30,000 in fixed costs. How much total contribution margin does it have to generate in order to break even?

$$\text{Total contribution} - \text{Fixed costs} = \text{Net profit}$$
$$\text{Break-even total contribution} - \text{Fixed costs} = £0$$
$$\text{Break-even total contribution} - £30{,}000 = £0$$
$$\text{Break-even total contribution} = £30{,}000$$

Here, too, at the break-even point, total contribution equals fixed costs of £30,000. Now suppose a company has contribution per unit of £6 and fixed costs of £600. What's the break-even point in units?

$$(\text{Sales volume} \times \text{Contribution per unit}) - \text{Fixed costs} = \text{Net profit}$$
$$(\text{Break-even sales volume} \times \text{contribution per unit}) - \text{Fixed costs} = £0$$
$$(\text{Break-even sales volume} \times £6) - £600 = £0$$
$$\frac{£600}{£6} = \text{Break-even sales volume}$$
$$100 \text{ units} = \text{Break-even sales volume}$$

Another company has a contribution margin ratio of 40 per cent and fixed costs of £1,000. Sales price is £1 per unit. What's the break-even point in sales revenue?

$$(\text{Sales revenue} \times \text{C/S ratio}) - \text{Fixed costs} = \text{Net Profit}$$
$$(\text{Break-even sales revenue} \times \text{C/S ratio}) - \text{Fixed costs} = £0$$
$$(\text{Break-even sales revenue} \times 40\%) - £1{,}000 = £0$$
$$\frac{£1{,}000}{40\%} = \text{Break-even sales revenue}$$
$$£2{,}500 = \text{Break-even sales revenue}$$

You can express break-even point in units or revenue. If your formula gives you units and you want revenue, multiply the number of units by the sales price. If your formula gives you revenue and you want units, just divide by the sales price. This tip works only for single-product companies.

Modifying to Achieve a Target Profit

If you have set a specific goal for net profit (called your *target profit*), contribution analysis can help you calculate the sales volume needed.

To calculate target profit, just adapt one of the three net income formulas from the earlier section 'Meeting Net Profit Targets with Cost-Volume-Profit Analysis'.

- Total contribution – Fixed Costs = Net Profit
- (Sales volume × Contribution per unit) – Fixed Costs = Net Profit
- (Sales revenue × C/S ratio) – Fixed Costs = Net Profit

Then simply plug target profit into one of these formulas as net profit:

$$\frac{(\text{Total fixed cost} + \text{target profit})}{\text{Contribution per unit}} = \text{Sales volume required}$$

$$\frac{(\text{Total fixed cost} + \text{target profit})}{\text{C/S ratio}} = \text{Sales revenue required}$$

Say a company is pushing to earn £20,000 in profit and has to pay £10,000 in fixed costs. How much total contribution does the company need to generate in order to make its target profit of £20,000?

$$\text{Net income} = \text{Total contribution margin} - \text{Fixed costs}$$
$$£20{,}000 = \text{Total contribution margin}_{\text{Target}} - £10{,}000$$
$$£30{,}000 = \text{Total contribution margin}_{\text{Target}}$$

Total contribution of £30,000 results in £20,000 worth of net profit.

Now suppose a company has set its target profit for £2,000, earns contribution per unit of £5 and incurs fixed costs of £500. How many units must the company sell?

$$(\text{Sales volume} \times \text{Contribution per unit}) - \text{Fixed costs} = \text{Net Profit}$$
$$(\text{Target sales volume} \times \text{Contribution per unit}) - \text{Fixed costs} = £2{,}000$$
$$(\text{Target sales volume} \times £5) - £500 = £2{,}000$$
$$\frac{£2{,}500}{£5} = \text{Target sales volume}$$
$$500 \text{ units} = \text{Target sales volume}$$

If the company wants to earn £2,000 in profit, it needs to sell 500 units.

Consider another company with a C/S ratio of 40 per cent and fixed costs of £1,000. The company is looking to earn £600 in net profit. How much does that company need in sales?

$$(\text{Sales revenue} \times \text{C/S ratio}) - \text{Fixed costs} = \text{Net Profit}$$

$$(\text{Target sales revenue} \times \text{C/S ratio}) - \text{Fixed costs} = £600$$

$$(\text{Target sales revenue} \times 40\%) - £1{,}000 = £600$$

$$\frac{£1{,}600}{40\%} = \text{Target sales revenue}$$

$$£4{,}000 = \text{Target sales revenue}$$

Don't confuse pounds with units. The formula that uses contribution per unit gives you sales in units, but the formula that uses the C/S ratio gives you sales revenue.

Feeling Secure: Margin of Safety

The *margin of safety* is the difference between your actual or expected profitability and the break-even point. It measures how much breathing room you have – how much you can afford to lose in sales before your net profit is wiped out. When budgeting, calculate the margin of safety as the difference between the budgeted sales and the break-even point. Doing so helps you understand the likelihood of incurring a loss.

Turn to Chapters 14 and 15 for more information about budgeting.

Depicting margin of safety with a graph

Figure 9-7 shows you how to visualise margin of safety with a graph. In this example, the margin of safety is the difference between current or projected sales volume (60 units) and break-even sales volume (34 units), or 26 units. Sales would have to drop by 26 units for existing profit of £240 to dry up completely.

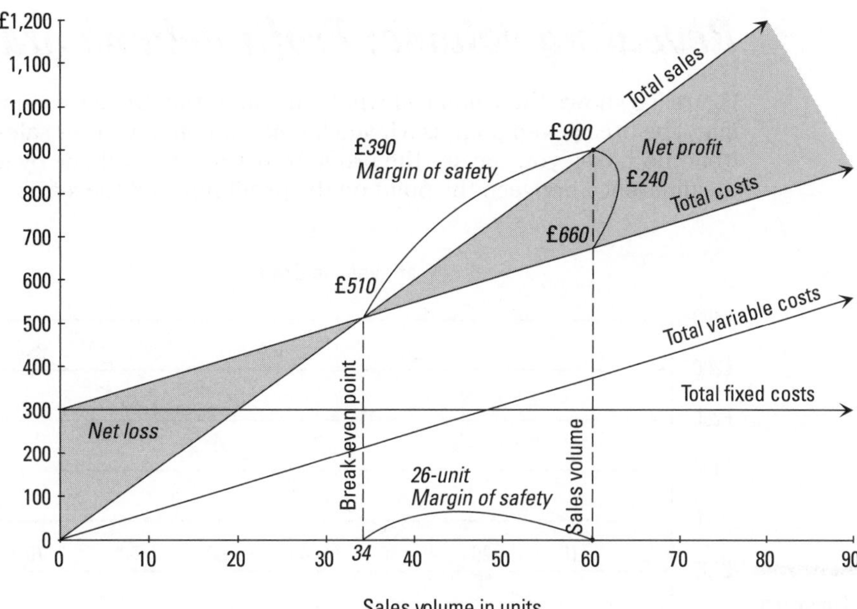

Figure 9-7: Graphing the margin of safety.

Making use of formulas

To find the margin of safety directly, without drawing pictures, first calculate the break-even point and then subtract it from actual or projected sales. You can use revenue or volume of units:

$$\text{Actual sales revenue} - \text{Break-even sales revenue} = \text{Margin of safety in revenue}$$

$$\text{Actual sales volume} - \text{Break-even sales volume} = \text{Margin of safety in volume (units)}$$

For guidance on finding the break-even point, check out the earlier section 'Bringing up Break-Even Analysis'.

You can calculate margin of safety in sales revenue or in units, but be consistent. Don't subtract break-even sales in units from the sales revenue!

Very often an exam question asks for the margin of safety. You need to know that some examiners award marks for the margin of safety (in units or revenue) *and* more marks for the margin of safety as a percentage of the forecast sales. The question may not explicitly ask for the margin of safety percentage, but some examiners are testing that you know to include it.

Revealing volume: Profit volume graph

Figure 9-8 shows the volume at which the operation breaks even with a single line. The break-even point is 34, and if you read off any other sales volume from the x-axis, you can see the profit or loss for that volume by looking at the difference between the point on the profit line and the x-axis.

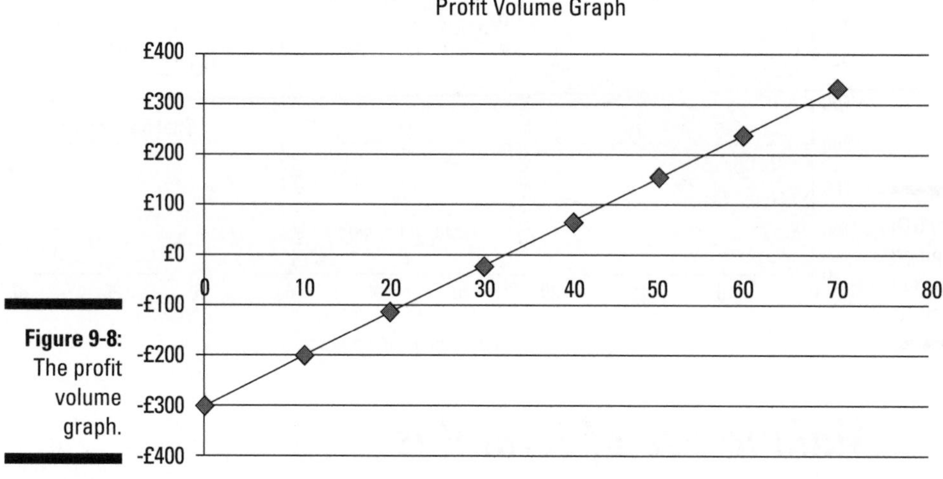

Figure 9-8: The profit volume graph.

Juggling Variable and Fixed Costs: Operational Gearing

Operational gearing measures how changes in sales can affect profit. For a company with high operational gearing, a relatively small increase in sales can have a fairly significant impact on profit. Likewise, a relatively small decrease in sales for that same company has a devastating effect on profit.

Operational gearing is driven by a company's blend of fixed and variable costs. The larger the proportion of fixed costs to variable costs, the greater the operational gearing. For example, airlines are notorious for their high fixed costs. Airlines' highest costs are typically depreciation, jet fuel and labour. They're all costs that are fixed in respect to the number of passengers on each flight. Their most significant variable cost is probably the cost of the airline food (judging from some recent flights we've been on, it wasn't very much!).

Therefore, airlines have ridiculously high operational gearing and unspeakably low variable costs. A small drop in the number of passenger-miles can have a very significant adverse effect on an airline's profitability.

Identifying decision points – when to invest in fixed cost production methods

In their day-to-day lives, people often face decisions about fixed and variable costs. Here's one that one of the authors currently faces: 'Shall I pay for a monthly season ticket on the train or pay daily?' From a management-accounting perspective, this dilemma is the same as a lot of fixed cost or variable cost decisions, or in the context of this section: what operational gearing to have.

A good idea is to consider such decisions by looking at the two alternatives and the difference. For example, a monthly ticket costs £63.60 and will lead to a saving (contribution) of £4.20 per day. By paying £63.60, all train journeys that month are free, but the traveller must use the train a minimum number of times for the season ticket to be worthwhile:

Increased fixed cost = Cost of season ticket (£63.60)

Extra contribution per unit = Saving each day (£4.20)

Therefore, the traveller must travel 15.14 (rounded up to 16) times per month to justify the cost of the season ticket. Each additional journey over 16 adds a £4.20 saving (or for a business, adds £4.20 to profit).

This approach would apply to a business deciding on the level of operational gearing to apply. Imagine that a caterer can buy a van to transport food to venues or hire a van each time a function requires a van:

$$\frac{\text{Increased fixed cost}}{\text{Extra contribution from the function}} = \text{Number of functions needed}$$

More figures may be needed than just the cost of two types of train ticket, but the principle is exactly the same.

This modified exam question concerns Royle Ltd, which manufactures stoves. The business has grown over recent years. Sales of the Handy Stove have grown to 900 per month. The board of directors is considering buying machinery and paying other fixed costs that would create a higher operational gearing. These costs would lead to variable cost savings on each stove, because some tasks currently carried out by workers would be mechanised. Here's the relevant information:

- Selling price of £220 per stove would not be affected by the decision.
- Variable costs of £180 per stove would fall to £120 if the fixed costs are increased.
- Fixed costs are currently £33,200 per month and would increase by £77,000 per month.

Your tasks are to:

- Find the break-even sales for each alternative.
- Find the level of sales needed to justify the higher gearing alternative.

Here's the process to follow:

1. **Find where the low operational gearing alternative breaks even, as follows:**

$$\frac{\text{Fixed cost}}{\text{Contribution per unit}} \quad \frac{£33,200}{£40} = 830 \text{ stoves}$$

2. **Find where the high operational gearing alternative breaks even:**

$$\frac{\text{Fixed cost}}{\text{Contribution per unit}} \quad \frac{£110,200}{£100} = 1102 \text{ stoves}$$

3. **Calculate the level of sales needed to justify the higher gearing alternative:**

$$\frac{\text{Additional fixed cost}}{\text{Additional contribution per unit}} \quad \frac{£77,000}{£60} = 1,283.33 = 1,284 \text{ stoves}$$

The low gearing alternative adds £40 to profit for every stove produced over the break-even number of 830. The high gearing alternative adds £100 to profit for every stove produced over 1,102. The high gearing alternative is making more contribution per stove, but it doesn't catch up with the low gearing alternative until production reaches 1,284.

This result would lead management accountants to discourage the board of directors from increasing the operational gearing.

Look out for the decision point (that is, where you'd recommend changing the operational gearing) when answering questions about spending more on fixed costs to save on variable cost per unit. Don't simply look for the two break-even points.

Deciding when to outsource products

Outsourcing decisions are a type of operational gearing question. The technique is the same, but it looks at saving fixed costs and incurring additional unit variable costs.

In this modified exam question, Floyd Ltd has developed a domestic wind turbine that it plans to produce and sell. The price has been set at £1,000 per unit. Costs are as follows:

- **Variable costs:**
  - Materials: £300 per unit
  - Labour: £200 per unit
- **Fixed costs:**
  - Production overheads: £3,000,000 (£1,950,000 specific to the manufacture of wind turbines; £1,050,000 general overheads)

Floyd Ltd could use a manufacturing company in Latvia to produce the turbines at £650 per unit. In addition to saving all the variable costs, the Latvian contractor would save £1,950,000 of fixed costs.

Your job is to answer this question: what level of sales would justify Floyd Ltd producing the domestic wind turbines themselves?

Additional fixed cost: £1,950,000 = 13,000 turbines

Additional contribution per unit £150

The result is as follows:

- The Latvian contractor should produce the turbines, if production and forecast sales are lower than 13,000.
- Floyd Ltd should produce the turbines themselves, if production and forecast sales are more than 13,000.

Graphing operational gearing

In a cost-volume-profit graph (see Figure 9-3 earlier in the chapter), operational gearing corresponds to the slope of the total costs line. The steeper the slope of this line, the lower the operational gearing.

Figure 9-9 compares the operational gearing for two different entities, Safe Co., which has lower operational gearing, and Risky Co., which has higher operational gearing.

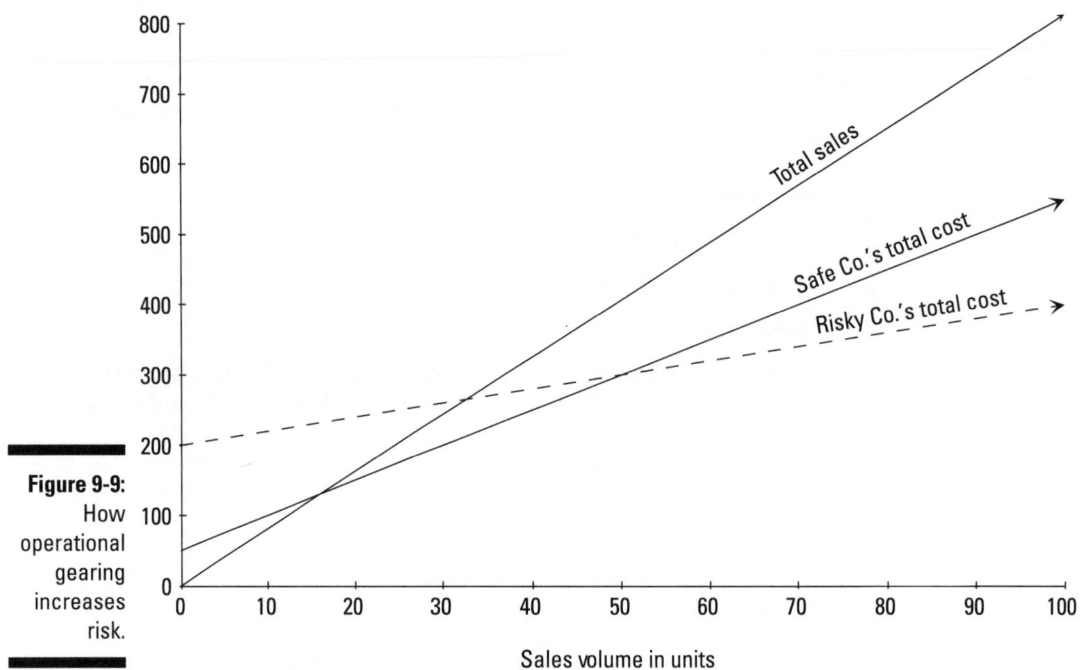

Figure 9-9: How operational gearing increases risk.

Risky has higher fixed costs and lower variable costs per unit than Safe. Therefore, Safe's total cost line is steeper than Risky's total cost line. Accordingly, Risky has the potential to earn much higher income with the same sales volume than Safe does. Because its fixed costs are so high, Risky also has the potential to incur greater losses than Safe does.

Looking at the operational gearing formula

The formula for operational gearing is as follows:

$$\frac{\text{Total contribution}}{\text{Net profit}} = \text{Operational gearing}$$

Continuing the example from the preceding section, suppose that Safe Co. and Risky Co. each earn sales of £400 on 50 units. Assume that on these sales, Safe has £150 contribution and Risky has £300 contribution. Safe has fixed costs of £50 and Risky has fixed costs of £200. Safe's profit comes to £100 (£150 – £50). At this volume level, Risky's profit also works out be £100. Look at the calculations:

$$\frac{\text{Total contribution}}{\text{Net profit}} = \text{Operational gearing}$$

$$\text{Safe Co.} = \frac{150}{100} = 1.5$$

$$\text{Risky Co.} = \frac{300}{100} = 3.0$$

According to these measures, Risky has twice the operational gearing of Safe. Although a 10 per cent increase in sales boosts Safe's profit by 15 per cent, a similar 10 per cent increase in sales for Risky increases that company's profit by 30 per cent!

That said, high operational gearing can work against you. For Safe, a 10 per cent decrease in sales cuts income by 15 per cent; for Risky, a 10 per cent decrease in sales reduces profit by 30 per cent.

Because automation replaces labour with machines, it usually replaces the variable costs (from direct labour) with fixed overhead (associated with running equipment). As such, automation tends to increase operational gearing. However, outsourcing usually has the opposite effect. Companies that close factories and pay other companies to make goods for them replace fixed costs (needed to run factories) with variable costs (used to pay other companies to make the goods).

Using contribution with a mix of products

Operational gearing provides an opportunity to analyse business performance by looking at the relative significance of the variable and fixed costs. Many businesses incur fixed costs when they produce and sell a mix of many different products. Dealing with a mix of products requires management accountants to carry out a modified analysis.

Sometimes exam questions test a pre-determined sales mix contribution. This approach overcomes one of the problems that businesses have where different products have different contribution margins, but it does set the sales mix and tends to rely on this figure not changing. A recent ACCA F5 exam tested sales mix contribution, and so we need to address it within this chapter for thoroughness.

Lawson Ltd produces three products, dolls named Maureen, Kathy and Jean (see Table 9-2).

Table 9-2 Data for the Lawson Ltd Example

	Maureen	*Kathy*	*Jean*	*Company as a Whole*
Price	£140.00	£200.00	£160.00	
Sales volume	15,000	16,500	19,500	
Variable costs	£56.00	£130.00	£120.00	
Fixed costs				£750,000

Weighing in with the weighted average C/S ratio

Each product within a sales mix has its own C/S ratio. Some products sell more than others. To identify an overall C/S ratio for a mix of different products, the calculation needs to treat the C/S ratios of the higher selling products with higher weightings than the C/S ratios of the lower selling products. The overall C/S ratio of the sales mix as a whole is called *the weighted average C/S ratio*. A quick way to find the weighted average C/S ratio is to calculate the individual product contributions and sales revenues, then total all the contributions and total all the sales revenue. Next, divide the company contribution by the company sales revenue (see Table 9-3).

Table 9-3 Lawson Ltd Example Weighted Average C/S ratio

	Maureen	Kathy	Jean	Company as a Whole
Price	£140.00	£200.00	£160.00	
Variable costs	£56.00	£130.00	£120.00	
Contribution per unit	£84.00	£70.00	£40.00	
Sales volume	15,000	16,500	19,500	
Total contribution	£1,260,000	£1,155,000	£780,000	£3,195,000
Total revenue	£2,100,000	£3,300,00	£3,120,000	£8,520,000
C/S ratio				0.375 (37.5%)

Having found the C/S ratio for all three products, you can use it to find the sales revenue needed to break even. Using the weighted average C/S ratio assumes a sales mix in the same proportion as the original budget. In the case of Lawson Ltd you use the C/S ratio 37.5% calculated in Table 9-3.

$$\frac{\text{Fixed costs}}{\text{Weighted average C/S ratio}} \quad \frac{\text{£}750{,}000}{0.375} = \text{£}2{,}000{,}000 \text{ revenue}$$

Breaking even across the mix

To complete a graph of the mix, you need to identify the individual C/S ratio of each product (see Table 9-4).

Table 9-4 Lawson Ltd Weighted Average C/S Ratio Calculated Using Total Values

	Maureen	*Kathy*	*Jean*	*Company as a Whole*
Total contribution	£1,260,000	£1,155,000	£780,000	£3,195,000
Total revenue	£2,100,000	£3,300,00	£3,120,000	£8,520,000
C/S ratio	0.60	0.35	0.25	0.375 (37.5%)

We recommend constructing the graph with the assumption that sales take place, taking the products in order of those achieving the highest C/S ratio. In this case, the order is Maureen, Kathy and Jean (see Figure 9-10).

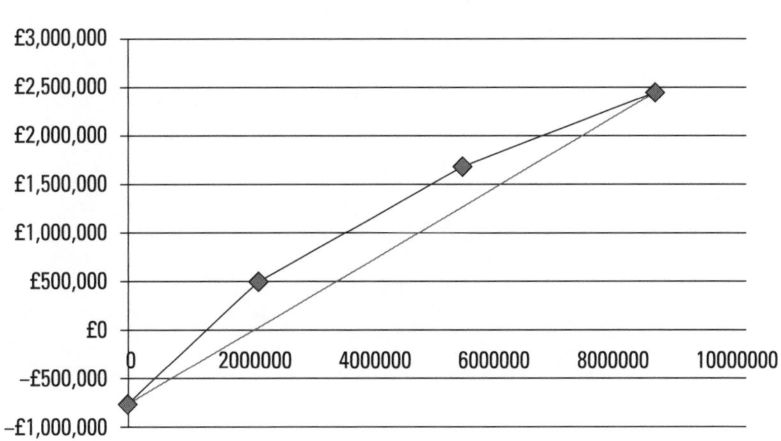

Figure 9-10: Lawson Ltd graph showing the profit from the sales mix of dolls.

The figure starts with a loss of £750,000 if no sales are made. Then, if sales of Maureen take place first, the first (and steepest thicker line) takes the profit to £510,000. Then sales of Kathy take the profit to £1,665,000, and further sales of Jean take the profit to £2,445,000. The thicker lines are progressively less steep as the C/S ratios fall.

If the first £1,250,000 of sales were all for Maureen products, these sales would be sufficient to break even.

The additional thinner straight line assumes the sales are made in the budgeted mix, and crosses the break-even line (£0) at £2,000,000 sales, which is the same value we found using the formula in the earlier section 'Weighing in with the weighted average C/S ratio'.

Selling loss-making products as part of the mix

Management accountants often look at a complete mix of products. Sometimes they support the continued sale of products even though they don't make a profit or even make a loss, when qualitative reasons exist for continuing to sell loss-making products as part of a wider policy. Examples may be:

- New products, which can be expected to make a profit when sales grow.
- Products that customers want to buy, if when they buy these, they also buy other products that do offer a profit.

Chapter 10

Decision-Making within the Reality of Limited Capacity

In This Chapter

- Maximising profit when facing limited capacity
- Identifying relevant costs to specific decisions
- Putting aside costs that aren't relevant

Welcome to the reality of running a business. Most companies sell many products – often hundreds or even thousands of different models – and yet usually have *limited capacity* (only enough machinery, space and workers to produce a restricted amount of finished goods during a time period).

In this chapter, we address the issue of limited capacity, identify relevant and irrelevant costs, and explain how to determine which products to make when limited capacity prevents you from producing as much as you can sell.

Understanding the Reality of Limited Resources

To quote the Rolling Stones, 'you can't always get what you want'. The fact is that companies usually have limited resources, whether that's limits on space, on the number of workers or even on the machine capacity needed to produce goods. This reality means that in order to best use limited production capabilities, managers have to choose which products to make and sell — and management accountants need to provide the necessary information for those decisions.

Coping with limited capacity

Perhaps the most common limit businesses have to cope with is the number of hours in a day: too many jobs to do and not enough time to do them all. Firms have many competing priorities and objectives, and so assuming profit maximisation as your priority can help with business decisions.

A plastic food container business (PlasticFantastic) produces Round and Square containers (see the data in Table 10-1).

Table 10-1 Data for the PlasticFantastic Example

	Round	Square	Total
Maximum sales	150,000	250,000	
Machine hours required	300	2,000	
Sales revenue	£135,000	£200,000	
Total variable cost	£70,500	£145,000	
Total fixed costs for both products			£95,600
Total machine hours available			2,100 hours

Producing the maximum sales would require 2,300 machine hours, but only 2,100 hours are available, so you need to allocate those hours as profitably as possible

The best approach is to use a table that shows the contribution each product generates per unit of the limiting factor. For this example, you need to find the contribution per machine hour (see Table 10-2).

Table 10-2 Calculating Contribution per Machine Hour for the PlasticFantastic Example

	Round	Square	Company as a Whole
Sales revenue	£135,000	£200,000	
Total variable cost	£70,500	£145,000	
Total contribution	£64,500	£55,000	
Total machine hours	300	2,000	
Contribution per machine hour	£215.00	£27.50	

The contribution per limiting factor has been calculated by dividing the total contribution by the total hours needed to generate that contribution. For example, £64,500 divided by 300 machine hours gives £215 per machine hour.

An alternative approach would find the same value using a unit basis. In that case, you find the contribution per unit and divide by the limiting factor per unit.

Contribution per limiting factor is used as a basis for ranking the products: here, Round containers generate £215 per machine hour, whereas the Square containers generate £27.50 per machine hour.

This factor is used to allocate the limited number of machine hours. Round units are allocated all the hours needed to achieve the maximum Round sales, and the remaining hours are allocated to Square production (see Table 10-3).

Table 10-3 Allocating Machine Hours for the PlasticFantastic Example

	Round	*Square*	*Company as a Whole*
Rank	1	2	
Machine hours available			2,100
Machine hours allocated	300	1,800	

Based on the hours allocated, you can identify the production mix. In this case, you require only one calculation. The maximum sales of Round units are 150,000 and require 300 hours (see Table 10-1). The production mix will include 150,000 Round units. Only 1,800 hours are allocated to Square production; this figure requires a calculation to find the number of units that will be produced.

Table 10-1 shows that 2,000 hours are needed to make 250,000 Square units. You need to find the number of hours needed to make one Square container.

Each Square container requires:

2,000 hours ÷ 250,000 units = 0.008 hours per unit

You now need to find how many units can be produced in the 1,800 hours allocated to Square container production.

Divide the total hours allocated by the hours per unit to obtain the number of units that can be produced:

1,800 hours ÷ 0.008 hours = 225,000

Your next task is to multiply the number of units to be produced by the contribution per unit, to find total contribution. When you add these together you can identify the total for the company. Then just deduct the fixed cost to find the profit (see Table 10-4).

Table 10-4 Profit Statement for the PlasticFantastic Example

	Round	*Square*	*Company as a Whole*
Production mix	150,000	225,000	
Contribution per unit	£0.43	£0.22	
Total contribution	£64,500	£49,500	£114,000
Total fixed costs			£95,600
Profit			£18,400

Sap 'n' Suds Ltd has a limited amount of raw material. Three of the company's products use the same rare plant extract as part of their manufacture. The sole supplier informs Sap 'n' Suds that, due to flooding at its South American facility, they can supply only 6,000 kilograms of the plant extract next month. It's decision time!

Figure 10-1 shows the budget information about the three affected products for next month.

	Bath Oil	*Hand Cream*	*Soap*	*Total*
Contribution	£26,400	£34,600	£48,204	£109,204
Fixed costs				£30,780
Profit				£78,424
Maximum demand (units)	6,600	6,920	16,068	
Kilograms of material per unit	2,640	1,730	8,034	

Figure 10-1: Data for the Sap 'n' Suds Practice.

Your task is to complete Figure 10-2, so that you can advise the firm's managers how many packs of each product to produce next month in order to maximise profits during this period.

Product	*Bath Oil*	*Hand Cream*	*Soap*	*Total*
Contribution/pack (£)				
Kilograms of material per unit				
Contribution per kilogram (£)				
Product ranking				
Kilograms available				
Kilograms allocated product				
Production mix				
Total contribution earned (£)				
Less: Fixed costs (£)				
Profit/loss made (£)				

Figure 10-2: Discovering the number of packs that Sap 'n' Suds needs to produce.

Identifying limiting factors

The company Balls R Us (BRU) has a factory in Southbourne and manufactures balls for various sports. All their balls go through three different processes:

- Ball moulding
- Ball painting/finishing
- Packing

Different skills are needed in each department, and employees who work in one department are unable to complete work in other departments. One week BRU has a problem: several of the staff aren't able to work during the week ending Sunday 18 April (they were arrested by the police for excessive bouncing, charged with disorderly conduct and bail was denied).

The manager, Kristine, is very concerned that the number of hours available isn't going to be sufficient for the production that has been scheduled for that week (see Table 10-5).

Table 10-5 Types of Ball — Labour Hours per Product for BRU Practice

Department	Squash Ball	Tennis Ball	Beach Ball
Moulding	0.08	0.18	0.20
Painting/finishing	0.05	0.11	0.12
Packing	0.04	0.07	0.07

The scheduled production per product and the available trained staff hours in each department are shown in the following two mini-tables:

	Squash Ball	*Tennis Ball*	*Beach Ball*
Forecast production per product in week ending 18th April	400	350	180

Department	*Labour hours available*
Moulding	132
Painting/finishing	82
Packing	52

Bearing this information in mind, Table 10-6 identifies a possible limiting factor during the week ending 18 April 2010.

Table 10-6 Identification of Possible Limiting Factor during the Week in Question: BRU Practice

Department	Labour Hours Required	Labour Hours Available	Limiting Factor (Yes or No)
Moulding	131	132	No
Painting/finishing		82	
Packing		52	

The hours required are shown in Table 10-7.

Table 10-7 Hours Required: BRU Practice

Department	*400 Squash Balls*	*350 Tennis Balls*	*180 Beach Balls*	*Total Hours*
Moulding	0.08 × 400 = 32 hours	0.18 × 350 = 63 hours	0.20 × 180 = 36 hours	131 hours
Painting/finishing	0.05 × 400	0.11 × 350	0.12 × 180	
Packing	0.04 × 400	0.07 × 350	0.07 × 350	

Copy the process you used for moulding: hours per unit × units for each of the three types of ball, and then add up the total hours required. Apply this to the painting/finishing department and to the packing department.

Then go back to Table 10-6. Compare the hours required and the hours available, and identify whether the labour time in each department is a limiting factor.

For moulding, 131 hours are required and 132 hours are available, so labour hours are not a limiting factor for the moulding department.

Does a limiting factor exist? If so:

- In which department(s)?
- How should you determine the production mix that maximises profits?

A useful management tool called the theory of constraints, which we describe in Chapter 19, provides more advanced techniques to help managers maximise the benefits from limited resources. Take a look.

Focusing on Relevant Costs

In the earlier section 'Coping with limited capacity', we look at cost descriptions, based on how total costs of particular types of expenditure vary based on the number of units produced, to identify fixed and variable costs. In

Chapter 3, we looked at the differences between direct costs and indirect costs based on whether they can be directly attributed to a product. Surely that's enough? Well, no! You need to see costs from yet another angle when decisions are being made in the short run. To do so you look at *incremental costs.* Incremental means extra; incremental costs are the extra costs a business incurs when it makes a particular decision. These are called *relevant costs,* because they're the costs that change depending on which alternative you choose. Other costs don't change and so are irrelevant to the decision (as we discuss in the later section 'Ignoring Certain Costs Safely: Irrelevant Costs').

If you're driving home from work and you give your neighbour a lift, the incremental cost you incur from having your neighbour in the car compared to having an empty seat is minimal. The vast majority of the costs of the petrol, the wear and tear on the tyres and road tax are the same as they would have been if you drove home alone.

Distinguishing the relevant costs

When you look at relevant costing you need to switch off the financial accounting part of the brain and think in a practical way. For example, suppose that your car doesn't pass the MOT and you're deciding what to do now. The price you paid to buy the car originally and how long you've had it aren't relevant. But your neighbour, who's a keen amateur mechanic and offers £150 to purchase the car, *is* relevant.

Now (the present moment) is key to discerning relevant costs, such as the cost to make the necessary adjustments to pass the MOT, a second fee you may incur to take the MOT and the amount the car is going to be worth when the work is done.

Here's a simple example:

- The neighbour offers you £150 now.
- The repair estimate is £280.
- The extra MOT costs £35.
- With an MOT in place, similar cars are selling for £390–410.

Use these numbers as follows:

Relevant costs if you repair	**£**
Repair charge	280
MOT	35
Income from sale to neighbour forgone	150
Total relevant cost	465
Resale value (approximately)	400

Based on this set of figures, your best approach is to sell without repairing. Assuming that you do need a car, selling now raises £150, which you can put towards the cost of a car costing around £400, a net additional cost of £250. If you can manage without a car, repairing and MOTing costs £315, but only increases the sales value from £150 to £410 at the most – paying out £315 for a £260 return.

Now consider the other costs that you ignore:

- Car parking
- Car washing
- Insurance
- Petrol
- Road tax

They're just not relevant in this case and not needed for the incremental analysis that you carry out to make the decision. The scenario is straightforward because it looks at similar cars, and so all these costs are the same whether you drive the same car after repairs or another one.

'Just the relevant facts, ma'am'

This question isn't about having a car or not having a car: it looks only at what to do with the car you already have. You may quite rightly say, 'well, if I sell now, I can claim back part of the road tax'. But as far as the sell-or-repair question is concerned, road tax isn't relevant. If you sell, the replacement car needs road tax; if you don't sell, the car being repaired needs road tax.

The question 'should I have a car at all?' demands a similarly disciplined assessment of relevant costs, but in that case you'd need to look at car usage and how you'd replace that with walking, bicycles, public transport and taxis. And we haven't even mentioned sentimentality.

As a management accountant, you look (at least at the start of this analysis) at the costs you can measure. No doubt Oscar Wilde's character Lord Darlington would be pleased to see his definition of a cynic ('a man who knows the price of everything and the value of nothing') being re-enacted!

Brrrrr: It's perishing in here!

Service businesses such as hotels, theatres, aeroplanes and buses have a common problem of *instant perishability.* A shop can put unsold stock into the store at the end of the day and then bring it out again to sell the next day. Even if an apple stall is concerned that some apples lose their attractive sheen if they aren't sold one day, they may still be bought by a customer willing to cut out the odd bruise and make apple pies or crumbles the next day.

But the minute an aeroplane takes off with an empty seat, the opportunity to sell that seat has gone (perished). Time moves quickly for a lot of service products: when hotel nights have completely gone, they've gone, and can't be stored to be sold the next day.

Relevant costing requires clarity on the precise decision you're addressing, and a cost analysis that looks only at the costs that will change as a result of the decision.

As a management accountant, incremental costs come up as you encounter these sorts of decisions.

This example looks at the question of accepting special orders (or not). A hotel isn't fully booked for tonight. At 11 p.m., a mysterious stranger approaches the counter, offering to pay just £20 for a room. The rooms normally go for a minimum of £100 a night. Do you take the money or turn the stranger down?

You start by considering some of the incremental costs:

- Electricity to power the heating, TV and any light bulbs.
- Gas to heat water for the shower and to power the laundry to clean the towels and bed linen.
- Chocolate mints for the pillows and sachets of coffee, tea, milk and sugar.

You can forget about housekeeping expenses, because you pay your housekeepers the same wage every day, regardless of how many rooms they clean. The relevant cost is less than £20 for the night. Take the money and direct the guest to his room.

Don't even think about the original cost when making relevant-cost decisions, because you aren't ever going to see that money again and it's irrelevant. Only think about the future alternatives and the different costs and revenues of each option.

Accounting for opportunity costs

Sometimes choosing one alternative over another means losing money, because you turned down another possibility.

A shop may choose to allocate more shelf space to salad items and allocate less space to fruit and vegetables one day. That's a choice: the alternatives include having more vegetables on display and having more fruit on display. Every alternative would make some money, but the shop has chosen to allocate the space to salad items because the manager considers this will make more than any of the alternatives.

Management accountants look at the alternatives and identify the amount of money the shop would make from them. Whichever one is the second best is important. Because this *wasn't* chosen, it represents a profit forgone (or denied to the shop). By putting salad items on a shelf that could have been used for fruit, the contribution towards overall profit that the fruit would have produced has been forgone. The second best choice profit forgone is called the *opportunity cost* of the alternative chosen.

Take a look at the selling your car example in the preceding section. If you keep the car, no money changes hands just because you said no to selling the car to your neighbour. You simply deny yourself the opportunity of receiving £150 for handing over the car: hence, it's an opportunity cost.

In fact, we can be more precise. Even if someone else offers you £120 for the car, because only one car is available for sale, you can accept only one offer (if any).

Opportunity cost is the value you turn down by not taking the second best alternative. So, you need to look at all the various alternatives and choose the second best alternative and treat any contribution towards profit it would have generated as a cost in relevant costing. After all, choosing to not use that alternative costs the business lost contribution, and the alternative you do choose needs to generate more than you have forgone.

At Sofi's bakery, a potential customer has requested a special cake that requires a rare ingredient. Sofi must assess the relevant cost of the rare ingredient. She has enough of this ingredient in stock, but uses it for one of the other cakes that she sells on a daily basis.

The rare ingredient has a lot of alternative cost values:

- The current stock value of the ingredient is £15 per kilogram.
- The ingredient would cost £21 per kilogram to replace.
- The ingredient is part of a cake where the price Sofi charges means that each kilogram of the ingredient that's used adds £9 to her profit.
- Another baker has offered to pay Sofi £20 per kilogram for the ingredient.
- Amateur bakers are willing to pay £3 per 100 grams for small bags of the ingredient, which have an additional cost of £0.10 to put together.

What price per kilogram should Sofi use for the rather special cake when she calculates its cost?

The current stock value is a historic cost and, because the ingredient is in regular use, you can ignore this figure. (This is true even if the replacement cost is lower).

The replacement cost appears the most likely figure to use, because the order is extra and the replacement material would be bought specifically for the order.

If Sofi was unable to buy this ingredient from a supplier, she'd have to stop producing the cake she sells on a daily basis to enable her to make the special one. This option would cause her to lose sales of the other cake, and so she'd have to add the £9 loss of extra profit to the cost of the ingredient. In other words, she has to forgo the profit she would have made by accepting the order, and so the order needs to make up this lost profit.

Consider these steps:

1. Producing the special cake means production of another cake is reduced.
2. Not producing the other cake prevents this cake being sold.
3. Every kilogram of the rare ingredient taken away from the other cake causes Sofi to lose £9 of profit.

Sofi incurs an opportunity cost of $9 for each kilogram of the rare ingredient that is taken away from making the other cake and reallocated to the special cake. This cost needs to be added to the relevant cost of making the special cake.

The other baker's offer of $20 is lower than the $21 Sofi would have to pay to buy in more. She has this ingredient in regular use, and so she should ignore the other baker's offer.

Selling the ingredient on its own in 100 gram packs for $3 per pack generates an extra $2.90 per pack after the additional cost. $2.90 per pack is equivalent to $29 per kilogram. If a plentiful supply exists for Sofi to buy at $21 per kilogram, she can ignore this figure. In fact, she may want to make up some bags and sell them; she'd be adding $8 per kilogram to her profit. If the supply is very low, however, Sofi needs to compare this option with the third alternative of not producing the other cake. The other cake adds $9 per kilogram to her profit and selling the 100 gram bags adds $8 to her profit. Therefore, the other cake is a better alternative.

Sofi needs to check how much of the rare ingredient she can buy at $21. If enough is available for her special order, her existing cake order and selling the 100 gram bags, she should treat the rare ingredient as costing $21 per kilogram in her costing calculation. But if the amount available isn't enough, and she has to stop making the other cake, by using the ingredient to make the special order cake she incurs the $21 cost charged by the supplier plus another $9 per kilogram opportunity cost for the lost sales of the other cake. Therefore, Sofi should charge $30 per kilogram on the order.

The decision needs to be based on how much saying 'yes' is going to cost.

In business, opportunity costs commonly arise from the reality that firms have limited resources. For example, if an arcade decides to replace an old pinball machine with a new video game, the income lost from the old pinball machine represents the opportunity cost arising from this decision.

Very many businesses have to take account of exactly this concern. In fact, one of the authors (Sandy) worked for a cosmetics company in the UK where the term 'cannibalisation' was used and calculated. Whenever a new product was launched, the company knew that the outcome of the promotion and development of that product would be that existing product sales would decrease. Effectively some sales of existing products were being eaten up by the sales of the new product. This amount is one of the opportunity costs of the new product.

Ignoring Certain Costs Safely: Irrelevant Costs

In the earlier section 'Focusing on Relevant Costs', we talked about how the vast majority of the costs of giving a neighbour a lift home from work are not much more than the costs of driving home alone. The road tax, for example, would be absolutely the same in either case. Road tax has to be paid just for driving on the road; once it's been paid it ceases to be an issue to consider if the question 'should I give my neighbour a lift?' arises. The road tax is a cost that's already been paid – a *sunk cost.*

Diving into sunk costs

Sometimes you wish you hadn't incurred certain costs in the past. For example, you may have purchased an office building that's too large to suit your needs, or made repairs to a piece of equipment that later needed to be replaced anyway due to obsolescence.

Such costs incurred in the past are called *sunk costs.* When making decisions in the context of the incremental costs, you can ignore sunk costs because they can't be changed. They're the same whether your decision to go ahead is a 'yea' or a 'nay'.

One of the most significant sunk costs is the original cost of your factory and equipment. You've already purchased these items and can't sell them; as a result, you can ignore these sunk costs completely and any depreciation on them.

Suppose that you spend £5,000 to repair a piece of equipment. A week later, your suppliers introduce a more powerful model that allows you to produce more units at a lower cost. When deciding whether to replace the machine with the new model, you ignore completely the £5,000 from the repair, because it's a sunk cost.

Considering committed costs

Other costs that form no part of a relevant cost-based decision are *committed costs.* Rather like the sunk cost in the preceding section, a committed cost is something that you decided on before the decision you now have to take arose. An example of these costs is the contractual obligations to pay instalments on a piece of machinery or vehicles.

Even though the cash hasn't changed hands yet, you've made the commitment. Therefore, that decision has no impact on the total incremental cost of a decision. The committed cost remains the same whether you decide to go ahead or not, and for that reason it's irrelevant.

Chapter 11

Deciding on Long-Term Purchases: Capital Budgeting

In This Chapter

- Receiving payback
- Understanding that value changes over time
- Estimating internal rate of return
- Considering qualitative factors

Companies invest in capital projects – buying large items such as factories, equipment, vehicles and even other businesses – to earn profits and a return on their investment. Therefore, managers need tools and techniques to evaluate different capital projects and decide which ones to invest in and which ones to avoid.

When managers commit to a major project, they agree to the vast majority of the costs before the project starts. They can't change their minds and have committed to making payments for years ahead. Clearly, therefore, in this situation, planning is vital. Managers need to estimate the future cash flows that the project will bring in and come to a reasonable determination that the project's cash inflows will exceed its cost. In this context, you need to understand which cash flows will change if the project goes ahead.

In this chapter, we discuss this aspect and show you three techniques for making decisions about whether to pursue long-term capital projects, as follows:

- **Payback:** Reveals how long the business is going to take to earn the cash to cover the investment in the project.
- **Net present value (NPV):** This is the effect that deciding to go ahead with a project is going to have on the value of the business right now. This takes into consideration the *time value of money*.

If you're new to the concept of time value of money, read this chapter in order. Each section takes a step towards helping you understand this important topic.

- **Internal rate of return:** Shows what percentage return the project generates.

Also, we remind you that some projects have values that go beyond finance, and managers have to look at these qualitative factors, such as product safety or employee loyalty, when making decisions about capital investment.

Identifying Incremental and Opportunity Costs

When faced with a capital-spending decision (in other words, whether to buy something or not) – and whatever decision-making technique you choose to use – two types of costs are of central importance:

- **Incremental costs** are those extra costs that you incur by doing something. If you buy a new washing machine, the machine's price is an incremental cost; if you didn't buy it, you wouldn't incur the cost.

  If that machine uses less electricity than your old one and less soap powder, these costs are also relevant. The *difference* between the electricity cost of the old machine and the electricity cost of the new one is an *incremental saving,* and the same applies to the saving in soap powder costs. But note that the saving isn't the cost of the electricity you need, just the difference between how much the electricity is going to be in the future compared to what it would've been if you didn't take the decision to buy the new washing machine.

- **Opportunity costs** are what it will cost the business if a capital project goes ahead. This is a very broad definition of cost and includes lost incomes from existing activities. We discuss opportunity cost in Chapter 10 and define it as the next best alternative foregone. For example, say you're approached by three firms asking you to do three hours' work on a Saturday afternoon. One will leave you £100 better off, another £75 better off and the third £50 better off. By choosing to use the three hours on Saturday to improve your wealth by £100, you turn down the other offers. The better of those offers was £75, making that job the best of the foregone alternatives: the *opportunity cost* of taking the £100 job.

  Capital investment appraisal only considers the costs and revenues or savings that arise directly as a result of deciding to go ahead with a decision, including lost revenues.

Imagine that the management at a hotel decides to open a new restaurant, which will cause sales in their own coffee shop to fall. In this case, the lost coffee shop contribution is a cost to include when evaluating the viability of opening the restaurant. This figure is an *opportunity cost* to the hotel.

The lost contribution cost would be the value of the lost sales in the coffee shop less the variable costs that would be incurred to generate those sales (for example, lost sales value of croissants less the cost of the ingredients needed to make them). When considering decisions to invest in long-term projects, one of the most significant opportunity costs is how much you could've earned by investing your money elsewhere.

When analysing for incremental costs (and especially for opportunity costs), remember that they're expected to happen in the future. That's how you know that you can't include *sunk costs* (costs that you incurred in the past) or *committed costs* (costs that you will pay anyway, irrespective of the decision to go ahead, because you've previously agreed to pay them). Sunk and committed costs (which we cover in Chapter 10) aren't incremental and you can ignore them when evaluating capital-investment projects.

Getting Your Money Back: The Payback Technique

One decision-making tool for evaluating capital projects is the *payback method*, which estimates how long a project will take to recover ('pay back') its original investment. In this technique, you look at the net cash inflow the project generates to spot the point where it matches the money paid out on investing in the project. Managers can use the payback method to reduce the number of possible projects by setting a maximum payback period before considering any project for investment.

Although it's quick and easy, the payback method doesn't account for the full profitability of the project; it ignores any cash flows after the payback period ends. However, it's useful for filtering all the possible projects and identifying those which pay back within the company's required time limit. Once this filtering has been completed, a more sophisticated model tends to be used. The net present value technique builds in the time value of money, and we describe how to use it in the later section 'Understanding Time Value of Money and Net Present Value (NPV)'. This helps the investing company to select which projects to fund.

Using the payback method

As a simplified introduction to the payback method, we assume that the capital investment project will lead to an increase in the cash coming into the business by exactly the same amount each year. Based on this assumption, we use the following formula to compute how long a given project will take to pay for itself:

$$\text{Payback period} = \frac{\text{Cost of Investment}}{\text{Annual net cash flow}}$$

When computing the payback period, annual net cash flow should include all forecast incremental cash receipts arising from the new project less all expected incremental cash payments. Note that *net cash flows* mean that you're subtracting cash outflows from cash inflows. Only the cash flows that arise because of the particular capital investment should be considered. Others, which would happen anyway, are ignored. When preparing this computation, the net cash flow is likely to vary each year. If so, just forecast the net cash flow that you expect for each year. Then add a running total (or cumulative net cash flow).

Paul is considering running a taxi service. He's identified the forecast cash flows for the next five years based on the time he'll have available (see Table 11-1).

Here are the costs that he has to incur before he starts:

Acquisition of suitable car: £18,000

Other start-up costs: £4,000

Table 11-1 Forecast Cash Flows for Paul's Taxi Example

Expected Revenue from Customers	*Expected Costs of Running the Taxi Service Each Year*
During year 1: £50,000	During year 1: £35,000
During year 2: £65,000	During year 2: £45,000
During year 3: £80,000	During year 3: £55,000
During year 4: £85,000	During year 4: £59,000
During year 5: £90,000	During year 5: £62,000

Additional cash flows at the end of five years:

Sale of car: £1,500

Finding the payback period

Continuing the taxi example from the preceding section, here's the procedure for discovering the payback period:

1. **Draw up a table to show all the cash flows for each year.** Treat each year as a single period of time and the cash flow as taking place on the last day of the year. Describe any cash flows at the start of the project as taking place in year 0 (see Table 11-2).
2. **Add an extra column to show the cash running total.** Look for the first year that this becomes a positive value (see Table 11-3).

Table 11-2 Forecast Cash Flows Showing the Annual Net Cash Flow: Paul's Taxi Example

Year	*Investment (£)*	*Revenue (£)*	*Running Costs (£)*	*Net Cash Flow (£)*
0	(22,000)*			(22,000)
1		50,000	(35,000)	15,000
2		65,000	(45,000)	20,000
3		80,000	(55,000)	25,000
4		85,000	(59,000)	26,000
5	1,500**	90,000	(62,000)	28,000

**Total start-up costs payable on day one*

*** Cash received from sale*

Table 11-3 Adding a Running Total Column: Paul's Taxi Example

Year	*Investment (£)*	*Revenue (£)*	*Running Costs (£)*	*Net Cash Flow (£)*	*Running Total (£)*
0	(22,000)			(22,000)	(22,000)
1		50,000	(35,000)	15,000	(7,000)
2		65,000	(45,000)	20,000	13,000*
3		80,000	(55,000)	25,000	
4		85,000	(59,000)	26,000	
5	1,500	90,000	(62,000)	28,000	

** The investment has paid back by the end of year 2*

If the cash flows for revenue and for running costs accrue evenly in year 2, you can suggest that this business will pay back in one year plus £7,000/£20,000 of the second year (1.35 years). But even if the cash flows don't accrue evenly in year 2, you know that this project pays back within two years. This length of time can be compared with the company's target maximum payback period.

When computing net cash flows, ignore non-cash transactions such as sales on credit (until the payment is received) and depreciation (the latter expense doesn't require cash payments).

Understanding Time Value of Money and Net Present Value (NPV)

Over time, the value of money changes. Given the choice between receiving £1,000 today and receiving £1,000 a year from now, most people would take the cash now because the value of money decreases with time. The later the cash flow, the less it's worth.

Understanding and estimating how the value of money changes over time is the premise for evaluating the *time value of money,* an extremely important financial tool for making investment decisions.

The central concept in this area is net present value (NPV), and the crucial word at its heart is 'present': now. *Net present value* concerns how much going ahead would be worth to the business *now* if it decides to make a particular investment.

This idea is crucial to understanding the NPV method of evaluation. The decision now to invest in a project will increase (or decrease) the value of the business by that amount *instantly.* The decision to invest is what adds the NPV of a project to the value of a business, rather than the subsequent activities of the project.

If you want to build an extension onto your house, you must apply for planning permission. The split second that planning permission is granted is the point at which your house is worth more.

When you're discussing the present value of a cash flow or a series of cash flows, remember that you mean 'how much is that cash flow worth *now*? What is its *present* value?' Net present value means 'what's the combined total of all the different annual present values?' The answer gives the overall value of the project now.

Watching for instant effects

A few years ago, Sandy was aware that the Finance Director of the company that owned a particular cola brand was going to make a presentation to stockbrokers to inform them of a very significant contract to supply a chain of supermarkets. In his class, he opened a computer screen to show students how the share value of the company rose when this information was announced: it was almost instantaneous.

Homing in on NPV and decision-making

You may be wondering why a contract with a major customer, like the one we relate in the earlier sidebar 'Watching for instant effects', increases the value of a company. The answer is that a contract is effectively an agreement to supply the customer with a lot of product for many years *and* for the customer to provide the supplier with cash flows.

To find the NPV, you discount each annual cash flow to its present value and add them together. The result is the value to the company of the contract.

Think about building a house extension. If you decide to go ahead and add an extension so that you can sell the extended house, you need time: you have to consider your incurred costs and the time it takes to sell. So the extra cash you receive from the buyer will come after the extra cash you have to spend on materials, builders, advertisements and anything else you need to help clinch the sale. So when you calculate how much that decision to go ahead is worth, you need to forecast how much you'll be able to sell the house for when you've added the extension, discounted to its present value.

Then you look at all the costs and when you incur them. Add up all the costs in each time period, and discount them to their respective present values – *and* include the current selling price of the house. Remember that investment appraisal includes opportunity costs (check out the earlier section 'Identifying Incremental and Opportunity Costs'). If you decide to extend the house now, you're also deciding to forgo the opportunity of selling it now.

Take a look at Table 11-4; you need three full years to extend the house (and think of all that brick dust!).

Table 11-4 Finding the NPV for the Extending a House Example

Year	*Costs*	*Net Cash Flow (£)*	*Present Value (£)*
0 (Now)	Not selling the house now	(200,000)	(200,000)
1	Builders, materials, costs of the inconvenience and so on	(75,000)	(71,429)
2	Further costs	(40,000)	(36,281)
3	Final costs and sales revenue	400,000	345,535
Net Present Value			**37,825**

We explain how a net cash flow becomes a present value in the next section 'Calculating the present value'.

Based on Table 11-4, your decision would be to go ahead. The decision to carry out this extension project instantly adds £37,825 to the value of the house. You're relying on the accuracy of all the forecast values, but in an example like this you have to make assumptions.

Calculating the present value

Assume that you need to know the cost of the capital a business has, which is generally the rate of interest the bank charges on any overdrafts the business takes out.

When you have that rate, you can use it to discount the future cash flows. This rate is generally called the *discount rate,* although the following terms all mean the same thing: cost of capital, weighted average cost of capital, hurdle rate, present value rate and required rate of return.

Many businesses use their overdraft rate as the discount rate for its cash flows. It saves the management accountant making some calculations as the bank will have assessed how risky the business and its projects are and decided on a rate of interest that will compensate the bank for the risk. On advanced finance courses other ways exist to calculate the rate, which look at all the various sources of finance a business uses, not just the overdraft.

When you have a discount rate, you use it to find the present value. The calculation is just like compound interest, but in reverse. If the bank offers you 10 per cent interest on a deposit of £1,000 (some chance!), Table 11-5 shows how you can calculate how much it's going to be worth in the future.

Table 11-5 Compound Interest on a Bank Deposit

Value at Start of the Year (£)	*Effect of the Interest*	*Value at End of the Year (£)*
Deposit 1,000	At the end of the year, the amount is worth the same as it was worth to start with, plus the interest it earns (10 per cent more): that is, 110 per cent of the deposit (or in decimals 1.10 × the deposit).	1,100
Now worth 1,100	You're now adding 10 per cent to the value that already includes last year's interest: that is, £1,100 × 110 per cent (or £1,100 × 1.10).	1,210

The table reveals that when you compound £1,000 at 10 per cent it's worth £1,210 after two years, because:

£1,000 × 110% × 110% = £1,210

We prefer to calculate using decimals rather than percentages as follows, which does exactly the same:

× 1.1 × 1.1

In fact, you can write $110\%^2$ (1.1^2), because multiplying a number by itself is the same as squaring it. Three years would be 1.1^3 ($110\%^3$), and so on.

£1,000 × 1.1^2 = £1,210 (this is compounding)

Discounting is the opposite to compounding.

So, you know what to do if you have £1,000 to invest now: you multiply it by 1 + the interest rate to the power of the length of time you want to deposit it, and then find how much you can withdraw at the end of that time.

But say that you're promised £1,210, but won't receive it for two years. You can put the same compounding process into reverse. Instead of multiplying you divide, as follows:

Value in 2 years' time	***Divide by***	***Present value***
£1,210	1.1^2 ($110\%^2$)	£1,000

There are different ways to show the 'divide by' value, but the principle remains the same. Here 'divide by' is a division sum – the value in two years' time divided by 1.1^2 – but you can also ‘divide by’ using a multiplication sum. The £1,210 would be multiplied by the reciprocal of 1.1^2; in other words, a value found by dividing 1 by 1.1^2.

If you divide 1 by 1.1^2, you get a value of 0.82644628, which you can use in the same way except that you multiply instead:

Value in 2 years’ time	*Multiply by*	*Present value*
£1,210	0.82644628	£1,000

In exams that test NPV, tables are often provided that have already calculated the discount rates, to show the discount rate value you multiply by the cash flow to find the present value. For an example, see Figure 11-1.

PRESENT VALUE TABLE

Present value of £1, where r = discount rate and n = number of periods until cash flow takes place $\frac{1}{(1+r)^n}$ which can be written as $1/(1+r)^n$

Period	Discount rates (r)									
Year (n)	1%	2%	3%	4%	5%	6%	7%	8%	9%	10%
1	0.990	0.980	0.971	0.962	0.952	0.943	0.935	0.926	0.917	0.909
2	0.980	0.961	0.943	0.925	0.907	0.890	0.873	0.857	0.842	0.826
3	0.971	0.942	0.915	0.889	0.864	0.840	0.816	0.794	0.772	0.751
4	0.961	0.924	0.888	0.855	0.823	0.792	0.763	0.735	0.708	0.683
5	0.951	0.906	0.863	0.822	0.784	0.747	0.713	0.681	0.650	0.621
6	0.942	0.888	0.837	0.790	0.746	0.705	0.666	0.630	0.596	0.564
7	0.933	0.871	0.813	0.760	0.711	0.665	0.623	0.583	0.547	0.513
8	0.923	0.853	0.789	0.731	0.677	0.627	0.582	0.540	0.502	0.467
9	0.914	0.837	0.766	0.703	0.645	0.592	0.544	0.500	0.460	0.424
10	0.905	0.820	0.744	0.676	0.614	0.558	0.508	0.463	0.422	0.386
11	0.896	0.804	0.722	0.650	0.585	0.527	0.475	0.429	0.388	0.350
12	0.887	0.788	0.701	0.625	0.557	0.497	0.444	0.397	0.356	0.319
13	0.879	0.773	0.681	0.601	0.530	0.469	0.415	0.368	0.326	0.290
14	0.870	0.758	0.661	0.577	0.505	0.442	0.388	0.340	0.299	0.263
15	0.861	0.743	0.642	0.555	0.481	0.417	0.362	0.315	0.275	0.239
16	0.853	0.728	0.623	0.534	0.458	0.394	0.339	0.292	0.252	0.218
17	0.844	0.714	0.605	0.513	0.436	0.371	0.317	0.270	0.231	0.198
18	0.836	0.700	0.587	0.494	0.416	0.350	0.296	0.250	0.212	0.180
19	0.828	0.686	0.570	0.475	0.396	0.331	0.277	0.232	0.194	0.164
20	0.820	0.673	0.554	0.456	0.377	0.312	0.258	0.215	0.178	0.149

Figure 11-1: Present value table to show the present value of £1.

In some advanced exams, you have to discount at rates not given in the tables. In those exams, you have to know the formula as well.

In the earlier section 'Using the payback method', we use the example of Paul's Taxi to examine the payback method, and here we employ the same information (from the earlier Table 11-2) to help understand the NPV method.

We add two columns onto Table 11-2 (in exams, you're normally told the rate to use). For this example, discount at 5 per cent using Table 11-6.

Table 11-6 Finding the NPV for the Paul's Taxi Example

Year	*Investment (£)*	*Revenue (£)*	*Running Costs (£)*	*Net Cash Flow (£)*	*Discount Factor 5%*	*Present Value (£)*
0	(22,000)			(22,000)	1.000	(22,000)
1		50,000	(35,000)	15,000	0.952	14,280
2		65,000	(45,000)	20,000	0.907	18,140
3		80,000	(55,000)	25,000	0.864	21,600
4		85,000	(59,000)	26,000	0.823	21,398
5	1,500	90,000	(62,000)	29,500	0.784	23,128
Net Present Value						**76,546**

You follow the same process as for the house extension in 'Homing in on NPV and decision-making', earlier in this chapter. As the NPV for Paul is positive we recommend that he should go ahead. The split-second when he decides to go ahead will then add £76,546 to the value of his business.

Working that NPV

After you've calculated the NPV – by finding the annual cash flows and listing net cash flow on a year by year basis, discounting these cash flows to produce a present value for each annual cash flow and adding up all the cash flows to find the net cash flow – you may be wondering about how to use it.

Well, you don't need a company policy. Although the payback method tells you the time needed to pay back your investment, you can go ahead only if that payback period was shorter than the company policy period. But the

NPV provides an absolute decision. If the NPV is a positive value it increases the value of the business; if it's negative it reduces the value of the business. So say yes to positive NPVs, they're worth the investment!

Putting Payback and NPV into Practice

We have a good look at the payback and NPV methods in the earlier sections 'Getting Your Money Back: The Payback Technique' and 'Understanding Time Value of Money and Net Present Value (NPV)', respectively, and if you're itching to practise them yourself (and even if you're not!), here's your chance.

For AAT exams payback is examined at level 3 and NPV at levels 3 and 4. Typically, AAT questions give candidates most of the information without requiring a lot of calculations for the net cash flows. They always provide the discount rates.

Task the first: Payback

See how you get on with the following task.

The company Macho Machines ('making mechanisms for real men') has the opportunity to manufacture a new product that involves an initial capital investment of £380,000. The product has an expected life of three years, and at the end of this period the equipment bought as part of the initial investment will be sold (a disposal) for £60,000. Table 11-7 shows the estimates of capital expenditure, sales and costs that the company has produced.

Table 11-7 Information for the Macho Machines Payback Example

Year	*Capital Expenditure/ Disposal (£000)*	*Sales Income (£000)*	*Operating Costs (£000)*	*Net Cash Flow (£000)*	*Running Total (£000)*
0	(380)				
1		310	(148)		
2		380	(170)		
3	60	250	(90)		

Use the information to find the payback period in the following two cases:

- On the assumption that you don't know how evenly the cash flows accrue during the year:

  This project pays back within .... years.

- On the assumption that the cash flows occur evenly each year:

  This project takes ....years to pay back.

Task the second: NPV

Take a look at the data in Table 11-8.

Table 11-8 Additional Information for Task 2: Macho Machines Example

Year	*Capital Expenditure/ Disposal (000)*	*Sales Income (000)*	*Operating Costs (000)*	*Net Cash Flows (000)*	*Discount Factors (000)*	*Present Value (000)*
0	(380)					
1		310	(148)			
2		380	(170)			
3	60	250	(90)			
Net Present Value						

The company's cost of capital is 10 per cent, as follows:

Year	*10%*
0	1.000
1	0.909
2	0.826
3	0.751

Please carry out the following tasks:

- Calculate the net present value for the proposed new capital investment.
- Recommend whether the proposed new capital investment should be made (based on your calculations of the NPV and the payback period).

Compounding the problem of interest

In this section's examples, we apply the time value of money based on periods of a whole year, designating the variable *n* to measure the number of years. The general approach can be applied to any time period: *n* would be the number of months or even days. The discount rate, or *r,* always measures the rate per period. Therefore, if *n* equals one year, an annual discount rate of 12 per cent is appropriate. But if *n* equals one month, you should also express the discount rate by months – say, as 1 per cent per month (12 per cent divided by 12 months).

Bankers call this *monthly compounding.* To try daily compounding, where *n* equals one day, express the discount rate in days. For example, 12 per cent divided by 365 days equals 0.0329 per cent per day, so that $r = 0.000329$. Banks work out your overdraft interest in this way.

Tackling tax

For a capital investment project, annual cash flows are affected by tax in two ways:

- Capital expenditure on equipment, such as machinery, is eligible for tax depreciation (in the UK called *capital allowances*), which reduces the tax payable by a company – and tax itself is a cash flow. Tax has to be paid to the government, so should be part of the calculation just as much as the other cash payments needed for the project, such as purchases of raw materials.
- Profits made from an investment are subject to tax. If a capital investment project leads to the company making more profit, the company has more tax to pay. If it leads to the company making less profit, the company has less tax to pay. These cash flows are relevant because they're cash payments and arise because of the capital investment.

The Operational Cash Flows from the investment and the tax implications

A capital investment project is an activity that has annual revenues and annual expenditures. You must identify all the cash flows that occur year by year. These tell you the annual net cash flow from running the investment project. You can also calculate the tax that will be incurred (or saved) on the operations based on the annual net cash flow.

Again, we make use of the Paul's Taxi example, which we introduce in the earlier section 'Using the payback method'.

You're only interested in the operations and so the investment and disposal parts aren't required. The net cash flow column is now an operating profit and two tax columns are added (see Table 11-9).

Typically tax is paid after the end of the year when the profit has been made. In this example, we assume that tax is levied at 30 per cent of the profit. We also assume that the government collects half of the tax liability in the year the profit is made and half in the following year.

Table 11-9 Operating Costs and Tax Cash Flow from Operations

Year	Revenue (£)	Running Costs (£)	Operating Profit (£)	Tax on Profit 30% (£)	Tax Cash Flow (£)
1	50,000	(35,000)	15,000	4,500	2,250
2	65,000	(45,000)	20,000	6,000	5,250*
3	80,000	(55,000)	25,000	7,500	6,750
4	85,000	(59,000)	26,000	7,800	7,650
5	90,000	(62,000)	28,000	8,400	8,100
6					4,200

**Tax cash flow is half in the year the tax is incurred and half from the previous year. For example, in year 2: £3,000 from year 2 and £2,250 from year 1.*

The Tax Cash Flows arising from capital allowances on non-current assets

Governments allow the cost of acquiring non-current assets to be used to reduce taxable profits. Typically such assets last for several years, and in many cases governments spread the cost over several years. The effect of reducing the taxable profit is that the company has less tax to pay. This is important in the context of investment appraisal. The reduction in the tax payable is effectively a tax saving. By saving tax, a project could become worth an investment when it might not be worthwhile without the tax saving.

Table 11-10 shows the carrying value at the end of each year after the capital allowance is taken off – the investment is an asset of the business and so it's shown here as a positive value. Tax depreciation (or capital allowance) is typically calculated as a percentage of the carrying value, that is, using the reducing balance; it's set by the tax authority in a particular country (for example, the UK government). In this example, we use a 25 per cent capital allowance (tax depreciation) on the reducing balance. Tables 11-10 and 11-11 show the same layout. Table 11-10 shows the investment value at the start and the subsequent values after deducting the *written down allowance* (where you can claim to reduce or 'write down' any remaining balance of capital expenditure on plant and machinery that you haven't already claimed a capital allowance for).

These subsequent values are called *carrying values* as they represent the value the company tax accounts allocate to the investment. This is how much it is worth on a tax basis.

Table 11-10 Tax Savings Based on Capital Allowances – Layout

Year	*Investment – Carrying Value (£)*	*Written Down Allowance (£)*	*Tax Saved at 30%*	*Tax Cash Flow (£)*
0	22,000			
1	16,500	5,500		
2	12,375	4,125		
3	9,281	3,094		
4	6,961	2,320		
5	1,500	5,461		
6				

If you have a conventional calculator (not a clever scientific one) you can key in the residual value percentage (in this case 0.75 or 75 per cent) and then press the times sign twice. Doing so tells the calculator to apply a constant multiplication value of 0.75 to each value. You then press 22,000 and the equals sign. First you get the 16,500; if you press the equals sign again you get 12,375 and so on. This tip saves a little time in an exam. To find the annual allowance values, you then do five take-away sums.

Also, make sure that you enter your disposal value at the point the asset is being sold, so that your allowance is based on the value for which it's expected to be sold. In other words, you disregard the tax allowance rate when you have a specific forecast resale value. Quite possibly (although it's unlikely) this figure may be a negative value. That's fine and this method of calculation allows your subsequent calculations to use a negative value. In the UK this amount is called a *balancing charge*, effectively because the asset has been sold for more than its carrying value. The reason that it's rare is that within this calculation the disposal value would have to be more than the carrying value one year earlier. In other words, you'd be selling the asset for more than its tax carrying value a year ago.

The tax saving and tax cash flow columns are completed in the same way as the tax on operating profit cash flows (see Table 11-11).

Table 11-11 Tax Savings Based on Capital Allowances – Complete

Year	Investment – Carrying Value (£)	Written Down Allowance (£)	Tax Saved at 30% (£)	Tax Cash Flow (£)
0	22,000			
1	16,500	5,500	1,375	688
2	12,375	4,125	1,031	1,203
3	9,281	3,094	773	902
4	6,961	2,320	580	677
5	1,500	5,461	1,365	973
6				683

The Net Present Value table

This table brings together the information from the table of Operational Cash Flows and their tax implications with the table of Tax Cash Flows arising from capital allowances.

Table 11-12 is based on the cash inflows and outflows provided by the Paul's Taxi project, and brings together the information from Tables 11-9 and 11-11. The second column is for the cash spent on the investment and the cash received when it's sold. The third is the cash inflow from the operation of the project (in this example, the taxi service). The fourth shows the tax cash payments due to the taxi service being profitable (from Table 11-9). The fifth shows the tax savings (from Table 11-11), and because this saves tax it's treated as an inflow. The sixth is the net cash flow for each year.

Table 11-12 Net Present Value Table for Paul's Taxi

Year	Investment and Disposal (£)	Operating Profit (£)	Tax Cash Flow on Profit (£)	Tax Cash Saving (£)	Net Cash Flow (£)	Discount Factor 5%	Present Value (£)
0	(22,000)				(22,000)	1.000	(22,000)
1		15,000	(2,250)	688	13,438	0.952	12,793
2		20,000	(5,250)	1,203	21,203	0.907	19,231
3		25,000	(6,750)	902	19,152	0.864	16,547
4		26,000	(7,650)	677	19,027	0.823	15,659
5	1,500	28,000	(8,100)	973	22,373	0.784	17,540
6			(4,200)	683	(3,517)	0.746	(2,624)
Net Present Value							**57,147**

This three-table approach suits exam candidates on ACCA F9 and CIMA P1. Many of the higher-level exams assume expertise in capital investment appraisal, and so you benefit from learning the approach so well that you understand it and can build up an analysis of an investment using the data your exam question provides.

This approach works for real-life investment decisions because, as Benjamin Franklin said, 'in this world nothing can be said to be certain, except death and taxes'. Your real-life investment decisions need to take account of this certainty.

Putting the three-table technique into practice

See how you get on with this task.

Paints and Poisons Ltd has identified an investment that reduces hazardous waste, produces a by-product that the company can sell and saves it fines for damaging the environment. The investment has a five-year life, after which it'll need to be replaced.

Table 11-13 shows the produced estimates of capital expenditure, sales, savings and costs.

Summing up the key components in NPV

If you track back from the value you find for the NPV of a project, you can see how specific key values contribute towards it:

- The incremental revenues each year
- Any incremental savings
- The incremental operating costs
- The investment cost and residual value
- The rate used to discount the cash flows
- The tax rate
- The tax allowance rate

Table 11-13 Figures for the Paints and Poisons Ltd Example

	£		£
Investment cost	45,000	Investment residual value (year 5)	10,000
Annual running costs	1,300	Waste disposal savings per year	5,000
Other annual operating costs	2,000	Fines saved per year	7,600
		By-product sales per year	4,500

The following figures apply:

- Tax depreciation of 25 per cent per year of the reducing balance carrying value, with a balancing adjustment in the year of disposal.
- Tax payable at 30 per cent of taxable profits: half is payable in the year when the profit arises, with the balance payable the following year.
- Cost of capital is 10 per cent per year to evaluate projects; you can ignore inflation.

Taking a sensitive approach

A project manager needs to look at the components in a specific NPV calculation and recognise those that may cause the project to fail to achieve the forecast NPV. This task requires sensitivity analysis, an aspect that's regularly tested in ACCA and CIMA exams.

Using the Paul's Taxi example, you can consider the expected cost of running the taxi service. You can carry out a *sensitive analysis* on this component to find the percentage change that would cause the NPV to fall to zero. (Sensitivity analysis attempts to predict how a model will react to changes.)

Your job is to discover by how much the running costs affect the NPV.

Table 11-14 Sensitivity Analysis for Paul's Taxi Example

Year	*Cash Outflow (£)*	*Tax Saving (£)*	*Tax Cash Flow (£)*	*Net Cost to Paul (£)*	*Discount Factor*	*Present Value (£)*
1	35,000	10,500	5,250	29,750	0.952	28,322
2	45,000	13,500	12,000	33,000	0.907	29,931
3	55,000	16,500	15,000	40,000	0.864	34,560
4	59,000	17,700	17,100	41,900	0.823	34,484
5	62,000	18,600	18,150	43,850	0.784	34,378
6			9,300	(9,300)	0.746	(6,938)
						154,737

Table 11-14 shows that the running costs have a present value (or more precisely a net present cost) of £154,737. In addition, the NPV of the whole project is £57,147 (taken from the earlier Table 11-12).

You find the sensitivity of the NPV to a component of the calculation as follows:

$$\frac{\text{NPV of the whole project}}{\text{Present value of running costs}}\ \frac{£57{,}147}{£154{,}737} = 37 \text{ per cent}$$

Therefore, the NPV of Paul's Taxi project will continue to be positive, but if the running costs increase by more than 37 per cent, that would be enough to change the decision to go ahead.

The lower the percentage change in a component that's needed to change an investment decision, the more the project is sensitive to that component. A figure of 37 per cent means that Paul doesn't need to be very worried about running costs.

Another component that can change the decision is the discount factor. In Paul's case the discount factor would have to be as high as 73 per cent before it would make the decision change from going ahead to rejecting it.

Investigating Internal Rate of Return (IRR)

In the preceding section's Paul's Taxi example, you see that if the discount rate is higher than your estimate it stops the investment being worthwhile. This situation is familiar to anyone asking for a mortgage to buy a house or who reads in the newspapers that businesses aren't investing.

The Internal Rate of Return (IRR) is defined as the discount rate that leads to a NPV of zero. The IRR is the maximum price of borrowing that a project can afford and is the subject of this section.

The price of borrowing is crucial. Paul's example is rare: in many cases the difference between a worthwhile investment and one that isn't worth taking can be a few per cent of interest. If you were able to borrow at 5 per cent per annum to buy your first home, no doubt you'd be more keen to go ahead than if the interest rate was 10 per cent.

The company Rum Financials, which has an unusual but lucrative business providing alcohol to accountancy firms, is considering a possible investment. The management hasn't investigated the company's cost of capital, but instead has calculated the NPV of the project using a 5 per cent discount rate (see Table 11-15).

The result shows a positive value of £1,276. At this level of return the project should go ahead and add the NPV to the overall value of the business.

Table 11-15 Net Present Value Table at 5% Discount Rate: Rum Financials

Year		*Net Cash Flow (£)*	*Discount Rate 5%*	*Present Value (£)*
0	Investment	(20,000)	1.000	(20,000)
1	Annual net cash flow	6,000	0.952	5,714
2	Annual net cash flow	6,000	0.907	5,442
3	Annual net cash flow	6,000	0.864	5,183
4	Annual net cash flow	6,000	0.823	4,936
Net Present Value				**1,276**

But when the company does exactly the same analysis using a discount rate of 10 per cent, the story is quite different: the NPV is negative (see Table 11-16). The same project would now reduce the value of the business by £981.

Table 11-16 Net Present Value Table at 10%: Rum Financials

Year		*Net Cash Flow (£)*	*Discount Rate 10%*	*Present Value (£)*
0	Investment	(20,000)	1.000	(20,000)
1	Annual net cash flow	6,000	0.909	5455
2	Annual net cash flow	6,000	0.826	4959
3	Annual net cash flow	6,000	0.751	4508
4	Annual net cash flow	6,000	0.683	4098
Net Present Value				**(981)**

This analysis agrees with the news reports about interest rates. When the interest rate goes up, people are less likely to buy a house and firms tend to reduce their investments in new equipment and machinery. When interest rates go down, however, more people are willing to buy houses and more firms are prepared to borrow to invest.

Figure 11-2 shows how the NPV falls as the discount rate rises.

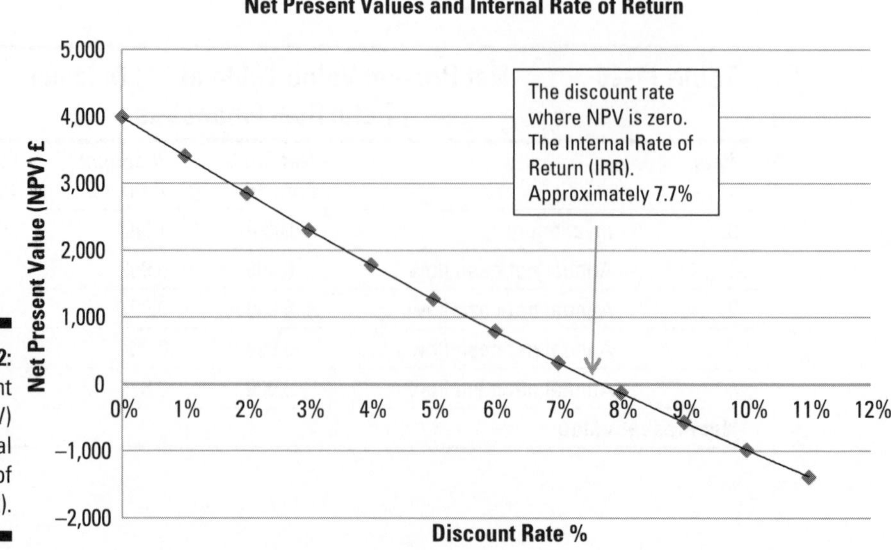

Figure 11-2: Net Present Value (NPV) and Internal Rate of Return (IRR).

The point at which the line joining the different net present values crosses the zero net present value shows the discount rate where the net present value is zero. This is the IRR value: approximately 7.7 per cent.

IRR takes into account the size of the investment, allowing you to compare different-sized projects alongside each other, and often a company's Board of Directors is more familiar with percentage comparisons than with absolute cash values. But NPV has the advantage in showing how a project will affect the value of the business.

In exams, the IRR can be found using a technique called *interpolation.* This approach involves identifying two different NPVs, ideally one that is positive and one that is negative.

Here's the formula:

$$\text{Lower discount rate} \left(\text{where NPV is positive}\right) + \frac{\text{Positive NPV}}{\text{Difference between the two different NPVs}} \times \text{Difference between the two percentage rates}$$

Using the Rum Financials example:

$$5\% + \frac{1{,}276}{1276-(981)} \quad \text{or} \quad \frac{1{,}276}{2.257} \times (10\% - 5\%) = 7.83\%$$

Some students make errors in the calculation of the difference between the two NPVs. Remember that if one is a negative value and the other is a positive value, the difference is the gap between them. In other words, you can ignore the negative sign and add the two values together.

In Rum Financials the fraction was 0.5654, and so the calculation is:

$$5\% + (0.5654 \times 5\%) = 7.83\%$$

This method is perfectly acceptable both at work and in exams. You may have noticed that we estimated 7.7 per cent from the diagram and found 7.83 per cent by calculation. Both values are fine. At work it is highly unlikely that a difference of 0.13 per cent would lead to accepting an investment project or not. All the figures are forecasts so precision is unlikely; we are merely recognising whether to invest.

Looking beyond the Numbers: Qualitative Factors

Capital investment projects can bring with them benefits that aren't necessarily best measured using the financial analyses we discuss in this chapter:

- **Increased customer loyalty:** The extra products the projects add can increase the prestige of the company and may lead to increased sales of other products. This is particularly true when customers purchase a basket of products and look for a single supplier. Having the opportunity to buy the full basket can attract these customers.
- **Stronger employee morale:** Staff retention can be improved by staff seeing that new projects are used and also from the promotional opportunities new projects offer.
- **The chance to test new markets:** A business may knowingly launch a project to supply a new market with a product that has a negative NPV, in the hope that the new market can become a place to sell other products.

Evaluating such qualitative factors when making decisions requires a measure of personal judgement, which is different for every decision-maker. When looking over the numbers for any capital project, think about other factors that the analysis doesn't account for but that you consider to be important.

Chapter 12

Naming Your Price: Approaches to Decision-Making

In This Chapter

- Addressing absorption costing
- Using cost-plus pricing
- Taking risks with relevant-cost pricing
- Aiming for target costing

On the popular game show *The Price is Right*, the host challenges contestants to estimate the prices of different pieces of merchandise. Guessing the right price wins them cash and all sorts of valuable prizes. Even if they get the price wrong, they still walk away with a novelty nametag and maybe a chance to spin a giant wheel. All good, clean fun.

But the stakes get a lot higher when you're naming prices in the real business world: set your prices too high and you risk scaring away customers; price too low and the losses may wipe out your business. Your prices have to be low enough to lure customers but high enough to cover your costs and help you earn a profit. Therefore, before setting a price, you need to understand the market forces and the cost structure of your business.

In this chapter, we explain how to use your knowledge of cost behaviour to make pricing decisions. We cover four approaches: absorption cost pricing (which takes into account all variable and fixed costs of manufacturing a product); cost-plus pricing (which adds a mark-up to the absorption cost); relevant-cost pricing (which only considers how the total costs of the business increase as a result of agreeing an extra sale); and target costing (which sets the product price from the outset and then forces managers to design and make products so that they can be sold profitably at that price). However much you might want to set a price based on the costs incurred making it, in the 21st century most of us don't have that luxury. Target costing is realistic in accepting that the price is out of your control and set by how much customers are prepared to pay, so this is the approach we talk about most.

Differentiating Products to Decide on Prices

Market analysts tend to split companies into two groups as regards setting selling prices for their products, depending on the extent to which the companies use *product differentiation.* This is what allows consumers to see differences among different companies' products and so decide to spend more money for some brands than for others. By looking at the differences a product has, you see the importance of customer perception. What the customer perceives as the value of a product is very important, and the price needs to be set at a level where the customer feels that he or she is paying for something that's worth buying. Every pricing method needs to take customer perception into consideration if the prices produced are going to lead to profitable sales.

- **Price makers:** These companies successfully differentiate their products and so are able to charge a higher price than competitors. For example, Apple has cleverly differentiated many of its products from competitors and customers often pay significantly more for them.
- **Price takers:** These companies don't differentiate their products and so need to use low prices instead to get a leg up on the competition. For example, customers usually have trouble seeing any difference among the products offered by different mainstream supermarkets. Therefore, all supermarkets are price takers and need to price their products competitively in line with each other.

Regardless of how well a company differentiates its products, its prices still need to take into account market forces *and* the company's own costs.

Taking All Costs into Account: Absorption Costing

Absorption costing (sometimes also called *full costing*) is the traditional method for costing goods that companies manufacture and sell. In fact, UK and international accounting standards require all companies to use absorption costing in their financial statements.

We look at how overheads are absorbed into products in Chapter 4. Absorption costs include all *product costs* (which we explain in Chapter 3):

- The costs of *direct materials* are raw materials that you can trace directly to the manufactured product. The same goes for *direct labour*, the cost of paying employees for the time they use to make your products.
- *Fixed overhead* costs are indirect and production overheads include the miscellaneous costs of running a factory, such as rent and supervisory salaries that can't be traced directly to products.

Absorption costing requires you to spread out the fixed costs over all units produced.

Suppose that your factory makes T-shirts. Each T-shirt requires £8 worth of variable costs (direct materials, direct labour and variable overhead), and your factory pays £100,000 for fixed costs each year for rent and utilities. This year, you plan to make 50,000 T-shirts. How much will each T-shirt cost?

According to absorption costing, the cost of a T-shirt includes variable and fixed components. You know that the variable component per shirt is £8, but the fixed component of £100,000 applies to all the shirts, and so you need to spread it out across each unit. To do so, you divide the total fixed costs of £100,000 by the number of units you plan to produce (50,000) to arrive at a fixed cost per unit of £2.

Therefore, each T-shirt has a total cost per unit of £10: £8 worth of variable costs and £2 worth of fixed costs.

As we explain in Chapter 5, businesses use total cost per unit to report the value of inventory on their balance sheets (Statements of Financial Position) and to calculate Cost of Goods Sold on their income statements.

Pricing at Cost-Plus

Retailers and manufacturers set their prices at *cost-plus* by adding a fixed mark-up to their absorption cost (which we describe in the preceding section). Cost-plus pricing ensures that prices are high enough to meet profit goals.

Figure 12-1 illustrates how cost-plus pricing calculates the sales price by adding mark-up to a product's fixed and variable costs.

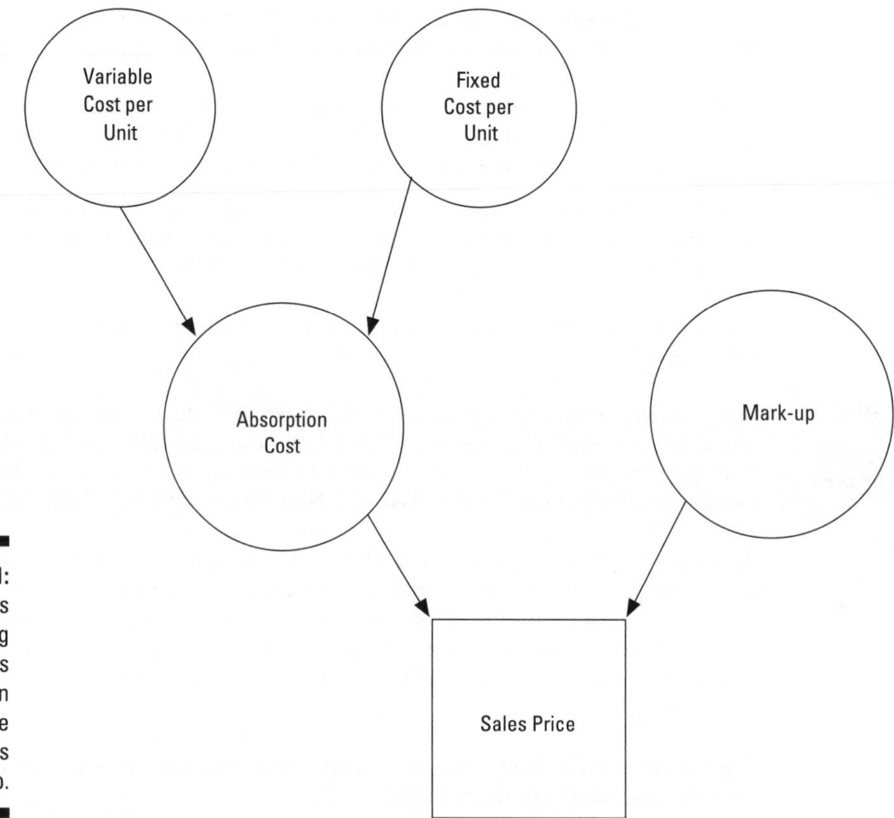

Figure 12-1: Cost-plus pricing includes absorption cost of the product plus a mark-up.

Calculating fixed mark-ups

To figure out the mark-up for cost-plus pricing, you divide total desired profit by the number of units produced.

Imagine that Saint Company wants to earn $100,000 on the production of 100 Model 51 robots:

$$\frac{\text{Desired profit}}{\text{Units produced}} = \text{Mark-up}$$

$$\frac{\$100{,}000}{100} = \text{Mark-up}$$

$$\$1{,}000 = \text{Mark-up}$$

Dividing the desired profit by units produced results in a planned mark-up of £1,000 per unit. To set the price, add this planned mark-up to the cost. Assume that Saint's cost to produce each robot is £4,000:

$$\text{Cost} + \text{Mark-up} = \text{Sales price}$$
$$£4{,}000 + £1{,}000 = \text{Sales price}$$
$$£5{,}000 = \text{Sales price}$$

If Saint Company wants to earn a total of £100,000, it needs to set the price at £5,000 per unit.

Setting a cost-plus percentage

Companies often sell many different products at different prices, and so they commonly use a *cost-plus percentage* or *percentage mark-up on cost* that applies to all their products. To work out this percentage, you divide the mark-up amount by the expected sales price. Then, to determine the products' sales prices, you apply this percentage to all products, or to different categories of products.

Assume that Saint Company's Model 51 robot (from the preceding section) has a £1,000 mark-up on a sales price of £5,000.

$$\frac{\text{Mark-up}}{\text{Sales price}} = \text{Cost-plus percentage}$$
$$\frac{£1{,}000}{£5{,}000} = \text{Cost-plus percentage}$$
$$20\% = \text{Cost-plus percentage}$$

Here, Saint earns a 20 per cent cost-plus percentage. The company can then apply the same cost-plus percentage to set the prices of other products. For example, another robot, Model 6, costs Saint Company £6,500 to produce. The mark-up on this robot amounts to £1,300 (£6,500 × 20 per cent), pricing it at £7,800 (£6,500 + £1,300).

Considering problems with cost-plus pricing

Cost-plus pricing works because it's easy to use, but it carries drawbacks:

- **Cost-plus pricing ignores market factors.**

  Just because you like to mark up your merchandise 20 per cent doesn't necessarily mean that your customers are willing to pay this price or that your competitors are going to co-operate with you by setting their prices even higher.

- **Cost-plus pricing relies on absorption costing, and so it treats fixed costs as though they're variable.**

  Saint Company wants to sell 100 Model 51 robots, which means it can distribute its fixed costs over 100 units. However, the fixed costs remain the same regardless of how many units Saint actually sells; if the company sells only 50 robots, the fixed costs are spread over fewer units (50 robots rather than 100), and the cost per unit rises. Here, if production drops to 50 robots, the cost per unit increases to £6,000 per unit. This change gives Saint a problem. Table 12-1 shows how this miscalculation causes Saint's profits to evaporate, leaving a £50,000 loss.

  Saint originally assumes that it will make and sell 100 units. Based on this assumption, it projects an average cost of £4,000 per unit, a mark-up of £1,000, and a sales price of £5,000. However, if Saint makes and sells only 50 units, the average cost balloons to £6,000 per unit. Stuck with a sales price of £5,000, Saint loses £50,000.

Table 12-1 Cost-plus Pricing Gone Wild

	The Plan	*What Actually Happened*
Number of units sold	100	50
Sales price	£5,000	£5,000
Cost per unit	£4,000	£6,000
Total sales	£500,000	£250,000
Cost of sales	£400,000	£300,000
Gross profit (loss)	£100,000	(£50,000)

Look on the bright side: if your sales volume is higher than you expected, it will have a disproportionately *positive* effect on income – delivering profits beyond your wildest dreams.

Short-Term Pricing Based on Relevant Costs

In Chapter 10 we look at deciding which costs are relevant when making business decisions. The only considerations are what the outcomes would be if you do or don't sell at a particular price; historic costs aren't always relevant. The only relevant costs are those that change as a result of the decision to supply a product or service now. For example, when an airline invites travellers to buy stand-by tickets half an hour before the plane takes off, the cost to the airline of each stand-by traveller is very low, and the alternative is to fly the plane with empty seats. This arrangement is fine in the short term and when considering a small part of an organisation. But overheads still have to be paid for, and even if one area of excess capacity can generate money using relevant costing, the organisation as a whole still has to cover all the direct and overhead costs and more if it's going to make a profit.

Management accounting courses often use hotels (as well as airlines) to provide examples of relevant costs. One of the authors (Sandy) has seen potential hotel guests milling around in London at around 9:00 p.m. because the word is out that a particular hotel is going to discount room prices from 9:30 p.m. onwards. Potential full-price sales are lost because a one-off short-term overcapacity solution turned into a routine and customer behaviour responded. Before deciding to use spare capacity by pricing using only the incremental cost of a sale (the relevant cost), think about the message it gives to customers. If long term sales at the normal prices might be lost to make a small number of sales at a price based on the relevant cost, those sales where the price is based on relevant cost may be worth forgoing.

Hitting Your Bull's-Eye: Target Costing

Many industries use *price points* – special price levels that customers expect to pay. You've probably seen these prices in shops: £99.99, £26.99, £19.95, and so on. Using an understanding of customer expectations and competitor pricing, manufacturers design products specifically so that they can be produced and sold at suitable price points.

Although traditionally firms design the product first and then set the price, target costing requires you to set the price before you design the product. After you know the price, you can engineer the product so that its costs are low enough to ensure that you earn the expected profit margin. Done right, target costing avoids problems caused by products that are priced too high for consumers or are too expensive to make. It engineers the price, the profit margin and the cost right into the product.

In the 21st century, most firms need to look to the market to decide on the price to charge. The target cost is the maximum cost to achieve a required profit.

Calculating your target cost

With target costing, you start with a market price and mark-up and use that information to figure out the product's cost and specifications. This approach is in contrast to cost-plus pricing, which starts with the product cost and desired profit and uses that information to set the price (refer to 'Pricing at Cost-Plus' earlier in the chapter).

To calculate the target cost, you subtract the desired profit from the market price:

Market price – Desired profit = Target cost

Figure 12-2 illustrates how this process works.

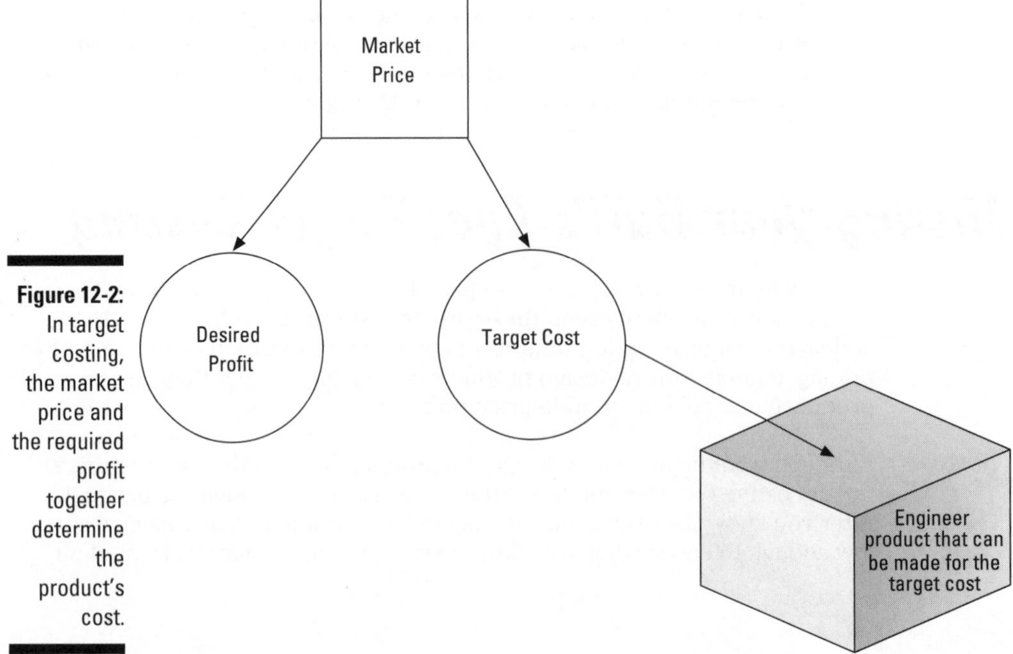

Figure 12-2: In target costing, the market price and the required profit together determine the product's cost.

Consider this true example, which demonstrates how target costing works in practice. One of the authors (Mark) went to Costco to buy a new desktop computer. Costco had four different desktop models, costing $599.99, $749.99, $999.99 and $1,299.99. Because Mark wanted to spend $750, he bought the $749.99 model.

At the time of writing, Costco's financial statements indicate that the company sets prices so that gross profit equals 10.51 per cent of the company's sales price. An inventory item that sells for $100 typically includes $10.51 worth of gross profit ($100 × 10.51 per cent), costing the company $89.49 ($100 – $10.51).

The company's desired profit on this computer model equals $78.82 ($749.99 × 10.51 per cent). Plug it into the formula:

$$\begin{aligned} \text{Market price} - \text{Desired profit} &= \text{Target cost} \\ \$749.99 - \$78.82 &= \text{Target cost} \\ \$671.17 &= \text{Target cost} \end{aligned}$$

The maths indicates that Costco should pay $671.17 for computers that it can sell for $749.99.

Target costing works for retailers (like Costco) and for manufacturers (like Hewlett-Packard (HP), maker of the new computer). Therefore, after Costco determines that it's willing to pay $671.17 for these computers, HP needs to figure out how to make computers with all the right bells and whistles that it can sell for $671.17.

Hewlett-Packard works to earn a 22.7 per cent profit margin on sales. Therefore, the company's desired profit equals $152.36 ($671.17 × 22.7 per cent):

$$\begin{aligned} \text{Market price} - \text{Desired profit} &= \text{Target cost} \\ \$671.17 - \$152.36 &= \text{Target cost} \\ \$518.81 &= \text{Target cost} \end{aligned}$$

After subtracting desired profit of $152.36 from its expected sales price of $671.17, HP works out that it needs to engineer and produce computers that cost $518.81. Armed with this knowledge, the engineers pick and choose various specifications and features to cook up a computer that costs exactly this amount.

Knowing when to use target costing

Target costing works especially well for companies whose products aren't well-differentiated (such as electronic accessories and economy cars), where price is often a key consideration for customers selecting which brand to buy. This technique ensures that the company can sell a competitive product with all the features – and the price – that customers expect.

AAT Financial Performance exams test target costing. It's one of two alternatives for task 9 on the computer-based exam, and so is well worth mastering.

Having set a target cost, achieving it can be difficult. For example:

- The product may have features that add costs but not value when it's sold.
- Processes used to make the product may include inefficiencies.

Exam questions can ask for definitions and for calculations. Here's an example.

The Saxby Company is in the process of engineering a new product. The company applies the principles of target costing and directors require that all new products make a profit margin of 20 per cent.

1. **The new product has an estimated sales price of £16.25 per unit. Calculate the total production cost per unit that the company will need to achieve in order to make a 20 per cent profit margin.**

   Hopefully this is fairly straightforward, as we show in Figure 12-3.

Figure 12-3: Calculating the total target cost per unit.

Market selling price		£16.25
Required profit margin	20% of price (20% × £16.25)	–£3.25
Total target production cost		£13.00

2. **The company expects the demand to be 15,000 units per month and the fixed production overheads are expected to be £75,000 per month. Calculate the target total variable costs per unit to achieve the desired profit margin.**

   Figure 12-4 shows the answer.

Total target production cost		£13.00
Forecast production overhead cost per unit	£75,000 per month ÷ 15,000 units	–£5.00
Target total variable cost per unit		£8.00

Figure 12-4: Calculating the variable target cost per unit.

The figure shows that the product is viable only if it can be produced costing a maximum of £8 per unit in variable costs.

3. **The material needed per product is 500 centimetres at a cost of £5 per metre. Labour rates would be £10 per hour. What is the maximum time that one new product can take to be made?**

Target total variable cost per unit		£8.00
Material cost per unit	500 cm × £5.00/m	–£2.50
Target labour cost		£5.50
Rate per hour	£10.00	
Maxiumum labour hours per unit	$\frac{\text{£5.50 per unit}}{\text{£10.00 per hour}}$	0.55 hours

Figure 12-5: The maximum time to make one product.

Figure 12-5 shows the answer and can be shown to management. This product would be viable at the market price, with the forecast fixed overhead costs, material costs and labour rate, provided that it can be produced in 0.55 hours (33 minutes) or less.

4. **What would the company have to do if the production department forecast that the time required was slightly more than the target time?**

   This situation would often happen. As the management accountant, you'd identify the maximum time for a product to be viable. As production engineers, they'd work out the time they think is needed to meet the quality standards.

Valuing the similarity

Unlike some people, we don't make a distinction between value engineering and value analysis. Although some writers distinguish the two, stating that value engineering is carried out at the design stage and value analysis is carried out within production, practising management accountants are more concerned with doing the analysis in the real world, and so tend to treat the two descriptions as meaning the same thing.

Boxing clever!

A folklore story about Swan Vesta matchboxes goes as follows. An employee approached the senior management and told them that he had a way to save millions of pounds in production costs. He held back from revealing it until a legal agreement was made that gave him a share of any savings. Then he told them to put the sandpaper on only one side of the matchbox.

The company saved millions, the employee received a substantial share and now boxes of Swan Vesta matches only have sandpaper on one side of the box.

At this point you could stop and say that the product isn't worth making. But the effort so far and the desire to produce this product ought to make you try to re-think. This brings in value engineering, which we discuss in the next section.

Carrying out value engineering

Value engineering demands that every process and every design characteristic of the product is evaluated to try to achieve the target cost.

Value engineering involves looking first at the product and the perception of the customer. Can aspects of the product be removed and not affect the level of customer satisfaction?

Value engineering reviews the production processes that are used to make the product and investigates whether inefficiencies exist. For example, many work benches now have electric tools on retractable cables to enable production workers to complete more jobs in the time available than their predecessors, who had to walk back and forward to a rack of tools.

Acting after value engineering is carried out

Following value engineering, the production engineers can re-cost the product. If the revised cost is no more than the target cost, the product can go into production. If not, it would be rejected on financial grounds.

In the Saxby Company example in the earlier section 'Knowing when to use target costing', the target costing question leads from a target total cost to identifying the maximum labour hours for the new product to be viable. Other questions may ask for:

- Maximum total fixed cost
- Maximum variable cost per unit and subsequent inputs and input costs
- Sales volume needed

Here's how we recommend answering these questions, with examples in Tables 12-2 to 12-4:

- **Maximum total fixed cost:**

  (Price × (1 – required profit margin) – variable cost per unit) × forecast sales volume

- **Maximum variable cost per unit:**

  (Price × (1 – required profit margin)) – (total fixed cost/forecast sales volume)

- **Sales volume needed:**

  Total fixed costs ÷ (price – required profit – variable cost per unit)

Table 12-2 Example on Finding the Maximum Total Fixed Cost

	Saxby 'Denise'	*Saxby 'Becky'*
Price	£15.00	£16.00
Forecast sales volume units	12,000	8,000
Required profit margin	20%	15%
Variable cost per unit	£8.00	£6.40

Table 12-3 Example on Finding the Maximum Variable Cost per Unit

	Saxby 'Denise'	*Saxby 'Becky'*
Price	£30.00	£36.00
Forecast sales volume units	10,000	12,000
Required profit margin	25%	20%
Total fixed cost	£105,000	£216,000

Table 12-4 Example on Finding the Sales Volume Needed to Achieve the Required Profit Margin Percentage

	Saxby 'Denise'	*Saxby 'Becky'*
Price	£15.00	£12.00
Variable cost per unit	£5.00	£4.00
Required profit margin	10%	12.50%
Total fixed cost	£11,900	£5,200

Chapter 13

Doing Deals between Company Divisions: Transfer Prices

In This Chapter

- Understanding why transfer prices are necessary
- Letting divisions haggle over their own transfer prices
- Basing transfer prices on the selling division's manufacturing cost
- Taking the guesswork out of transfer pricing by using market value

One of the authors (Mark) has three sons who love to cut deals. The other day, Levi sold David three action figures, payable whenever David collects the money that Aaron owes him for his old watch. Aaron, meanwhile, is still waiting for the balance from Levi for an old, torn-up *Harry Potter* book.

These deals often require complex computations involving not only time value of money (cash paid today is worth more than cash paid tomorrow), but also adding up the cost of acquiring the item, market value that it can be sold for (to someone outside the family!) and opportunity costs. Negotiations can stretch on for days or even weeks and sometimes involve tactics that probably wouldn't hold up in court. The boys attach great importance to these prices, because they can substantially increase their net worth.

Similarly, divisions within large companies sometimes need to haggle in order to make deals to buy and sell merchandise between each other. For example, if a company owns a retail shop and a factory that sells its wares to the retailer, someone somewhere has to set a price, called the *transfer price*.

In this chapter, we explain how to set transfer prices and describe the most commonly used technique: having the divisions negotiate a transfer price between themselves. We also explain how to use other transfer-pricing techniques, such as cost-based pricing and market-based pricing.

Pinpointing the Importance of Transfer Pricing

Large companies usually organise themselves into divisions that provide different goods or services and often do business with each other. For example, a clothing retailer may own several clothing factories, with the retailer and each factory being treated as separate divisions, sort of like companies within a company. Similarly, separate divisions of an oil company may produce, refine and sell petrol. Many large entertainment companies own film studios, cinemas, and satellite and cable networks, the cinemas and networks featuring movies and shows that the film studio produces.

In order to manage these divisions, most larger companies *decentralise*, treating each division as its own business earning its own profit. The use of divisions is highly beneficial in giving decision-making autonomy to divisional managers and the opportunity for rewards through improved performance. Sometimes, however, the motivation to improve profitability in one division can lead managers to disregard the other divisions and the company as a whole. When these different divisions do business with each other, buying and selling different products, the transfer prices they set play a critical role in determining how they share the company's overall profits.

Transfer prices need to be set to benefit the organisation as a whole.

Setting out the problem

Suppose that Jeffrey and Sandy are employed by Dorothy. Jeffrey works manufacturing T-shirts. Sandy retails the T-shirts to customers. In business terms, Dorothy is the overall company and Jeffrey and Sandy are two separate divisions. Each T-shirt costs Jeffrey £5 in variable costs per unit and £30,000 worth of fixed costs a year (check out Chapter 8 for more about fixed and variable costs). Sandy sells each shirt to the end-customer for £10. To do so, however, she has to pay an additional £1 commission per shirt and £25,000 a year in fixed costs. Sandy expects to sell 50,000 shirts to outside customers.

The question is: at what price should Jeffrey sell Sandy the shirts? To illustrate the problem, we pick a number to test out: £8 per T-shirt. Figure 13-1 uses contribution, as explained in Chapter 9, to describe how this price impacts both divisions' profits. Remember that the Marginal Costing income statement starts with sales and then subtracts variable costs, resulting in contribution. To arrive at profit, you then subtract fixed costs.

	Jeffrey (makes shirts)	Sandy (sells them)
Jeffrey's sales price (comes from Sandy)	**£8.00**	
Sandy's sales price (comes from customers)		£10.00
Jeffrey's variable cost	(£5.00)	
Sandy's variable cost of buying shirts from Jeffrey		**(£8.00)**
Sandy's variable cost of sales commissions		(£1.00)
Contribution margin per unit	£3.00	£1.00
Volume	50,000 shirts	50,000 shirts
Total contribution margin	£150,000	£50,000
Total fixed costs	(£30,000)	(£25,000)
Net profit	£120,000	£25,000

Figure 13-1: The effect of selling the T-shirts at a transfer price of £8.

Figure 13-1 indicates that at a price of £8 per unit, Jeffrey enjoys contribution per unit of £3, leaving Sandy with only £1 per unit. Now multiply this contribution per unit by total sales volume for each division and then subtract fixed costs. Jeffrey gets £120,000 worth of net income, whereas Sandy gets just £25,000.

Try a different sales price per unit: £5.50. Figure 13-2 shows what happens. With a per shirt price of £5.50, the shoe is on the other foot (to mix our clothing references!). Jeffrey is going to be disappointed to discover that he earns only £0.50 in contribution per unit, while Sandy earns £3.50 per unit. Jeffrey incurs a £5,000 net loss and Sandy earns £150,000 in net income for the year.

	Jeffrey (makes shirts)	Sandy (sells them)
Jeffrey's sales price (comes from Sandy)	**£5.50**	
Sandy's sales price (comes from customers)		£10.00
Jeffrey's variable cost	(£5.00)	
Sandy's variable cost of buying shirts from Jeffrey		**(£5.50)**
Sandy's variable cost of sales commissions		(£1.00)
Contribution margin per unit	£0.50	£3.50
Volume	50,000 shirts	50,000 shirts
Total contribution margin	£25,000	£175,000
Total fixed costs	(£30,000)	(£25,000)
Net profit (loss)	(£5,000)	£150,000

Figure 13-2: How a transfer price of £5.50 affects Jeffrey and Sandy's profits.

The purpose of testing different unit sale prices in this way is to show you that higher transfer prices shift profits from the purchasing division (Sandy) to the selling division (Jeffrey). This discrepancy can lead to discord between the different divisions of a company.

For clarity, throughout this chapter we use the terminology of a *selling division* that sells product to a *purchasing division*, as illustrated in Figure 13-3.

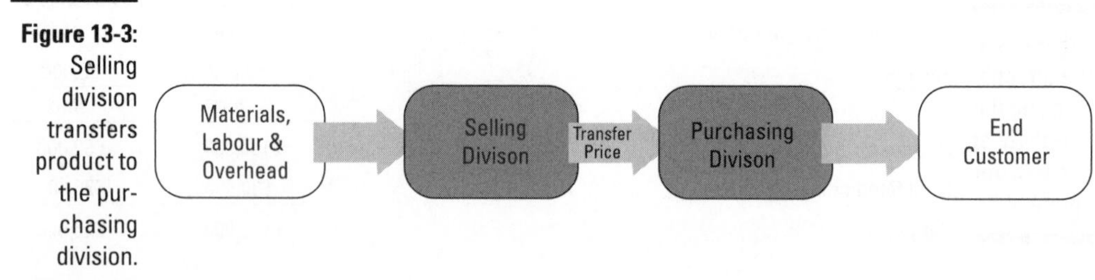

Figure 13-3: Selling division transfers product to the purchasing division.

Resolving discord and creating harmony

As the preceding section reveals, the fundamental problem is how to set the transfer price so that the two divisions split profits fairly. A higher price gives more profit to the selling division, whereas a lower price gives a larger share of profit to the purchasing division.

Here are a few different approaches for addressing this problem:

- **Negotiation:** Let the selling and purchasing divisions fight over a price (as we discuss in the next section 'Negotiating a Transfer Price').
- **Cost-based transfer price:** The overall company boss (Dorothy, in the preceding section's T-shirt example) sets the transfer price equal to the selling division's variable cost or total cost and adds a reasonable mark-up (for details, check out the later section 'Transferring Goods between Divisions at Cost').
- **Market-based transfer price:** The company boss sets the transfer price equal to the T-shirts' market value, the amount for which the selling division can sell them to outside customers (flip to 'Positioning Transfer Price at Market Value', later in this chapter).

Centralising control

Most managers think of transfer pricing of some sort as a necessary evil, without which they can't run their business, even though it often creates new problems that encourage managers to make decisions that aren't in the best interest of the company.

In fact, no hard-and-fast rule requires companies to evaluate each division based on profit. Another approach is to centralise control. In other words, the boss declares martial law, does away with all transfer-pricing schemes and no longer computes separate profit for each division. Instead, she evaluates the selling division based on its total expenses and evaluates the purchasing division on its total sales.

Managers may also choose to evaluate selling divisions on their costs, eliminating the need for transfer prices that set revenues and net income. Similarly, evaluators may gauge purchasing divisions based on sales to outside customers and ignore their expenses (which would be based on the transfer price), at least for evaluation purposes. A company can also combine different divisions, eliminating the need for any transfer prices.

Many companies don't employ the centralising approach because divisional directors have responsibility and accountability for the profits they generate. It's possible to measure how well a division and those managers in charge of it have performed by counting the profit it has made. This profit can be compared to profits from previous years and to profit from other divisions. Without divisions, individual managers aren't as easily assessed in terms of how well they're adding to overall company profitability.

Negotiating a Transfer Price

To negotiate a transfer price between two divisions, you lock the managers of the selling and purchasing divisions into a room and don't let them out until they agree on a number or discover that no mutually beneficial price is possible.

Of course, these negotiations aren't based on numbers the purchasing and selling divisions pull out of thin air. Each side does its research first. In order to prepare itself with a minimum transfer price, the selling division needs to consider carefully its cost structure and other sales opportunities. Similarly, the purchasing division has to figure out the maximum transfer price that it's willing to pay. The negotiated price winds up falling somewhere in the middle.

As long as both divisions do the necessary preparation, this approach is a good one, although inevitably it leads to a result in which the better negotiator gets a better deal. The two divisional managers may not need negotiation skills to the same extent in other aspects of their work, and so one of them can be at an advantage.

In the following sections, we ask you to assume that the following conditions apply:

- Selling and purchasing divisions have to do business together.
- The selling division doesn't have the option of selling its goods to an outside buyer.
- The purchasing division has no choice but to buy from the selling division.

Finding the selling division's minimum transfer price

The selling division's primary objective needs to be to add more money to its *contribution* (the difference between sales revenue and total variable cost), as we explain in Chapter 9. Therefore, as long as the selling division has excess capacity, it should be willing to sell its wares to the purchasing division for any value that gives it a contribution of zero or higher – a price that doesn't hurt its profits. The minimum transfer price should equal the total variable cost incurred by the selling division. The selling division is willing to transfer goods to the purchasing division as long as the transfer price is equal to or exceeds this value.

In the T-shirt example (in the earlier section 'Setting out the problem'), Jeffrey has a variable cost of £5 per T-shirt. Any transfer price over £5 results in a positive contribution and increases Jeffrey's profits. At a minimum, Jeffrey must cover his variable costs on the deal. Ideally, however, he wants to earn more – enough to cover his fixed costs and earn a healthy profit.

Setting the purchasing division's maximum transfer price

Like the selling division, the purchasing division doesn't want to lose money on any deal. Therefore, the purchasing division has to be willing to pay any price that results in a contribution greater than or equal to zero.

In the T-shirt example (see the earlier 'Setting out the problem' section), Sandy's sales price to customers is £10 per shirt. Sandy refuses to pay any variable cost that results in a negative contribution, and as a result she needs to figure out where to draw the line on price, so that contribution equals zero:

Sales price per unit	–	Variable costs per unit	=	Contribution
£10	–	£1	=	£9

Sandy can afford to pay no more than £10 in variable costs. Remember that she also needs to pay £1 commission for each T-shirt sold, a variable cost. Therefore, she has a maximum of £9 left to pay Jeffrey (£10 – £1). Her maximum sales price therefore comes to £9.

This price is so high that, although it allows Sandy's sales price to cover all the variable costs, it doesn't cover her fixed costs. Sandy certainly prefers to pay a lower price so that her revenues cover her variable *and* fixed costs.

Trying to meet in the middle

The selling and purchasing departments sit down and talk. Both divisions play a role in setting prices that make each of them – and the company as a whole – profitable. In the T-shirt example, Jeffrey knows that he can't sell the T-shirts for any amount less than £5 and Sandy isn't going to pay more than £9.

If the seller's minimum price exceeds the purchaser's maximum price, both parties agree to *no* deal. After all, neither of them wants to lose money. For example, if Jeffrey's minimum transfer price is £5 but Sandy's maximum transfer price is only £3, a sales price of £2 would make Sandy happy but force Jeffrey to lose £3 per shirt. A sales price of £7 would make Jeffrey happy but cause Sandy to lose money. A compromise of £4 would force both divisions to lose money. They'd have to abandon the deal, a decision that's in the best interest of the company as a whole.

Negotiated prices may be unduly affected by each party's ability (or inability) to negotiate, causing divisions led by weak negotiators to have lower profits than divisions led by more aggressive negotiators. Furthermore, clashing egos or a lack of trust between negotiating partners can cause divisions to avoid transactions that would have been profitable for the company as a whole. Management accountants need to be aware of these human weaknesses, and review transfer prices for the benefit of the company rather than individual divisional managers.

Managing with full capacity

If the selling division is operating at maximum capacity and has only a limited number of goods to sell, any goods sold to another division mean giving up sales to an outside customer. This scenario entails *opportunity costs* – the cost of losing profits because you choose a different alternative (turn to Chapter 10 for more on this topic). Therefore, the selling division's minimum transfer price in this scenario equals the total variable cost it would have incurred plus any contribution it would've earned from existing customers (that is, the opportunity cost of not selling to other customers).

Sylvia farms corn and her business partner Herbert runs a restaurant. Corn costs £1 per ear to grow and sufficient demand exists, which means that Sylvia has no problem selling her entire crop. Sylvia must choose whether to sell to her partner Herbert for his restaurant or to a local dealer. She can sell corn to the local dealer for £2 per ear as long as she pays additional variable sales commissions of £0.20 per ear.

Sylvia's minimum price when negotiating with Herbert equals her unit variable cost plus the contribution she'd earn from existing customers. If she sells to the corn dealer, her contribution equals £0.80 (see Figure 13-4): £2 per ear less £1 variable cost to grow and £0.20 variable sales commission. Therefore, her minimum transfer price for the deal with Herbert equals £1.80 (£1 cost plus £0.80 contribution earned from existing customers).

Sales price (per ear)	£2.00
Variable costs:	
Cost of growing corn	(£1.00)
Sales commissions	(£0.20)
Contribution	£0.80

Figure 13-4: Sylvia's contribution when selling to the outside customer.

Selling to another division rather than selling to an outside customer can also affect variable costs. For example, suppose that fictional company Big Paper has two divisions: one manufactures raw paper and the other makes paper bags out of raw paper. When selling to other divisions, the raw-paper division's usual cost of £100/roll drops to £95/roll because of savings in shipping costs. This saving in unit variable cost reduces the raw-paper division's minimum transfer price by £5.

However, selling to another division can increase costs instead, for example if the internal purchasing division demands higher quality materials than an outside customer.

Transferring Goods between Divisions at Cost

Establishing standard and agreed-upon guidelines for transfer pricing can help managers avoid arbitrary or expensive negotiation. After all, separately negotiating every transaction increases the amount of costly and cumbersome paperwork. One such approach to cutting out negotiation is to base the transfer price on the selling division's own manufacturing cost. The following sections offer a few options.

Setting the transfer price at variable cost

One simple approach to setting £ transfer price is to use the item's variable cost. After all, in a negotiation, this amount would have been the seller's minimum price anyway (see the earlier section 'Finding the selling division's minimum transfer price').

Suppose that Caroline's Dairy has two divisions: Milk and Ice Cream. The Milk division produces milk for a variable cost of £3 per litre. The Ice Cream division processes milk into ice cream for an additional variable cost of £1 per litre. Its ice cream sells for £6 per litre.

Variable cost gives Caroline's Dairy a transfer price of £3 per litre. Figure 13-5 shows how this price affects the two divisions' contributions.

	Milk	Ice Cream
Milk's sales price (the transfer price)	**£3.00**	
Ice Cream's sales price (to customers)		£6.00
Milk's variable cost	(£3.00)	
Ice Cream's variable cost of buying product from Milk		**(£3.00)**
Ice Cream's variable cost of sales commissions		(£1.00)
Contribution per unit	£0.00	£2.00

Figure 13-5: Caroline's Dairy sets the transfer price at variable cost.

Figure 13-5 shows how setting the contribution at Milk's unit variable cost of £3 shifts all the profits from the Milk division to the Ice Cream division, such that Milk earns no contribution per unit (left column) whereas Ice Cream earns £2 per unit (right column). If Caroline's Dairy evaluates the Milk division on its profitability, the Milk division needs to find a better customer than the Ice Cream division – one that provides more contribution. Selling to an outside customer for a slightly higher price would improve Milk's profitability.

Establishing the transfer price at variable cost plus a mark-up

In order for both divisions to share profits more equally, managers may prefer to set the transfer price at unit variable cost plus a mark-up. At Caroline's Dairy (introduced in the preceding section), Managing Director Caroline decides to set the transfer price at unit variable cost plus a £1 mark-up, resulting in a transfer price of £4 (£3 unit variable cost plus £1 mark-up). To see how the Milk and Ice Cream divisions now share profits, take a look at Figure 13-6. Fair is fair, and now the two divisions split their contributions equally: £1 goes to each.

Figure 13-6: Caroline's Dairy sets the transfer price at unit variable cost plus mark-up.

	Milk	Ice Cream
Milk's sales price (the transfer price)	**£4.00**	
Ice Cream's sales price (to customers)		£6.00
Milk's variable cost	(£3.00)	
Ice Cream's variable cost of buying product from Milk		**(£4.00)**
Ice Cream's variable cost of sales commissions		(£1.00)
Contribution per unit	£1.00	£1.00

Setting the transfer price at unit variable cost plus mark-up can lead to problems, though. Suppose that the Ice Cream division receives a special order to supply a local college with 1,000 litres of ice cream. Competitors offer to sell ice cream for £4.80 per litre. How low can Caroline's Dairy Ice Cream division go?

The Ice Cream division calculates that its unit variable cost equals the £4 transfer price plus another £1 in sales commissions. That makes £5, well over the competitors' price of £4.80. Therefore, the Ice Cream division probably miss out on this opportunity.

But if you consider the real cost of the ice cream, Caroline's Dairy would have been better off if the Ice Cream division had cut its price. After all, because making a litre of milk costs the Milk division only £3, total cost for the ice cream is really £4 (£3 unit variable cost to the Milk division plus £1 sales commission). Caroline's Dairy could've bid £4.75 per litre on the college account and still earned £0.75 contribution on each litre sold.

Setting the transfer price at unit variable cost plus a mark-up, therefore, can lead to decisions that aren't in the best interest of the company as a whole. To avoid this scenario, the Milk division must share its information about the real cost of the milk, even if that cost is lower than the transfer price. Furthermore, divisions sometimes need to forgo their own profits in order to do what's most profitable for the whole company.

Basing transfer price on full cost

A company may set the transfer price at *full cost* (also known as *absorption cost*): the sum of variable and fixed costs per unit. In order to ensure that the selling division earns a profit, it can also add a mark-up.

Suppose that the HOO Water Company produces spring water and soft drinks. The Clor division produces spring water and the Shpritz division makes soft drinks. HOO managers encourage Clor and Shpritz to work together so that the Shpritz division uses Clor's spring water to make its soft drinks. However, the Clor division also sells its water to outside customers for £0.75 per gallon. In order to minimise costs, Shpritz can also buy water from suppliers other than Clor.

This year, the Clor division plans to produce 100,000 gallons of spring water but has the ability to produce more water if it can sell it. Clor's water carries a variable cost of £0.30 per gallon and the division must cover fixed costs of £40,000.

Shpritz plans to make 60,000 gallons of soft drinks; it can buy the water from Clor or from an outside supplier. In addition to the cost of the water, Shpritz must pay £0.40 per gallon for flavourings and other additives to produce each gallon of soft drink. Shpritz also pays fixed costs of £30,000 per year. Shpritz's soft drink sells for £2 per gallon.

To set a transfer price that will benefit the HOO Water Company rather than individual divisions, you start by computing Clor's full cost. Fixed costs amount to £40,000 needed to produce 100,000 gallons of spring water. The fixed cost per unit, then, comes to £0.40 per gallon (£40,000 ÷ 100,000 gallons). Clor's variable costs equal £0.30 per gallon; you add that to the fixed cost per unit to get a total cost of £0.70 per gallon: this number is the transfer price.

Figure 13-7 explains what happens when Clor supplies Shpritz with 60,000 gallons' worth of spring water for a transfer price of £0.70 per gallon and the rest to outside customers for £0.75 per gallon.

	Clor	Shpritz
Clor's sales to outside customers (40,000 gallons x £0.75)	£30,000	
Clor's sales to Shpritz (60,000 gallons x £0.70)	**£42,000**	
Shpritz' sales of soft drinks (60,000 gallons x £2.00)		£120,000
Clor's variable costs (100,000 gallons x £0.30)	(£30,000)	
Shpritz's variable costs of buying spring water from Clor (60,000 gallons x £0.70)		**(£42,000)**
Shpritz's variable costs of flavourings and other additives (60,000 gallons x £0.40)		(£24,000)
Total contribution margin	£42,000	£54,000
Fixed costs	(£40,000)	(£30,000)
Net profit of each division	£2,000	£24,000
HOO Water's total net profit		£26,000

Figure 13-7: Best case scenario: Clor sells spring water to Shpritz for £0.70 per gallon.

Here, Clor receives £30,000 in revenues from outside customers and £42,000 in revenues from Shpritz. Subtracting Clor's variable costs of £30,000 and fixed costs of £40,000 results in net profit of £2,000. Shpritz takes in revenues of £120,000 from its soft drinks. Of this amount, it must pay £42,000 to Clor and £24,000 in other variable costs. Shpritz must also pay £30,000 worth of fixed costs, resulting in net profit of £24,000 for Shpritz. HOO Water, which owns both divisions, earns a total profit of £26,000 from both products.

Decisions to base transfer price on full cost can trick division managers into making bad decisions that hurt the overall company's profitability. Suppose that another company, outside supplier Malcolm Water, sells water for £0.65 per gallon. (In case you're wondering, Malcolm Water can charge less money for its water because it's of poorer quality.) The Shpritz division needs to choose between paying £0.70 per gallon to Clor or £0.65 per gallon to Malcolm.

On the face of it, you may think that HOO should buy the water from the cheaper outside supplier and save £0.05 per gallon. After all, why pay £0.70 a litre when you can pay £0.65 to buy it from Malcolm?

But the situation isn't that simple, and not just because of loyalty (both divisions sharing the same parent company). Figure 13-8 illustrates the fiasco that occurs when Shpritz attempts to save money by buying its water from Malcolm.

Shpritz's decision to try to cut costs reduces HOO Water's overall profitability by £21,000. Certainly Shpritz's profitability goes up: the decision to outsource reduces the variable cost of buying water from £42,000 to £39,000, and the net profit of Shpritz rises to £27,000.

	Clor	Shpritz
Clor's sales to outside customers (40,000 gallons x £0.75)	£30,000	
Shpritz's sales of soft drinks (60,000 gallons x £2.00)		£120,000
Clor's variable costs (40,000 gallons x £0.30)	(£12,000)	
Shpritz's variable costs of buying spring water from Malcolm (60,000 gallons x £0.65)		(£39,000)
Shpritz's variable costs of flavourings and other additives (60,000 gallons x £0.40)		(£24,000)
Total contribution margin	£18,000	£57,000
Fixed costs	(£40,000)	(£30,000)
Net profit of each division	(£22,000)	£27,000
HOO Water's total net profit		£5,000

Figure 13-8: Shpritz buys water from an outside supplier for £0.65 per litre.

But Shpritz's decision hurts Clor and ultimately reduces HOO Water's total profitability. Clor's sales to Shpritz of £42,000 completely dry up (no pun intended). Its variable costs also drop from £30,000 to £12,000. However, Clor's fixed costs of £40,000 remain the same, forcing Clor to suffer a loss of £22,000. HOO Water's overall profits fall from £26,000 to just £5,000. Basing the transfer price on full cost leads Shpritz to make decisions that hurt the company's overall profitability.

Positioning Transfer Price at Market Value

Setting the transfer price at market value solves many of the problems that crop up with the negotiation and cost-based transfer price methods (that we describe earlier in the 'Negotiating a Transfer Price' and 'Transferring Goods between Divisions at Cost' sections, respectively). If an outside market exists for the transferred goods, managers can set the transfer price equal to the listed market value of the goods. This value is often readily available through listings published on an industry-by-industry basis. These published listings eliminate the need for negotiations.

When the selling division operates at full capacity, market pricing usually encourages both divisions to do what's in the best interest of the whole company. When the transfer price equals market value:

- The selling division doesn't care who it sells to, as long as the sale maximises its revenue and profit.
- The purchasing division doesn't care who it buys from; it also makes choices to earn the highest revenue and profit possible.

Your coffee may taste bitter

Towards the end of 2012, headlines appeared in UK newspapers as a result of the public disclosure that the UK-based Starbucks Company wasn't paying corporation tax in the UK.

They were using transfer pricing as follows:

- An intellectual property division was set up within the Starbucks Group, located in a low-tax country. The UK Starbucks division has to pay 6 per cent of total sales for the use of its 'intellectual property', such as its brand and business processes. These payments reduce taxable income in the UK. Starbucks says it abides by the 'arm's length' principle (the buying and selling divisions of different companies set their prices without becoming entangled with one another).This has been questioned by the British media because it appears odd for Starbucks to want to continue to run a company that they claim is autonomous in the UK and for that company to not have been profitable.
- Starbucks buys coffee beans for the UK through a Swiss-based firm, Starbucks Coffee Trading Co. Before the beans reach the UK, they're roasted at a division that is based in Amsterdam but separate from the European HQ. Starbucks hasn't supplied details or commented on what the charges indicate about the price its roaster paid its Swiss unit for coffee beans. It also declines to say what profit the Swiss coffee-buying unit makes, although the company has said that it was 'moderately' profitable. Swiss law doesn't require the unit to publish accounts.
- These two transfer-pricing factors, together with inter-company borrowing by the UK division leading to interest charges being paid to other companies within the Starbucks Group of companies, has led to the consistent reporting of taxable losses in the UK.

As a management accountant you must look beyond the numbers and tax costs as you strive to increase the value of a company. Saving tax can cost a lot more in lost sales revenue, so saving tax may cost the company more than it saves. In the case of Starbucks, the publicity that the use of transfer pricing produced caused boycotts and threats that may well have resulted in much lower sales revenue in future years. Therefore, this situation created a public-relations angle. Unless Starbucks took action, its coffee sales in 2013 and onwards could've been adversely affected.

At the beginning of December 2012, the UK management of Starbucks pledged to pay £10 million tax in the form of a voluntary tax contribution each year for the next two years. The UK tax authorities hadn't found a breach in UK tax rules, but the public had taken against the company because of its arrangements. In recognition of the power of its customers, Starbucks made its pledge and customers appear happy to continue to hand over their money for coffee in Starbucks' UK coffee shops.

In this scenario, because each division maximises its revenues and profits, so too does the whole company.

When the selling division has excess capacity, however, making additional sales in-house to the purchasing division increases the selling division's revenues and helps cover its fixed costs. In this scenario, market-value pricing may encourage the purchasing division to buy cheaper goods from outside sources instead of buying higher-priced goods from the selling division. (The full-cost and mark-up pricing strategies earlier in the chapter in the sections 'Basing transfer price on full cost' and 'Establishing the transfer price at variable cost plus a mark-up' may also have this effect.) This move hurts the selling division's sales and profitability, possibly also damaging the whole company's performance.

Tax benefits and dangers

The discussion of prices has deliberately excluded tax considerations, but management accountants need to consider all aspects when assisting company managers. Multinational companies have divisions operating under different tax regimes. One way of contributing towards minimising the overall tax liability of a group of companies may be to use transfer pricing to:

- Reduce the profitability of the divisions (or subsidiary companies) in high-tax countries.
- Increase the profitability of the divisions (or subsidiary companies) in low-tax countries.

Changes in the transfer price can redistribute the pre-tax profit between divisions, although the group's overall pre-tax profit remains the same. This approach effectively moves profits from a subsidiary in a high-tax country into a subsidiary in a low-tax country and lowers the total tax liability of the group (see the earlier sidebar 'Your coffee may taste bitter').

Clearly tax authorities are very interested in preventing the loss of tax revenues by such actions. The expression 'arm's length' transaction is often used in these cases, though it's more formally called the *comparable uncontrolled price* (CUP). If a company is found to be using a transfer price deliberately to avoid tax, its actions wouldn't be at arm's length. Tax authorities tend to look at external market prices and apply some leeway above and below to account for the internal aspect when asserting the extent to which a transaction is at arm's length. Companies found guilty of abusing transfer pricing can be made to pay tax in both countries. The UK penalty is 100 per cent of any tax adjustment.

A company may safeguard its position by contacting the relevant tax authorities in advance and entering an Advanced Pricing Agreement (APA), which can avoid subsequent disputes and the costly penalty of double taxation and penalty fees. The accountants Ernst and Young report that the majority of companies are already doing so, or intend to do so. The UK Prime Minister David Cameron initiated international discussions in June 2013. These aim to make it more difficult for a company to make profits in one country but pay little or no tax there as a result of transfer pricing.

Chapter 14

Planning Budgets for the Future

In This Chapter

- Planning budgets for manufacturers
- Budgeting for retailers and service companies
- Considering alternatives to traditional budgeting

A couple of summers ago, one of the authors (Mark) took his three sons on a cross-country camping trip in the US, visiting Yellowstone, Yosemite and Grand Canyon national parks. Along the way, the family took detours through places as far afield as Chicago, Montana, San Francisco and Miami Beach (yes, really!).

The planning took four months. They started at the end of the trip and worked backwards, after some negotiation agreeing on the three primary destinations. Then they produced an itinerary spreadsheet that specified driving times, side trips and where they'd sleep every day over seven weeks. Mark used this itinerary to prepare a detailed budget, estimating the cost of food, petrol, campsites, motels and equipment. Finally, they booked the trip.

Don't worry; we're not going to force you to watch his photo slideshow! This story is to illustrate that whether you're taking a road trip or running a large company, you need to plan for the future. This chapter clues you in on how to prepare a *master budget* (which uses realistic sales goals to plan your company's production level, cash flow and profitability) for manufacturers, retailers and service companies.

Budgeting helps you to plan your business – by identifying your goals and how you're going to reach them – as well as control your business by measuring the likelihood that you'll be able to reach those goals. Budgeting does the following:

- Establishes measurable objectives for different parts of your company
- Signals when your company may get sidetracked by problems
- Motivates employees

- Co-ordinates different activities
- Determines whether you have adequate resources
- Helps you allocate resources throughout your business

In a large organisation, poor planning can cause fatal errors because your business may run out of inventory or cash.

Preparing a Manufacturer's Master Budget

Welcome to the world of Bizarro Accounting, where everything goes backwards. Normally, a business first buys materials, finds labour, pays overhead, makes goods and finally sells them. But in the world of Bizarro Accounting, where people prepare budgets, you move in the opposite direction.

In this section, we lead you through the master budgeting process for a manufacturer, but much of this information applies equally to retailers and service companies. We describe some differences and variations in the later section 'Applying Master Budgeting to Non-Manufacturers'.

Budgeting backwards

When budgeting, start with your sales. Don't use an accurate number based on actual receipts from the prior year. Instead, come up with a realistic estimate of next year's sales.

After you (sort of) know next year's sales, keep working backwards. To make all these sales, what quantity of goods does your factory need to produce? Then figure out the direct materials, direct labour and overhead needed to make all these goods.

From here, estimate your cash flows. Not last year's cash flows, but next year's cash flows:

1. **Start with cash payments.** How much do you need to pay in order to make all the goods that you plan to produce next year?
2. **Look at inflows.** Where will you generate the cash inflows needed to support production? Will you need to borrow money next year?
3. **Prepare the rest of next year's financial statements.**

If you're feeling a little lost in Bizarro Accounting, take a look at Figure 14-1. This figure provides a map of the master budget process we lay out in the rest of this section, starting with sales and then working its way down to a cash budget and other budgeted financial statements. Return to this figure to keep your bearings as you read this section.

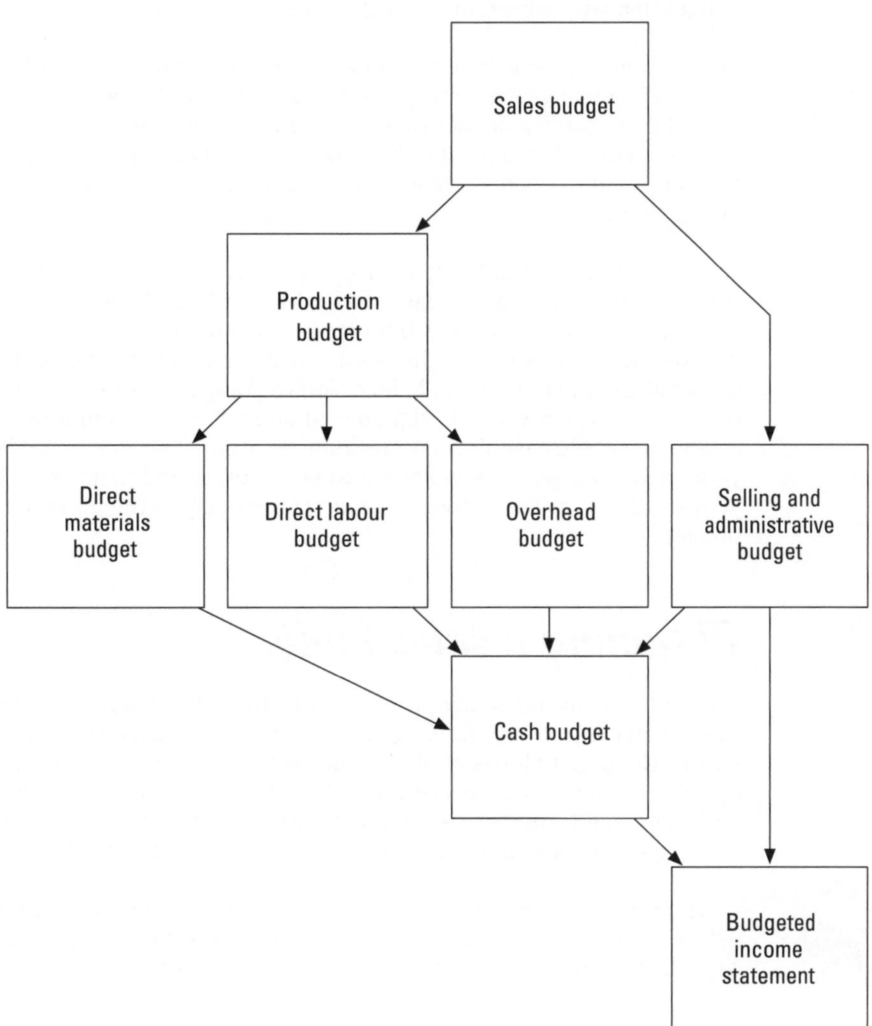

Figure 14-1: A budgeting road map.

When compared to budgeting, ordinary accounting is pretty cut and dried. In ordinary accounting, you record, classify and report what happened. No guesswork; boom, you're done. However, in order to create a master budget, different parts of an organisation need to negotiate and work out estimates and plans that co-ordinate all parts of the business. This process involves more than adding – different groups need to work together until they create a budget that works best for the organisation.

The accounting records run for financial reporting purposes only shows what has happened. The budget doesn't appear in the records. We're in the area of management accounting here, which feeds planning information to management rather than supplying the financial accountants with costs and revenues that happened. As a result, negotiation is needed within this planning process.

For example, a draft of the master budget may indicate that the sales budget is too low to make the company profitable. You may have to make the sales department rework the sales budget, perhaps increasing prices and lowering volume. Then you redo the whole master budget all over again to find out what's going to happen. In fact, you're going to need to do and redo the budget until you create a budget based on realistic assumptions that generates manageable cash flow and maximises profit. This document becomes your road map, and so you need it to be accurate and to mark a clear route to your destination. The following sections break down the parts of the master budget.

Obtaining a sales budget

You start the master budget process with the sales department, because sales is an example of a *limiting factor* (sometimes called the *principal budget factor*). Chapter 10 looks at other limiting factors, but the process here based on sales is similar with any other limiting factor, in putting that budget first and using that budget to develop the subsequent budgets. The *sales budget* uses expected sales in the coming period to project total sales revenue.

Consider the case of Forever Tuna, a company that processes and cans tuna fish. A single case of Forever Tuna sells for £100. Table 14-1 provides the sales department's projection of the next four quarters' sales.

Table 14-1 Projected Sales of Forever Tuna

Quarter	*Expected Unit Sales*
1	4,000
2	5,000
3	6,000
4	7,000

To create a sales budget that projects total sales for the next year, multiply expected unit sales by the sales price as shown in Figure 14-2.

Forever Tuna, Ltd.
Sales Budget
For the Year Ended 31 December, 2013

	Quarter 1	Quarter 2	Quarter 3	Quarter 4	Year
Expected unit sales	4,000	5,000	6,000	7,000	22,000
Sales price	£100	£100	£100	£100	£100
Total sales	£400,000	£500,000	£600,000	£700,000	£2,200,000

Figure 14-2: How much is Forever Tuna going to sell next year?

Generating a production budget

If you plan to sell inventory, you need some inventory to sell. That's why you need a production budget.

The *production budget* is a calculation of the number of units the company needs to produce in order to meet its sales budget. To prepare a production budget, you estimate how much inventory the company wants to keep in stock at the end of each period. This figure forms the opening inventory to enable sales in the next period.

To prepare a production budget, start with the formula for inventory flow. Note the sequence in Table 14-2.

Table 14-2 Preparing a Production Budget to Find Units Sold

	In Money	*In Physical Stock*
Opening Inventory		
+ Purchases		
= Sub-total		
– Closing Inventory		
	Cost of Sales	Units Sold

Chapter 5 shows you how to apply this formula to calculate the number of units sold, the number of units manufactured, Cost of Goods Sold and Cost of Goods Manufactured.

But in master budgeting, you know the outputs (how many units you need) – just check out the sales budget. And you can find the opening and closing number of units on the company's estimates of inventory needed at the end of each period. As a result, the missing number you're after in the production budget is inputs: how many units do you need to make? The physical stock is your priority. Therefore, you rearrange the formula as shown in Table 14-3.

Table 14-3 Rearranging the Formula to Calculate Purchases

	In Physical Stock
Sales (or the material needed to make the sales)	Material requirement to meet the forecast sales
+ Closing Inventory	+ the inventory needed at the end of the period
= Sub-total	
– Opening Inventory	– the inventory expected (or forecast) at the start of the period
= Purchases	= The purchases needed

Don't be put off by the 'sales or' aspect of the top line. Bear in mind that a retailer buying frozen pies or sausage rolls to warm up and sell only needs sales numbers, whereas a manufacturer buying 2 kilograms of material to make a finished product needs to multiply the sales units by the 2 kilograms per unit to find the material requirement.

Plug the numbers in for Forever Tuna's first quarter. According to the sales budget in the earlier Figure 14-2, the company plans to sell 4,000 units in the first quarter and 5,000 units in the second quarter. Managers keep inventory equal to 10 per cent of the following period's sales. The company starts its first quarter in 2013 with 400 units. At the end of the first quarter, it needs 500 units (that is, 5,000 units projected to be sold in the second quarter times 10 per cent).

$$\text{Production units} = \text{Sales} + \text{Closing inventory} - \text{Opening inventory}$$
$$\text{Production units} = 4{,}000 + 500 - 400$$
$$\text{Production units} = 4{,}100 \text{ units}$$

The company needs to produce 4,100 units.

A full-blown production budget computes this information for a whole year. As indicated in the sales budget shown in Table 14-1, Forever Tuna projects unit sales of 4,000 in Quarter 1 of 2013. The production budget is shown in Figure 14-3.

Figure 14-3: How much inventory does Forever Tuna need to make next year?

Forever Tuna, Ltd.
Production Budget
For the Year Ended 31 December, 2013

	Quarter 1	Quarter 2	Quarter 3	Quarter 4	Year
Expected unit sales	4,000	5,000	6,000	7,000	22,000
Add: Closing inventory	500	600	700	750	2,550
Less: Opening inventory	(400)	(500)	(600)	(700)	(2,200)
Production required	4,100	5,100	6,100	7,050	22,350

The number of opening units in one period always equals the closing units in the previous period. Similarly, the cost of opening inventory always equals the cost of closing inventory in the previous period.

Setting a direct materials budget

If you're making inventory, you need to get direct materials (as well as direct labour and overhead, which we cover in the later sections 'Working on a direct labour budget' and 'Building an overhead budget'). To start, tackle the *direct materials budget,* which specifies the amount of direct materials that the company needs to buy in order to meet its production budget. To prepare this document (using the budget formula we introduce in the preceding section), you need to know the following:

- **Level of production:** You find this info in the production budget.
- **Opening direct materials inventory:** To get this information, go to the production budget for the most recently completed period.
- **Closing direct materials inventory the company wants:** Set this target at a level that ensures you have enough direct materials to meet the production requirement in the next period.
- **Direct materials that go into your products:** Base this figure on how you design your products.
- **Cost of direct materials:** Obtain this projected price from the purchasing department.

The outputs are the level of production already noted in the existing production budget. For Forever Tuna's level of production, use the production budget in Figure 14-3. Assume the company starts its first quarter with 2,460 kilograms of direct materials inventory. Managers like to have 10 per cent of the following period's direct materials in inventory at the opening of each period. Because the company estimates that it's going to need 40,000 kilograms of direct materials in the first quarter of 2014, it requires a closing inventory of 4,000 kilograms of direct materials at the end of the fourth quarter (which is 10 per cent of 40,000). Six kilograms of tuna fish go into every case of Forever Tuna. The company pays £10 per kilogram for tuna fish.

To compute the direct materials needed for production, multiply the number of finished goods units to be produced by the cost per unit. This calculation gives you the total direct materials needed for production. Next, following the budget formula, add desired closing direct materials and subtract opening direct materials, to get the total direct material purchases needed. Multiply this amount by the cost of the direct material units to arrive at the total cost of direct materials. Figure 14-4 provides the direct materials budget for Forever Tuna.

This direct materials budget indicates that the company needs to purchase £252,000 worth of direct materials in the first quarter, £310,200 in the second quarter, £371,700 in the third quarter and £420,700 in the fourth quarter.

Working on a direct labour budget

In order to convert direct materials into finished goods, you need direct labour. The *direct labour budget* tells you how many direct labour hours of work you're going to need, indicating whether you have enough workers or need to hire more.

Forever Tuna, Ltd.
Direct Materials Budget
For the Year Ended 31 December, 2013

	Quarter 1	Quarter 2	Quarter 3	Quarter 4	Year
Units to be produced (from Production Budget)	4,100	5,100	6,100	7,050	
Direct materials per unit (kgs)	6	6	6	6	
Total direct materials needed for production (kgs)	24,600	30,600	36,600	42,300	
Add: closing direct materials (kgs)	3,060	3,660	4,230	4,000	
Less: opening direct materials (kgs)	(2,460)	(3,060)	(3,660)	(4,230)	
Direct material purchases (kgs)	25,200	31,200	37,170	42,070	
Cost per kg	£10.00	£10.00	£10.00	£10.00	
Cost of direct material purchases	£252,000	£312,000	£371,700	£420,700	£1,356,400

Figure 14-4: What quantity of materials does Forever Tuna need to buy next year?

To prepare a direct labour budget, multiply the number of units to be produced (from the production budget) by the direct labour time needed to make each unit. Then multiply that result by the average direct labour rate per hour.

In the Forever Tuna example from the preceding sections, the company's production budget (Figure 14-3) indicates the number of units to be produced. Assume that making a single case of Forever Tuna takes half an hour of direct labour. The company pays, on average, £12 per direct labour hour. The direct labour budget in Figure 14-5 multiplies the number of units produced each quarter by the direct labour time per unit, by the direct labour cost per hour.

Forever Tuna, Ltd.
Direct Labour Budget
For the Year Ended 31 December, 2013

	Quarter 1	Quarter 2	Quarter 3	Quarter 4	Year
Units to be produced (from Production Budget)	4,100	5,100	6,100	7,050	
Direct labour hours per unit	½	½	½	½	
Total direct labour hours needed	2,050	2,550	3,050	3,525	
Direct labour cost per hour	£12.00	£12.00	£12.00	£12.00	
Cost of labour	£24,600	£30,600	£36,600	£42,300	£134,100

Figure 14-5: How much does Forever Tuna need to pay workers next year?

The direct labour budget indicates that the company can expect to pay a total of £134,100 for direct labour next year.

Building an overhead budget

The *overhead budget* estimates the coming year's total overhead costs and sets an overhead absorption rate. (As we explain in Chapter 4, *overhead* consists of the costs of making products above and beyond direct materials and direct labour.) To prepare it, you need detailed information about the company's overhead, including an analysis of fixed and variable components of the overhead.

Chapter 4 explains how accountants absorb overhead into products by spreading overhead costs out over all the units produced, like peanut butter and banana on sandwiches. To find the *overhead absorption rate,* divide total budgeted overhead by the total budgeted value for the chosen *cost driver,* a factor that you expect to vary with overhead. For the overhead budget, set the number of direct labour hours as the cost driver:

$$\text{Overhead absorption rate} = \frac{\text{Estimated total overhead}}{\text{Estimated total direct labour hours}}$$

Then, for each product, multiply the overhead absorption rate by the direct labour hours required.

Don't confuse the overhead absorption rate with variable overhead per unit or per direct labour hour. Variable overhead per unit is used to compute variable cost per unit when calculating contribution margin (see Chapter 9).

For the earlier Forever Tuna example, assume that the company has variable overhead equal to £4 per direct labour hour. The company needs to pay an additional £200,000 per year in fixed overhead. Use the number of direct labour hours from the direct labour budget (in Figure 14-5 earlier in the chapter) to estimate total variable costs. Then add in fixed costs of £50,000 per quarter (£200,000 divided by four quarters) as shown in Figure 14-6.

Adding up the product cost

A critical step in the budgeting process is to compute *projected product cost,* which is how much you expect making each unit to cost during the budgeted period. (Turn to Chapter 3 for more on product costs.) To calculate Forever Tuna's projected product cost, add together the costs of direct materials per unit, direct labour per unit and overhead per unit, as shown in Figure 14-7.

Forever Tuna, Ltd.
Overhead Budget
For the Year Ended 31 December, 2013

	Quarter 1	Quarter 2	Quarter 3	Quarter 4	Year
Direct labour hours (from Direct Labour Budget)	2,050	2,550	3,050	3,525	
Variable overhead per unit	£4	£4	£4	£4	
Total variable overhead	£8,200	£10,200	£12,200	£14,100	
Total fixed overhead	£50,000	£50,000	£50,000	£50,000	
Total overhead	£58,200	£60,200	£62,200	£64,100	£244,700
Number of direct labour hours	2,050	2,550	3,050	3,525	11,175
Overhead allocation rate per direct labour hour (£244,700 / 11,175 hours)					£21.90
Number of units produced (from Production Budget)					22,350
Overhead cost per unit (£244,700 / 22,350 units)					£10.95

Figure 14-6: How much overhead is Forever Tuna going to pay next year?

Direct materials per unit	£60.00	From Direct Materials Budget	(6 kgs. x £10 each)
Direct labour per unit	6.00	From Direct Labour Budget	(½ hour x £12 each)
Overhead per unit	10.95	From Overhead Budget	
Total cost per unit	£76.95		

Figure 14-7: Forever Tuna's product cost per unit.

On average, each unit costs £76.95 to make.

Product cost per unit helps you to prepare the budgeted income statement. Furthermore, this information is very useful for setting prices (see Chapter 12).

Fashioning a selling and administrative budget

Sales don't happen by themselves, especially with canned seafood product. If you plan to sell 22,000 cases of vacuum-packed tuna, you can't just sit around waiting for customers. Instead, you need a sales force, paid with a combination of salaries and commissions. You may also have to pay freight to ship goods to customers. And then you have advertising, office salaries and all the costs that come with running a sales office.

The *selling and administrative expense budget* predicts the amount of selling and administrative expenses (abbreviated S&A) needed to generate the sales forecast in the sales budget. To prepare this budget, you need detailed information about the company's S&A; you then divide S&A costs into fixed and variable components.

Forever Tuna plans to sell 22,000 cases of product, as projected by the sales department in Table 14-1 earlier in the chapter. Suppose an account analysis indicates that Forever Tuna has variable S&A costs of £5 per unit. The company pays fixed S&A costs equal to £90,000 per year (£22,500 per quarter). Figure 14-8 shows how to combine fixed and variable S&A expenses to create an S&A budget.

Forever Tuna, Ltd.
Selling and Administrative Budget
For the Year Ended 31 December, 2013

	Quarter 1	Quarter 2	Quarter 3	Quarter 4	Year
Budgeted sales in units (from Sales Budget)	4,000	5,000	6,000	7,000	
Variable S&A per unit	£5	£5	£5	£5	
Total variable S&A	£20,000	£25,000	£30,000	£35,000	
Total fixed S&A	£22,500	£22,500	£22,500	£22,500	
Total S&A	£42,500	£47,500	£52,500	£57,500	£200,000

Figure 14-8: Forever Tuna's S&A budget.

The S&A budget indicates that Forever Tuna's managers expect to pay £200,000 worth of S&A expenses next year.

Creating a cash budget

The *cash budget* summarises all your cash inflows and outflows for the period, adding cash receipts and subtracting cash payments. Positive cash projections assure you that your company has enough cash to get through the next period.

If your cash budget comes out negative, though, you may have to start all over again from the beginning. Do not pass go, do not collect £200!

Before you can prepare a cash budget, you need to do some homework to estimate cash receipts and cash payments. We walk you through the cash budgeting process in the following sections.

A cash flow forecast is exactly the same as a cash budget, and so don't be confused if you're asked to prepare a cash flow forecast for a manager to take to the bank and a cash budget for the board of directors. The same document would cover both requests.

Predicting cash receipts

Some customers pay their bills quickly, but others take advantage of the credit you give them, paying more slowly. This delay means that predicted sales, as calculated in the production budget (refer to the earlier section 'Generating a production budget'), don't always translate immediately into cash flows.

Forever Tuna's accountants estimate that, on average, the company collects 40 per cent of sales in the same month as the sale, 35 per cent in the following month and the remaining 25 per cent two months after the sale. The company has £230,000 worth of Accounts Receivable on 31 December, 2013, of which it collects £155,000 in the first quarter and the remaining £75,000 in the second quarter. Figure 14-9 provides a schedule of expected cash receipts, which computes when the company expects to receive payments for each quarter's sales.

Forever Tuna, Ltd.
Schedule of Expected Cash Receipts
For the Year Ended 31 December, 2013

	Sales	Quarter 1	Quarter 2	Quarter 3	Quarter 4
Accounts Receivable, 31/12/2013		£155,000	£75,000		
Quarter 1	£400,000	£160,000	£140,000	£100,000	
Quarter 2	£500,000		£200,000	£175,000	£125,000
Quarter 3	£600,000			£240,000	£210,000
Quarter 4	£700,000				£280,000
Total collections	£2,200,000	£315,000	£415,000	£515,000	£615,000

Quarter 1 sales collected in Quarter 1: £400,000 x 40% = £160,000;
Quarter 1 sales collected in Quarter 2: £400,000 x 35% = £140,000;
Quarter 1 sales collected in Quarter 3: £400,000 x 25% = £100,000;
Quarter 2 sales collected in Quarter 2: £500,000 x 40% = £200,000;
Quarter 2 sales collected in Quarter 3: £500,000 x 35% = £140,000;
Quarter 2 sales collected in Quarter 4: £500,000 x 25% = £125,000;
Quarter 3 sales collected in Quarter 3: £600,000 x 40% = £240,000;
Quarter 3 sales collected in Quarter 4: £600,000 x 35% = £210,000;
Quarter 4 sales collected in Quarter 4: £700,000 x 40% = £280,000.

Figure 14-9: Forever Tuna's predicted cash receipts.

The schedule of expected cash receipts indicates that Forever Tuna will probably receive £315,000 from its customers in the first quarter; £415,000 in the second quarter; £515,000 in the third quarter; and £615,000 in the fourth quarter.

Predicting cash payments

Just as you give customers the luxury of paying their bills over several quarters, your suppliers probably give you time to pay them.

Forever Tuna's policy is to pay half its Accounts Payable in the same quarter as the purchase and half in the following quarter. The company pays 75 per cent of its S&A expense in the same quarter and 25 per cent in the following quarter. The company has £105,375 worth of accounts payable on 31 December, 2012, and pays that entire amount in the first quarter of 2013. The direct materials budget in Figure 14-4 earlier in the chapter provides the amount of direct materials that the company plans to purchase next year, and the S&A budget in Figure 14-8 indicates how much the company plans to spend on S&A.

For the company's schedule of estimated cash payments, look at Figure 14-10, which computes the payments to be made for purchases and S&A next year.

This schedule of expected cash payments indicates that Forever Tuna expects to pay £263,250 in the first quarter; £328,250 in the second quarter; £393,100 in the third quarter; and £452,450 in the fourth quarter for purchases and S&A.

Piecing together your cash budget

To prepare a cash budget, combine information about every cash inflow and outflow from the schedule of estimated cash receipts, the schedule of estimated cash payments and any other budgets that involve cash flows (such as the direct labour budget, the overhead budget and/or tax payment info).

In addition to the cash flows listed in Figures 14-9 and 14-10, Forever Tuna has to pay for direct labour and overhead, which it does immediately, as incurred. The company also needs to make quarterly tax payments of £5,000. It starts the year with £50,000 worth of cash. The cash budget culminates this project, as shown in Figure 14-11.

Forever Tuna, Ltd.
Schedule of Expected Cash Payments
For the Year Ended 31 December, 2013

		Quarter 1	Quarter 2	Quarter 3	Quarter 4
Accounts payable, 31/12/2012	£105,375	£105,375			
Quarter 1	Purchases £252,000	£126,000	£126,000		
	S&A £42,500	£31,875	£10,625		
Quarter 2	Purchases £312,000		£156,000	£156,000	
	S&A £47,500		£35,625	£11,875	
Quarter 3	Purchases £371,700			£185,850	£185,850
	S&A £52,500			£39,375	£13,125
Quarter 4	Purchases £420,700				£210,350
	S&A £57,500				£43,125
Total payments		£263,250	£328,250	£393,100	£452,450

Quarter 1 purchases paid in Quarter 1: £252,000 x 50% = £126,000;
Quarter 1 purchases paid in Quarter 2: £252,000 x 50% = £126,000;
Quarter 1 S&A paid in Quarter 1: £42,500 x 75% = £31,875;
Quarter 1 S&A paid in Quarter 2: £42,500 x 25% = £10,625;
Quarter 2 purchases paid in Quarter 2: £312,000 x 50% = £156,000;
Quarter 2 purchases paid in Quarter 3: £312,000 x 50% = £156,000;
Quarter 2 S&A paid in Quarter 2: £47,500 x 75% = £35,625;
Quarter 2 S&A paid in Quarter 3: £47,500 x 25% = £11,875;
Quarter 3 purchases paid in Quarter 3: £371,700 x 50% = £185,850;
Quarter 3 purchases paid in Quarter 4: £371,700 x 50% = £185,850;
Quarter 3 S&A paid in Quarter 3: £52,500 x 75% = £39,375;
Quarter 3 S&A paid in Quarter 4: £52,500 x 25% = £13,125;
Quarter 4 purchases paid in Quarter 4: £420,700 x 50% = £210,350;
Quarter 4 S&A paid in Quarter 4: £57,500 x 75% = £43,125

Figure 14-10: Forever Tuna's predicted cash payments.

Forever Tuna, Ltd.
Cash Budget
For the Year Ended 31 December, 2013

	Quarter 1	Quarter 2	Quarter 3	Quarter 4
Opening cash	£50,000	£13,950	£4,900	£23,000
Cash receipts (from Schedule of Estimated Cash Receipts, Figure 14-10)	£315,000	£415,000	£515,000	£615,000
Cash payments for purchases and S&A (from Schedule of Estimated Cash Payments, Figure 14-11)	(£263,250)	(£328,250)	(£393,100)	(£452,450)
Cash payments for direct labour (from Direct Labour Budget, Figure 14 -6)	(£24,600)	(£30,600)	(£36,600)	(£42,300)
Cash payments for overhead (from Overhead Budget, Figure 14-7)	(£58,200)	(£60,200)	(£62,200)	(£64,100)
Cash payments for income taxes	(£5,000)	(£5,000)	(£5,000)	(£5,000)
Closing cash	£13,950	£4,900	£23,000	£74,150

Figure 14-11: Forever Tuna's cash budget.

Note how the amount of closing cash at the bottom of each column of the budget rolls forward to become opening cash in the next quarter (at the top of the budget).

This cash budget indicates that Forever Tuna is cutting things pretty close. Although the company starts with £50,000 worth of cash, its cash reserves drop to £4,900 by the end of the second quarter. This reserve level means that an error or some unexpected cash payment greater than £4,900 would cause the company to run out of cash in the middle of the year. Forever Tuna may even have a shortage of cash if all the predicted figures are correct. Look again at the second quarter and consider the worst case scenario of all payments being made at the start of the quarter but all receipts coming in at the end of the quarter.

Quarters are periods of around 90 days, not single points in time. Cash needs to be managed on a daily basis to ensure the business can survive.

Constructing a budgeted income statement

A key test of a budget is the *budgeted income statement.* Here, you can check to see whether all the predictions and assumptions you made about sales, materials, direct labour, overhead and S&A are going to bear fruit next year and generate a profit.

Like the cash budget, a budgeted income statement that predicts a loss indicates that you need to take the master budget back to the drawing board.

A budgeted income statement looks like any other income statement, except that it's for next year rather than last year. After all, you're still in the backwards Bizarro Accounting world of budgeting.

Figure 14-12 illustrates Forever Tuna's budgeted income statement, drawing figures from the other budgets prepared throughout this chapter. The company's income tax rate is 28 per cent. Following the multi-step format (which we describe in Chapter 9), the budgeted income statement starts with sales revenue and then subtracts Cost of Goods Sold to arrive at Gross Profit. You then subtract S&A expenses to arrive at Operating Profit before tax. Finally, you subtract Tax to arrive at Profit for the year.

Forever Tuna, Ltd.

Budgeted Income Statement

For the Year Ended 31 December, 2013

Sales	£2,200,000	*(Sales Budget, Figure 14-2)*
Cost of goods sold	£1,692,900	*(See below)*
Gross profit	£507,100	
Selling and administrative expenses	£200,000	*(S&A Budget, Figure 14-8)*
Operating profit	£307,100	
Tax	£85,988	*(307,100 x 28%)*
Profit for the year	£221,112	

Computation of Cost of goods sold:

22,000 units x £76.95 each

22,000 units comes from the Sales Budget, Figure 14-2

£76.95 cost per unit comes from Figure 14-7

Figure 14-12: Forever Tuna's budgeted income statement.

Whew! The Budgeted Income Statement indicates that, if all the assumptions of the budget hold true, Forever Tuna will report £221,112 profit for next year.

Many companies also prepare a Budgeted Statement of Financial Position based on the previous year's Statement of Financial Position and the budgets for next year.

Applying Master Budgeting to Non-Manufacturers

Manufacturers aren't the only companies that need master budgeting. Retailers and service providers have to plan ahead, too. This section provides tips on how you can adapt the process from the earlier section 'Preparing a Manufacturer's Master Budget' for other industries.

Budgeting for a retailer

Unlike a manufacturer, a retailer doesn't make goods, it buys and sells them. Therefore, it operates shops and possibly warehouses, not factories.

Even without all the burdens of manufacturing, retailers still have to prepare budgets. However, their *merchandise purchases budget* replaces the need for a production budget, direct materials budget and overhead budget (flip to the earlier sections 'Generating a production budget', 'Setting a direct materials budget' and 'Building an overhead budget', respectively). A retailer uses its merchandise purchases budget to prepare a schedule of cash payments in order to complete its cash budget.

The merchandise purchases budget uses the same budget formula as the manufacturer's budget does:

Opening inventory + Purchases – Closing Inventory = Units Sold

Here, the retailer wants to know inputs – how much merchandise to buy. The outputs equal the budgeted Cost of Goods Sold. Closing means the desired balance of inventory at the end of the accounting period, and opening reflects the existing balance of inventory at the beginning of the period. You can apply this formula in total, for separate quarters or months, or even for individual products.

Pickers Ltd owns a chain of shops that sells clothing in shopping centres. The company's inventory on 31 December, 2012, was £250,000. The company budgets show Cost of Goods Sold in 2013 of £325,000 and desired closing inventory on 31 December, 2013, of £210,000. Figure 14-13 shows how the company estimates the merchandise purchases needed for next year.

This merchandise purchases budget indicates that Pickers needs to purchase £285,000 worth of merchandise during the period.

Figure 14-13: Pickers' planned merchandise purchases.

Pickers, Ltd.
Merchandise Purchases Budget
For the Year Ended 31 December, 2013

Budgeted cost of goods sold	325,000
Closing merchandise inventory	210,000
Less: beginning merchandise inventory	(250,000)
Budgeted merchandise purchases	£285,000

Co-ordinating a service company's budget

Service companies, such as solicitors, limousine services and mobile phone companies, sell services rather than products. Like manufacturers and retailers, they also need to prepare budgets. However, service companies need to focus on their direct labour budgets, because direct labour usually comprises most of these companies' expenses (check out the earlier 'Working on a direct labour budget' section for details). Overstaffing can drag down profits. Understaffing can cause employees to work excessive overtime or even force the company to turn down business.

For a service company, the direct labour budget feeds right into the cash budget and the budgeted income statement (see the earlier sections 'Creating a cash budget' and 'Constructing a budgeted income statement', respectively). Service companies usually have no need for production or overhead budgets.

Moving Beyond Budgeting

Some commentators and business managers have challenged the traditional approach to budgeting that we describe in the preceding sections. Modern businesses need to be responsive to the changes in their external environments, flexible in their manufacturing, versatile when responding to the effects of short product life cycles and quick to react to changing customer preferences. These requirements conflict with planning and measuring performance in terms of the ability to carry out what the plan says. Managers at the high-profile business failure WorldCom claimed that meeting budget targets set by their chief executive were their key performance indicators. This approach may work in a static environment where the chief executive can accurately predict future trends, but the business world is no longer static and easy to predict.

Therefore, some organisations have responded with what's called *beyond budgeting.* This is a cultural change and incorporates many modern management practices within a general framework. It's a move away from the 'command and control' use of targets under traditional uses of budgeting.

Rolling forecasts and plans

Instead of setting budget targets for a year and trying to meet those targets, in the beyond budgeting approach the management accountant is involved in an annual forecast drawn up with key managers. This forecast is then rolled forward each month.

The earliest months in a forecast are the ones where the greatest amount of information is available, and so they tend to be the months that managers can more accurately predict. By re-writing the forecast each month (for the next 12 months) new data is incorporated and managers can build a better understanding of what the business will do during the year.

Moving away from tradition

The move away from the traditional 'command and control' management style often associated with budgeting systems means that decision-making becomes less centralised. This change leads to specific benefits in businesses that adopt beyond budgeting. Here are some of the general benefits claimed for the beyond budgeting approach:

- Faster response times to customer requests.
- Better innovation in working methods and technologies.
- Cost savings, because minimising costs instead of spending within a budget cuts out some inefficiencies.
- Improved relationships with customers and suppliers, because decision-making is taken by front-line teams.

Part IV

Using Management Accounting for Evaluation and Control

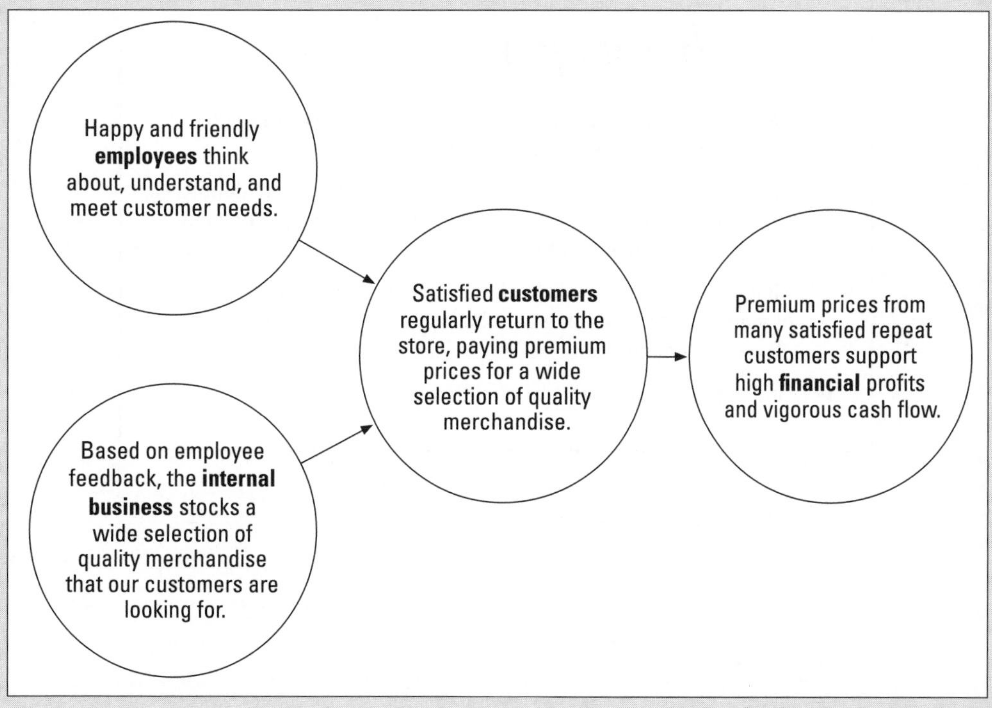
Happy and friendly **employees** think about, understand, and meet customer needs.
Based on employee feedback, the **internal business** stocks a wide selection of quality merchandise that our customers are looking for.
Satisfied **customers** regularly return to the store, paying premium prices for a wide selection of quality merchandise.
Premium prices from many satisfied repeat customers support high **financial** profits and vigorous cash flow.

web extras

Go to `www.dummies.com/extras/managementcostaccountinguk` for free online bonus content created especially for this book.

In this part . . .

- Get to grips with responsibility accounting — how to assign responsibility to different parts of the organisation.
- Understand variance analysis, a set of techniques that identify unexpected events, measure how they affect income and help assign responsibility for them.
- Meet the balanced scorecard, which uses a wide-ranging set of measures to determine whether a company's strategy is in place as planned.
- Find out about the theory of constraints.

Chapter 15

Using Flexible Budgets to Exert Control

In This Chapter

- Employing a budget to control your business
- Looking at variances and their causes
- Creating a flexible budget

In Chapter 14, we describe Mark's detailed planning for a cross-country camping trip with his sons. To tell you the truth, things didn't quite go as planned and his famed budget spreadsheet turned out not to be so accurate. A 30 per cent increase in the price of fuel added more than $1,000 to the cost of the trip, and although he timed the trip to drive 600 miles per day, he didn't take into account stops for coffee, toilets or travel sickness (the horror, the horror!).

In addition, changes in time zones gave the family three additional hours when driving west, which they lost on the way home. Plus, the youngsters didn't care for the *Power Rangers* films, a problem alleviated when the DVD player mysteriously disappeared somewhere in Indiana or Illinois. Needless to say, this loss caused further expenses (a new DVD player and film collection). Ho hum!

This chapter describes the importance of controlling your business and the problems of variances. Plus, as Mark's road trip attests, budgets don't have to be set in stone, and so we explain how to use flexible budgets to manage your business's operations.

Appreciating the Need to Control Your Business

Budgeting helps you plan your business's operations. However, you also need to *control* your business – that is, to monitor what's actually happening. Controlling involves constantly comparing real activity to your budget and carefully analysing and understanding any differences. To accomplish this task, you need budget reports that compare your budgets (what should have happened) to what really happened.

For example, suppose that your company budgeted £100,000 for sales in the first quarter. Actual sales for the quarter come up short, at only £70,000. Here's what to do:

1. **Call the sales manager to find out what happened.** In this case, a computer error accidentally caused cancelled customer orders.
2. **Take corrective action.** Fix your computer and call your customers to apologise.
3. **Adjust your future plans.** Perhaps cut next quarter's production estimates if the orders can't be added to next month's sales.

As we explain in Chapter 14, master budgeting provides the basic template for this analysis, offering projections for sales, expenses, production levels and cash flows to help you plan for future periods. A master budget's major flaw, however, is that it's *static* – it projects only one scenario based on a single set of sales estimates and it can't change.

Therefore, a £30,000 difference throws off more than just your sales budget. It also necessitates changing your production, purchases, direct labour, overhead costs and selling and administrative expenses, ruining the entire planning process and making future comparisons between your budgets and actual results almost impossible for you.

Enter the flexible budget. As activity levels change, you can easily adjust a flexible budget so that you can continue to use it to plan and control your business.

Common practice is to look at sensitivities at the planning stage (when a budget is drawn up initially; see Chapter 14) as well. Many firms draw up the budget, and then produce additional planning budgets to show the effect of key factors not being quite as forecast. For example, an original budget for a sandwich shop might have £300 as the forecast revenue for one day, but the owner might produce two more budgets based on the same assumptions, one showing £330 and another £270. These same assumptions might be that sandwiches sell for £3 each and cost £1.20 each and that the shop rent is £50 per day. The term used to describe the second and third budgets is *flexed*. Flexed means: take the basic assumptions from the first budget (the £300 sales revenue) and fleX them to the revised number of sandwiches. The X is deliberate because flexing is a multiplication sum!

Look at Figure 15-1 for the Sandwich Shop.

	Original Budget	***Assumptions***	***More Sales***	***Fewer Sales***
Sandwiches	100		110	90
	£	Sandwiches sell for £3 each, ingredients cost £1.20 per sandwich and the rent is £50 irrespective of how many sandwiches are sold.	£	£
Revenue	300		330	270
Ingredients	120		132	108
Rent	50		50	50
Profit	130		148	112

Figure 15-1: The Sandwich Shop.

Certainly, applications for bank finance require not only a realistic cash budget, but also budgets for 'what if' the sales volume actually achieved turns out to be 80 or even 60 per cent of the forecast.

Dealing with Budget Variances

What we've described so far are the planning benefits of flexing a budget. What if we sell more sandwiches? What if we sell fewer?

Flexing a budget is very useful for control purposes. At the end of an accounting period, management accountants can review what happened during that period. One part of that review is to compare what happened with the budget. If the original budget is flexed to the actual units produced and the actual units sold, the flexed budget that's produced is more useful for comparison purposes than the original one.

The difference between a budget cost and an actual cost is called a *variance*. Some companies compare the original budget cost of labour with the actual cost, but it's much more useful to compare the flexed budget cost of labour with the actual cost because both are based on the actual number of units produced.

The later section 'Implementing a Flexible Budget' gives you the lowdown on the budget flexing process, but here we go a little deeper into the issue of variances.

Always indicate whether a variance is favourable or adverse:

- **Favourable variance:** One that increases profit. So the variance is favourable when actual revenues exceed budgeted amounts or when actual expenses are less than budgeted expenses.
- **Adverse variance:** One that decreases profit. So the variance is adverse when actual revenues fall short of budgeted amounts or when actual expenses exceed budgeted expenses.

In terms of costs, each variance causing a difference between the budget flexed to actual sales, and the actual results, can be due to several factors. The analysis of these variances into the contributory parts forms the basis of Chapter 16.

The AAT Costs and Revenues exam includes task 9, which requires careful reading. Sometimes the questions ask for a comparison of actual cost with the planning budget, and other times they ask for a comparison with a flexible budget, as the next two sections show.

Example exam question 1: Comparing the fixed budget and the actual results

We use a fixed budget and compare it with the actual results for the period for the Devil's Kiss chilli sauce company. Figure 15-2 is drawn up as any income statement may be, but has three additional columns. These allow the budget and the actual results to be shown side by side, the difference between the two (the variance) and a description about how that variance affects the company's overall profitability. The variances are shown in bold, because they're calculated after completing the budget and actual columns.

'You say to-may-to and I say to-ma-to'

Accountants usually express favourable variances as positive numbers and adverse variances as negative numbers, which suits spreadsheet and other software-based reporting. Some accountants and management accounting textbooks avoid expressing any variance values as negative, but always notate whether a variance is favourable or adverse, which can help in an exam because the effect the variance has on profit is clear.

In the level 2 AAT costing exam, some of the exams used to call variances positive when the actual amount exceeds budget and negative when the actual amount falls short of budget. Here, a positive variance for sales would be favourable because sales were higher than expected. However, a positive variance for costs would be adverse because costs were higher than expected (reducing the profit). You need to be aware of this practice if you use these past papers in your preparation for future exams, but we advise you to use the adverse/favourable effect on profit approach whenever you're given a choice.

In this chapter, and in Chapter 16, we express variances as positive when they have a favourable effect on profit and negative when they have an adverse effect on profit.

Hot Chilli Sauce	***Budget***	***Actual***	***Variance***	***Adverse/Favourable***
Litres produced and sold	10,000	12,000	**2,000**	
Sales Revenue	£8,800	£10,400	**£1,600**	favourable
Costs				
Variable costs				
Direct materials	£1,200	£1,368	**£168**	adverse
Direct labour	£1,000	£1,160	**£160**	adverse
Overheads	£1,600	£1,912	**£312**	adverse
Fixed costs				
Indirect labour	£700	£720	**£20**	adverse
Overheads	£1,600	£1,650	**£50**	adverse
Total cost	£6,100	£6,810	**£710**	adverse
Profit	£2,700	£3,590	£890	favourable

Figure 15-2: Budgetary Control Statement for Devil's Kiss using the original budget.

Example exam question 2: Comparing a flexed budget and the actual results

In this example exam question, the comparison is based on the actual litres of sauce produced and sold. In other words, the budget has been flexed to match the actual units.

This time we use the budget and flex it before we compare it with the actual results for the period for the Devil's Kiss chilli sauce company. The table is drawn up in a similar way to the comparison with the fixed budget in the preceding section, but has an extra column (see Figure 15-3). It also has a different set of figures in the flexed budget column.

Here are some tips on how to proceed:

- The extra column is only used for budgeted costs and revenues that are variable, and shows the per unit values. For example, the sales revenue (price) for one unit is £0.88 (£8,800 budgeted revenue/10,000 budgeted sales) and the direct material cost £0.12 (£1,200 budgeted cost/10,000 budgeted production). You use only budgeted figures. Your flexed budget needs to be the budgeted revenue and costs based on your assumptions at the time the budget was written, but using the actual volume of sales and production. We cover the subject of flexing in Chapter 16 and use the name *flexed to output* for production costs.

  At this stage be very clear: you never use the actual column to calculate the budgeted unit price or the budgeted costs per unit.

- In the flexed budget column you copy whatever the actual sales and production volume are and use these figures. In this example, these are the same as each other. In this example, the 12,000 is multiplied by the variable values in the extra column: 12,000 × £0.88 = £10,560 and 12,000 × £0.12 = £1,440. But note that fixed costs, by definition, don't change due to a change in the volume of units sold. Copy the fixed costs from the original budget into the flexed budget.
- In the actual column, you can leave this exactly the same as for the previous example. In this example the production volume and the sales volume are the same as each other. If they aren't, one common approach is to only use sales volume, but this requires adjustments to the actual column. When you're given a question where the two volumes are different, divide each production cost by the units produced (only using actual figures) and multiply by the units sold to find the cost of sales effectively on an expense by expense basis.
- The variance columns show the variances and whether they're favourable or adverse in exactly the same way as they did for the example in the preceding section.

This example question compares like with like and is a good basis for a management report comparing the profit which should have been earned from a given sales revenue and the actual profit earned, and breaks down all the contributing factors that explain the difference.

Hot Chilli Sauce	*Budget*	*Flexed Budget*	*Actual*	*Variance*	*Adverse/ Favourable*
Litres produced and sold	One unit	12,000	12,000	**0**	
Sales Revenue	£0.88	£10,560	£10,400	**£160**	adverse
Costs					
Variable costs					
Direct materials	£0.12	£1,440	£1,368	**£72**	favourable
Direct labour	£0.10	£1,200	£1,160	**£40**	favourable
Overheads	£0.16	£1,920	£1,912	**£8**	favourable
Fixed costs					
Indirect labour		£700	£720	**£20**	adverse
Overheads		£1,600	£1,650	**£50**	adverse
Total cost		£6,860	£6,810	**£50**	favourable
Profit		£3,700	£3,590	£110	adverse

Figure 15-3: Budgetary Control Statement for Devil's Kiss using a flexed budget.

Dealing with variances

Management needs to investigate the cause of significant budget variances. Here are some possibilities:

- **Changes in conditions:** For example, a supplier may have raised prices, causing the company's costs to increase.
- **Quality of management:** Special care to reduce costs can result in favourable variances. On the other hand, management carelessness causes adverse variances.
- **Lousy budgeting:** An unrealistically ambitious budget is likely to cause negative variances.
- **Misposting:** Within the normal recording of posting of costs onto the accounting system, the miscoding and misposting of costs causes more variances than anything else.

If you find you have variances at work, before you start any major investigations of work practices, check the posting of costs in the accounts office. In our experience this is where most variances have been caused. Miss Posting and Miss Coding have a lot to answer for!

Don't be fooled into thinking that favourable budget variances are always good news. Cost-cutting measures reflected in a favourable variance may in fact hurt the quality of finished products. Senior managers may have preferred that the company spent more for better materials and sold higher quality goods.

Many managers use a system called *management by exception*, in which they investigate the largest variances, whether favourable or adverse, and ignore the rest. This strategy helps focus managers on potential problem areas in operations. Chapter 16 explains more about how to assign responsibility for budget variances.

Implementing a Flexible Budget

Creating a flexible budget is helpful to compute variances that can help you understand why actual results differed from your expectations. A *flexible budget* adjusts the master budget for your actual sales or production volume.

For example, your master budget may have assumed that you'd produce 5,000 units, when in fact you produced 5,100 units. The flexible budget rearranges the master budget to reflect this new number, making all the appropriate adjustments to sales and expenses based on the unexpected change in volume.

To prepare a flexible budget, you need to have a master budget, properly understand cost behaviour and know the actual volume of goods produced and sold.

Consider Kira, president of the fictional Skate Company, which manufactures roller skates. Kira's accountant, Steve, prepared the overhead budget shown in Figure 15-4.

Skate had a great year; actual sales were 125,000 units. Much to the disappointment of Steve and Kira, however, the overhead budget report, shown in Figure 15-5, reports major overruns. For each category of overhead, Steve computes a variance, identifying adverse variances in indirect materials, indirect labour, supervisory salaries and utilities.

Skate Company
Overhead Budget
For the Year Ended 31 December, 2013

Budgeted production	100,000	units
Indirect materials	£50,000	
Indirect labour	£40,000	
Supervisory salaries	£100,000	
Rent	£80,000	
Utilities	£40,000	
Depreciation	£20,000	
Total overhead	£330,000	

Figure 15-4: Skate's static overhead budget.

Skate Company
Overhead Budget Report
For the Year Ended 31 December, 2013

	Budget	Actual	Variance	Favourable/ Adverse
Production (units)	100,000	125,000		
Indirect materials	£50,000	£60,000	£10,000	Adverse
Indirect labour	£40,000	£45,000	£5,000	Adverse
Supervisory salaries	£100,000	£105,000	£5,000	Adverse
Rent	£80,000	£80,000	-0-	
Utilities	£40,000	£45,000	£5,000	Adverse
Depreciation	£20,000	£20,000	-0-	
Total overhead	£330,000	£355,000	£25,000	Adverse

Figure 15-5: Skate's overhead budget report.

Skate's total overhead exceeded budget by £25,000. He made the elementary mistake of treating variable costs as fixed. After all, portions of overhead, such as indirect materials, appear to be variable costs. If Skate increased production from 100,000 units to 125,000 units, these variable costs also increase. In other words, comparing the £60,000 actual cost of making 125,000 units to the £50,000 budgeted cost of making just 100,000 units makes no sense. You're comparing apples and oranges.

Instead, Steve needs to flex the budget to determine how much overhead he should have, assuming that the company makes 130,000 units. The following two sections show you how.

Separating fixed and variable costs

Some costs are *variable* – they change in response to activity levels – whereas other costs are *fixed* and remain the same. For example, direct materials are variable costs because the more goods you make, the more materials you need. On the other hand, some overhead costs, such as rent, are fixed; no matter how many units you make, these costs stay the same. To determine whether a cost is variable or fixed, think about the nature of the cost and evaluate it by using the techniques in Chapter 8.

For Skate, an analysis indicates that indirect materials, indirect labour, and utilities are variable costs. On the other hand, supervisory salaries, rent and depreciation are fixed. Steve recalculates variable costs with the assumption that the company makes 125,000 units, as shown in Figure 15-6.

	Original Budget	**Variable Cost per Unit**	**Flexible Budget**
		Original budget/ 100,000	Average cost x 125,000
Production	100,000 units		125,000 units
Indirect materials	£50,000	£0.50	£62,500
Indirect labour	£40,000	£0.40	£50,000
Utilities	£40,000	£0.40	£50,000
Total	£130,000	£1.30	£162,500

Figure 15-6: Flexing variable overhead costs.

In the original budget, making 100,000 units resulted in total variable costs of £130,000. Dividing the total cost of each category by the budgeted production level results in a variable cost per unit of £0.50 for indirect materials, £0.40 for indirect labour and £0.40 for utilities.

To compute the value of the flexible budget, multiply the variable cost per unit by the actual production volume. Figure 15-6 indicates that the variable costs of producing 125,000 totals £162,500 (125,000 units × £1.30).

Comparing the flexible budget to actual results

You combine the variable and fixed costs in order to prepare a new overhead budget report, inserting the new flexible budget results into it as shown in Figure 15-7.

Skate Company
Overhead Budget Report (Flexible)
For the Year Ended 31 December, 2013

	Flexible Budget	Actual	Variance	Favourable/ Adverse
Production (units)	125,000	125,000		
Variable Costs				
Indirect materials	£62,500	£60,000	£2,500	Favourable
Indirect labour	£50,000	£45,000	£5,000	Favourable
Utilities	£50,000	£45,000	£5,000	Favourable
Total variable costs	£162,500	£150,000		
Fixed Costs				
Supervisory salaries	£100,000	£105,000	£5,000	Adverse
Rent	£80,000	£80,000	-0-	
Depreciation	£20,000	£20,000	-0-	
Total fixed costs	£200,000	£205,000		
Total overhead	£362,500	£355,000	£7,500	Favourable

Figure 15-7: Skate's flexible overhead budget.

Look at that! After you adjust for the change in production level, Skate's variance is suddenly favourable. Actual overhead of £355,000 is £7,500 less than the £362,500 flexible budget.

Chapter 16

Variance Analysis: Flexing Standard Costs

In This Chapter

- Establishing standard costs
- Getting under the skin of variances
- Explaining and solving discrepancies with variances

When things don't go according to plan, inevitably you're left asking 'why?' To find the answer, you need to examine the factors that are under your control.

For example, we hate to diet and we don't like exercise. If you think that all accountants enjoy counting calories and logging walking distances with a pedometer, think again! No surprise, therefore, that checking our weight often leaves us asking the question 'why?', especially when we think that we've been careful during the week; but the scales don't lie (unfortunately). The fact is that the increase in weight comes down to three factors that are under our control: what we eat and drink; how much we eat and drink; and how much we exercise. Examining each of these factors in more detail helps us to change our routines so that we can diet more successfully in the future.

Variance analysis plays a similar role for businesses. When things go wrong, or even when they go more right than expected, variance analysis explains why. What caused higher-than-expected profits? What about unexpected losses? You can use all this information to improve future operations.

In this chapter, we look at standard costs, what variances are and how managers can use them productively to address a company's problems.

Setting Up Standard Costs

You can't measure variances without first setting *standard costs* or *standards* – predetermined unit costs of materials, labour and overhead. Standards are the building blocks of budgets; budgets predict total costs (as we explain in Chapter 14), but standards predict the cost of each unit of direct materials, direct labour and overhead.

Standard costs provide a number of important benefits:

- They help managers budget for the future.
- They help all employees focus on keeping costs down.
- They help set sales prices.
- They give managers a benchmark for measuring variances and identifying related problems.
- They simplify collecting and managing the cost of inventory.
- They provide useful information for variance analysis (which is the focus of this chapter).

Discovering the different types of standards

Implementing standards often forces managers to face a critical dilemma, because as we discuss in this section you can set standards in several different ways:

- **Ideal standards:** Can encourage employees to work hard to achieve rigorous goals. Ideal standards are the best that people can possibly achieve and can't be beaten. Therefore, they can be achieved only under the best possible conditions.

  Overly aggressive standards can unduly pressure employees, causing them to report false information or to just give up on the standards out of frustration, deeming them unattainable. Such behaviour tends to be a response to how senior managers react when performance is reported. If senior management are critical of very good performances by the operational managers because they produce small *adverse variances* in one period (that is, when actual costs exceeds the standard), these operational managers may be less inclined to make an additional effort in the next period.

No *favourable variances* (that is, when actual costs come in under standard costs) are possible with ideal standards. A nil variance is only just possible; adverse variances are pretty much inevitable.

- **Target standards:** Difficult to achieve, but don't require the perfect conditions essential for ideal standards. They tend to lead to adverse variances because of their difficulty, but favourable variances are possible. Just as for ideal standards, the success in using them depends on the reaction of senior management to small adverse variances. Provided senior management rewards good performance and effort, operational managers are likely to be motivated and work hard to improve performance.
- **Attainable standards:** Provide more accurate cost information and are less likely to lead to the kind of adverse variances that result in lower-than-expected income. However, attainable standards still need to be set as achievable rather than 'easy', to encourage employees to 'go the extra mile' to improve cost control and productivity. Attainable standards are assumed in most accounting exam questions and are the most widely used in business.
- **Basic standards:** Tend to become out of date or reflect a minimum performance level. If you accept that the ultimate purpose of a set of standards is to enable you to use them as a benchmark to assess actual performance then, to be honest, basic standards have no useful role. They're unrealistic and too easily achieved, and so often have a negative effect on motivation as they don't encourage managers to try that little bit harder.

Your standards have to include the cost and how much direct materials and direct labour is needed, as well as the amount of overhead required.

Here are a few points to bear in mind about standards in connection with the various accounting exams:

- CIMA CO1 doesn't specify the types of standard, but tends to assume the attainable standard within the calculations.
- CIMA P1 and ACCA F2 require an understanding in the context of setting and the behavioural implications.
- ACCA F5 specifies an understanding at the application and analysis level of the methods used to derive standard costs and the different types of cost possible.
- AAT Financial Performance requires an understanding of how standard costs can be established, the different types of standard (ideal, target, attainable, basic) and how the type of standard can affect the behaviour of the budget holder and workforce.

After you establish standards, you use them to compute variances, which can help explain why actual performance strayed from expectations.

Establishing direct materials standards

Direct materials are raw materials traceable to the manufactured product, such as the amount of flour used to make a cake.

To compute the direct materials standard price (SP), consider all the costs that go into a single unit of direct materials. Because several different kinds of direct materials are often necessary for any given product, you need to establish separate direct material standard prices and quantities for every kind of direct material needed.

Suppose that Band Books usually pays £10 per kilogram for paper. It typically pays £0.25 per kilogram for freight and another £0.10 per kilogram for receiving and handling. Therefore, as shown in Figure 16-1, total cost per kilogram equals £10.35.

Figure 16-1: Adding up direct material standard price (SP).

Cost	Per Kilogram
Purchase price	£10.00
Freight-in	0.25
Receiving and handling	0.10
Direct materials standard price (SP)	£10.35

Another standard to consider is the *direct materials standard quantity* (SQ) per unit. This number is the amount of direct materials needed to make a single unit of finished product. It includes not only the direct materials actually used, but also any direct materials likely to get scrapped or spoiled in the production process.

Variance costing involves juggling many different figures and terms. To simplify matters, use abbreviations such as SP (for direct materials standard price) and SQ (for direct materials standard quantity). Doing so makes remembering how to calculate variances easier.

For example, assume that Band Books needs 25 kilograms of paper to make a case of books. For every case, 3 kilograms of paper are deemed unusable because of waste and spoilage. Therefore, the direct materials SQ per unit equals 28 kilograms, as shown in Figure 16-2.

Figure 16-2: Computing direct materials standard quantity (SQ) per unit.

Cost	Quantity (Kilograms)
Required materials per unit	25
Waste and spoilage	3
Direct materials standard quantity (SQ)	28

Determining direct labour standards

Direct labour is the cost of paying your employees to make products. Proper planning requires setting standards with respect to two factors:

- The direct labour standard rate (SR)
- The direct labour standard hours (SH) per unit

To compute the *direct labour SR* (the hourly rate of direct labour), consider all the costs required for a single hour of direct labour. For example, suppose that Band Books usually pays employees £9 per hour. Furthermore, it pays an additional £1 per hour for payroll taxes and, on average, £2 per hour for fringe benefits. As shown in Figure 16-3, the direct labour SR equals £12 per hour.

Figure 16-3: Computing the direct labour standard rate (SR).

Cost	Per Hour
Average hourly wage	£9.00
Payroll taxes	1.00
Fringe benefits	2.00
Direct labour standard rate (SR)	£12.00

You also need to estimate the amount of direct labour time needed to make a single unit, the *direct labour SH per unit.* This calculation estimates how long employees take on average to produce a single unit. Include in this rate the time needed for employee breaks, clean-ups and set-ups.

For example, employees at Band Books need 3 hours to produce a single case of books, plus an average of 30 minutes of set-up time and 30 minutes of break time. Therefore, the direct labour SH per case of books is 4 hours, as shown in Figure 16-4.

Cost	Hours
Average production time	3.00
Break time	0.50
Setup time	0.50
Direct labour standard hours (SH)	4.00

Figure 16-4: Computing direct labour standard hours (SH).

Calculating the overhead rate

In addition to direct materials and direct labour (see the preceding sections), standard costs also need to account for *overhead* (the miscellaneous costs of running a business; refer to Chapter 4).

Overhead is much more difficult to measure than direct materials or direct labour standards, because the relationship between overhead and each unit produced is trickier to nail down. To assign overhead costs to individual units, you need to compute an overhead absorption rate, as explained in Chapter 4.

In Chapter 4 we show the steps needed to calculate the overhead absorption rate in detail. Here we simplify the steps to the final calculation:

1. **Compute the overhead absorption rate.**

   Divide the total budgeted overhead by the budgeted number of direct labour hours.

   For Band Books Company assume the total budgeted overhead is £100,000 and budgeted production is 1,000 cases of books.

   Figure 16-4 shows the SH per case is 4 hours. 1,000 cases x 4 SH per case gives 4,000 total budgeted direct labour hours.

   Divide the budgeted overhead cost by the budgeted labour hours as follows:

$$\text{Overhead allocation rate} = \frac{\text{Total overhead}}{\text{Total direct labour hours}} = \frac{\text{£}100{,}000}{4{,}000\text{ hours}} = \text{£}25.00$$

   Therefore, for every SH of direct labour needed to make books, Band Books applies £25 worth of overhead to the product. This is the standard overhead absorption rate per direct labour hour. As 4 SH are required per case, the standard overhead cost per unit (at Band Books a unit is a case of books) is 4 × £25 = £100.

2. **Apply overhead.**

   Multiply the overhead absorption rate by the number of direct labour hours needed to make each product.

   Suppose that a department at Band Books actually work 20 hours on a product. Apply £500 worth of overhead to this product (20 hours × £25).

Adding up standard cost per unit

To find the standard cost, you compute the cost of direct materials, direct labour and overhead per unit, as we explain in the preceding three sections, and then add up these amounts.

Figure 16-5 applies this approach to Band Books:

1. **Calculate the standard cost of direct materials.**

   Multiply the direct materials SP of £10.35 by the direct materials SQ of 28 kilograms per unit (as we describe in the earlier section 'Establishing direct materials standards'). The result is a direct materials standard cost of £289.80 per case.

2. **Compute direct labour standard cost per unit.**

   Multiply the direct labour SR of £12 per unit by the direct labour SH per unit of 4 hours (check out 'Determining direct labour standards' earlier in this chapter). The standard cost per unit is £48 for direct labour.

3. **Work out the standard cost of overhead per unit.**

   Multiply the overhead absorption rate of £25 per hour by the direct labour SH 4 hours per unit (see the earlier section 'Calculating the overhead rate' for details). Standard cost of overhead per unit is therefore £100.

4. **Calculate the standard cost per unit.**

   Add together direct materials, direct labour and overhead to arrive at £437.80, which is what making a single case of books costs Band Books.

Figure 16-5: Standard cost card for Band Books: One case of books.

Input	*Input required*	*Cost per unit of input*	*Cost per unit of output*
Paper	28 kilograms	£10.35/kilogram	£289.80
Labour	4 hours	£12.00/hour	£48.00
Overhead	4 hours	£25.00/labour hour	£100.00
Standard cost per unit produced			£437.80

The standard cost card uses the words input and output, which is an important distinction that lies at the heart of understanding variance analysis:

- **Inputs** go into production
- **Outputs** are what are produced

In Figure 16-6 a little later on in this chapter we identify variances, and we look at the total standard costs based on outputs and based on inputs.

Identifying Factors that Give Rise to Variances

In Chapter 15, we outline budgetary control variances using a table but we only look at the total cost variances for each type of expenditure. This section breaks the variances down into their constituent parts.

A *variance* is the difference between the actual cost and the standard cost that you expected to pay (we cover standard costs in the earlier 'Setting Up Standard Costs' section). When actual cost exceeds the standard, the resulting variance is considered *adverse* because it reduces profit. On the other hand, when actual costs come in under standard costs, the resulting variance is considered *favourable* because it increases profit.

Variances can arise from direct materials, direct labour and overhead. In fact, the variances arising from each of these three areas, when added together, should equal the total variance:

Total variance = Direct materials variance + Direct labour variance + Overhead variance

You can break down direct material variances further into price and usage variances to understand how changes in materials prices and materials quantities used affect overall profitability. Similarly, you can break down direct labour variances into labour rate and labour efficiency variances. You use the standard usage of material per unit SQ, the standard price per kilogram or litre of material SP, the standard hours per unit SH and the standard rate per hour SR to carry out this analysis.

Working out the direct materials variances usage and price

We need to flex (in other words, multiply) the standard cost of one unit of production (originally used in the planning budget; see Chapter 14) to find the standard material used and then the standard material cost of actual production. The standard material cost of actual production means exactly the same as the flexed budget material cost we calculate in Chapter 15.

To break down the total variance into the part due to the actual usage of material being different from the standard material needed for the actual production, you need to insert a column between the flexed to output (or the 'Standard cost per unit flexed to output') column and the 'Actual cost' column. Doing so enables you to flex the standard cost of a unit of input to the actual amount of material used.

Figure 16-6 shows the approach and names the values in each box. We use the example of Band Books (which we introduce in the earlier section 'Establishing direct materials standards') to complete the table in Figure 16-6. We employ the data from 'Setting Up Standard Costs' earlier in the chapter and add:

- **Actual production:** 900 cases of books.
- **Direct materials:** 30,000 kilograms purchased and used at a cost of £297,000.
- **Direct labour:** 3,450 hours worked at a total direct labour cost of £43,400.
- **Overhead cost:** £95,000.

	Original budget	*Standard cost per unit flexed to actual output*	*Standard cost per unit of output flexed to actual inputs*	*Actual cost*
Production (cases of books)	1,000	900		
Direct materials				
Kilograms per unit	28	28		
Total kilograms		Standard material used	Actual material used	
Cost per kilogram	£10.35	£10.35		
Cost	Budgeted cost	Standard material cost of actual production	Standard cost of material used	
Variances				

Figure 16-6: Variance Analysis Workings Sheet for Band Books showing where values should be entered to find the material variances.

Here are the necessary steps:

1. **Enter the information you have in the 'Original budget' column.** The budget was for 1,000 cases and so you enter this figure at the top of the column. Then enter the kilograms per case (28 kilograms) and the cost per kilogram (£10.35). No further calculations are needed.
2. **Enter the production of 900 cases in the 'Standard cost per unit flexed to output' column.** Then copy the standard values from the 'Original budget' column: 28 kilograms per unit and £10.35 per kilogram (see Figure 16-6).
3. **Add the actual materials used in the 'Standard cost per unit of input flexed to actual inputs' column: 30,000 kilograms.** Copy the cost per kilogram across into the column: £10.35. Add the actual cost in the 'Actual cost' column: £297,000.
4. **Carry out multiplication as follows (see Figure 16-7):**
   - **Standard cost flexed to output:**

     Total kilograms: 900 × 28 kilogram/unit = 25,200 kilograms

     Cost: 25,200 kilograms × £10.35/kilogram = £260,820
   - **Standard cost flexed to input:**

     Cost: 30,000 kilograms × £10.35/kilogram = £310,500
5. **Identify the variances:**
   - **Total variance:** Cost from the 'Standard cost per unit flexed to actual output' column less the 'Actual cost' column: £260,820 – £297,000 = £36,180 adverse. This approach is exactly the same as the budgetary control one (see Chapter 15).
   - **Material usage variance:** Cost from the 'Standard cost per unit flexed to actual output' column less the cost from the 'Standard cost per unit of input flexed to actual inputs' column: £260,820 – £310,500 = £49,680 adverse.
   - **Material price variance:** Cost from the 'Standard cost per unit of input flexed to actual inputs' column less the 'Actual cost' column: £310,500 – £297,000 = £13,500 favourable.

Examiners are familiar with the use of 'F' to indicate a favourable variance and 'A' to indicate an adverse variance. These abbreviations can save you having to write out the whole word when time is pressured.

Figure 16-7: Variance Analysis Workings Sheet for Band Books showing the material variances. (A means Adverse, F means Favourable.)

	Original budget	Standard cost per unit flexed to actual output	Standard cost per unit of input flexed to actual inputs	Actual cost
Production (cases of books)	1,000	900		
Direct materials				
Kilograms per unit	28	28		
Total kilograms		25,200	30,000	
Cost per kilogram	£10.35	£10.35	£10.35	
Cost	Budgeted cost	£260,820	£310,500	£297,000
Variances		Material variance £36,180 (A)		
		Usage £49,680 (A)	Price £13,500 (F)	

In this example, the material usage variance is caused by the 900 cases of books requiring 30,000 rather than 25,200 kilograms of paper. You don't know why such a significant difference exists, but you do know that it's a large variance.

Typical investigations would look at the accuracy of the posting of material costs, just in case a requisition for paper from the stores had been charged to book production when it was supposed to be for another product. Other investigations may ask whether a problem had occurred during the accounting period, which meant that a lot of paper was wasted; had a machine broken down and paper been scrapped? Had the paper been of a poorer quality than the normal paper, and had this led to more wastage? This list isn't exhaustive, but it provides the sort of questions a management accountant would ask.

The material price variance is favourable, which may indicate that a poorer quality, cheaper material was purchased and not the quality that the standard was based on. Investigations may show that this poorer quality paper caused the usage variance to be adverse.

Finding direct labour variances efficiency and rate

A *direct labour variance* is caused by differences between the standard labour hours produced and the actual hours worked and/or differences between the standard rate per hour and the actual rate paid.

You need to flex the standard cost of one unit of production (originally used in the planning budget; see Chapter 14) to find the standard labour hours produced and then the standard labour cost of actual production.

To break down the total variance into the part due to the actual hours worked being different to the standard hours produced for the actual production, you need a column between the 'Standard cost per unit flexed to actual output' column and the 'Actual cost' column just as with the material cost variances in the preceding section. You use the same approach, values and layout as for Figures 16-6 and 16-7. We continue to use Band Books to illustrate how to complete a variance analysis working sheet. The labour variance section is shown in Figure 16-8.

Here's the relevant additional data:

- **Actual production:** 900 cases of books.
- **Direct labour:** 3,450 hours worked at a total direct labour cost of £43,400.

Here's the process to follow:

1. **Enter the information you have in the 'Original budget' column (see Figure 16-8).** The budget was for 1,000 cases and so you enter this figure at the top of the column. Then enter the hours per case (4 hours) and the rate per hour (£12). No further calculations are needed.
2. **Enter the production of 900 cases in the 'Standard cost per unit flexed to output' column.** Copy the standard values from the 'Original budget' column: 4 hours per unit and £12 per hour.
3. **Add the actual hours worked in the 'Standard cost per unit of input flexed to actual inputs' column: 3,450 hours.** Copy the rate per hour across into the column: £12. Complete the 'Actual cost' column: £43,400.

	–	*Original budget*	–	*Standard cost per unit flexed to actual output*	–	*Standard cost per unit of output flexed to actual inputs*		*Actual cost*
Production (cases of books)		1,000		900				
Direct labour								
Hours per unit		4		4				
Total hours				Standard hours produced		Actual hours worked		
Rate per hour		£12.00		£12.00				
Cost		Budgeted cost		Standard labour cost of actual production		Standard cost of labour hours worked		
Variances								

Figure 16-8: Variance Analysis Workings Sheet for Band Books showing where values should be entered to find the labour variances.

4. **Carry out multiplication as follows (see Figure 16-9):**
   - **Standard cost flexed to output:**

     Total hours: 900 × 4 hours/unit = 3,600 hours

     Cost: 3,600 hours × £12/hour = £43,200
   - **Standard cost flexed to input:**

     Cost: 3,450 hours worked × £12/hour = £41,400
5. **Identify the variances:**
   - **Total variance:** Cost from the 'Standard cost per unit flexed to actual output' column less the 'Actual cost' column: £43,200 – £43,400 = £200 adverse. This approach is exactly the same as the budgetary control one.
   - **Labour efficiency variance:** Cost from the 'Standard cost per unit flexed to actual output' column less the 'Standard cost per unit of input flexed to actual inputs' column: £43,200 – £41,400 = £1,800 favourable.
   - **Labour rate variance:** Cost from the 'Standard cost per unit of input flexed to actual inputs' column less the 'Actual cost' column: £41,400 – £43,400 = £2,000 adverse.

	Original budget	*Standard cost per unit flexed to actual output*	*Standard cost per unit of input flexed to actual inputs*	*Actual cost*
Production (cases of books)	1,000	900		
Direct labour				
Hours per unit	4	4		
Total hours		3,600	3,450	
Rate per hour	£12.00	£12.00	£12.00	
Cost	Budgeted cost	£43,200	£41,400	£43,400
Variances		Labour variance £200 (A)		
		Efficiency £1,800 (F)	Rate £2,000 (A)	

Figure 16-9: Variance Analysis Workings Sheet for Band Books showing the labour variances. (A means Adverse, F means Favourable.)

Here, the labour efficiency variance is caused by the 900 cases of books requiring 3,450 rather than 3,600 labour hours. You don't know the reason for the difference, but you do know that it's a favourable variance.

As a management accountant, you'd need to look at the accuracy of the posting of labour costs and check that all hours worked had been charged to book production. Another possible cause may be errors at the time that 4 hours per case was set as the standard. Other investigations may ask whether more experienced employees had been working compared to the proficiency expected in the original budget, meaning that the work was completed more quickly than expected. Perhaps you can link the high usage adverse variance to the labour efficiency variance being favourable. Also, you may want to investigate whether the employees rushed this work, and in doing so had a very high level of paper wastage but completed the work in less time than the standard for the 900 cases of books produced.

The adverse labour rate variance has been caused by the average hourly rate being higher than the standard rate. This may link to the favourable efficiency variance if the staff working were more highly skilled and consequently paid at a higher rate.

The typical AAT Financial Performance exam tests your understanding of variances in task 6. In this question, one part of the task regularly asks for links between variances. Look for links between usage and price for materials and between efficiency and rate for labour; but links between labour efficiency and material usage, such as the one highlighted above, are also often worth looking for.

Calculating variable overhead variances

Band Books' overhead is treated as fixed, because that provides an opportunity to explain how the predetermined overhead rate is built into variance analysis. Band Books doesn't have variable overheads when producing cases of books.

The calculation process follows the same process as labour cost variances in the preceding section. In situations where labour hours are used to absorb variable overhead, the values also correspond to labour hours. The way in which the hours were used is called the *variable overhead efficiency variance* and the difference between the actual cost and the overhead absorbed based on the hours worked is called the *variable overhead expenditure variance.*

Where labour hours are used to absorb variable overhead, the two efficiency variances are either both adverse or both favourable.

The variable overhead efficiency variance shows exactly the same information as the labour efficiency variance (from the preceding section) whenever variable overhead is absorbed on a labour hour basis. The variable overhead expenditure variance shows either unexpected changes in the amounts charged for variable overheads, or errors in not accurately forecasting the variable overhead costs at the time the standards were set.

Figuring out fixed overhead variances

The process is similar to the material and labour cost variances. The total fixed overhead variance is the difference between the standard fixed overhead cost for actual production and the actual cost incurred. This figure is the same as the under-/over-absorbed overhead value from Chapter 4.

In Chapter 4, we explain that the overhead absorbed is hours worked multiplied by the overhead absorption rate per hour. Under standard costing, overheads are absorbed on the basis of standard hours produced, not actual hours worked. The calculation of absorbed overhead is different. One reason to use standard costing is to simplify the routine tasks as the work is carried out and then reconcile the actual hours at the end of the accounting period. Standard hours produced are calculated; units of output × standard hours per unit don't require collecting the record of actual hours worked as production takes place.

The total fixed overhead variance can be broken down into two sub-variances to start with:

- **Expenditure variance:** Difference between budgeted overhead and actual overhead incurred.
- **Volume variance:** Difference between the standard fixed overhead for actual production and the budgeted overhead.

Some exams also break the volume into the part caused by having more or less time (capacity variance) and how well the time was used (efficiency variance).

We continue to use Band Books to illustrate how to complete Figure 16-10. Here's the relevant additional data:

- **Actual production:** 900 cases of books.
- **Direct labour:** 3,600 hours were worked at a total direct labour cost of £46,800.
- **Overhead cost:** £95,000.

Follows these steps:

1. **Enter the information you have in the 'Original budget' column.**

   The budget in this case was for 1,000 cases, which you enter at the top of the column. Then enter the hours per case (4 hours) and the absorption rate per hour (£25). You can also add the total budgeted overhead cost of £100,000 (from the earlier section 'Calculating the overhead rate'). No further calculations are needed yet.

2. **Enter the production of 900 cases in the 'Standard cost per unit flexed to output' column.**

   Copy the standard values from the 'Original budget' column: 4 hours per unit and £25 per hour.

3. **Add the actual hours worked in the 'Standard cost per unit of input flexed to actual inputs' column: 3,450 hours.**

   Copy the rate per hour across into the column: £25. Complete the 'Actual cost' column: £95,000.

	–	*Original budget*	–	*Standard cost per unit flexed to actual output*	–	*Standard cost per unit of input flexed to actual inputs*		*Actual cost*
Production (cases of books)		1,000		900				
Fixed overheads								
Hours per unit		4		4				
Total hours				Standard hours produced		Actual hours worked		
Rate per hour		£25.00		£25.00				
Cost		£100,000		Standard fixed overhead cost of actual production		Standard fixed overhead cost of the hours worked		Actual fixed overhead cost
Variances								

Figure 16-10: Variance Analysis Workings Sheet for Band Books showing where values should be entered to find the fixed overhead variances.

4. **Carry out multiplication (see Figure 16-11):**
   - **Standard cost flexed to output:**

     Total hours: 900 × 4 hours/unit = 3,600 hours

     Cost: 3,600 hours × £25/hour = £90,000
   - **Standard cost flexed to input:**

     Cost: 3,450 hours × £25/hour = £86,250
5. **Identify the variances:**
   - **Total variance:** Cost from the 'Standard cost per unit flexed to actual output' column less the 'Actual cost' column: £90,000 – £95,000 = £5,000 adverse. You can also call this figure the *under-absorbed overhead.*
   - **Fixed overhead expenditure variance:** Cost from the 'Original budget' column less the cost from the 'Actual cost' column: £100,000 – £95,000 = £5,000 favourable.
   - **Fixed overhead volume variance:** Cost from the 'Standard cost per unit flexed to actual output' column less the 'Original budget' column: £90,000 – £100,000 = £10,000 adverse. (Note how this arrow

points in the opposite direction (right to left) compared to all the other variances calculated so far which all point from left to right.)

- **Sub-variances of the fixed overhead volume variance:** These add up to the same value, but show the two key causes of a volume variance):

  Fixed overhead capacity variance: Cost from the 'Standard cost per unit of input flexed to actual inputs' column less the 'Original budget' column: £86,250 – £100,000 = £13,750 adverse.

  Fixed overhead efficiency variance: Cost from the 'Standard cost per unit flexed to actual output' column less the cost from the 'Standard cost per unit of input flexed to actual inputs' column: £90,000 – £86,250 = £3,750 favourable.

	–	*Original budget*	–	*Standard cost per unit flexed to actual output*	–	*Standard cost per unit of input flexed to actual inputs*		*Actual cost*
Production (cases of books)		1,000		900				
Fixed overheads								
Hours per unit		4		4				
Total hours				3,600		3,450		
Rate per hour		£25.00		£25.00		£25.00		
Cost		£100,000		£90,000		£86,250		£95,000
Variances		Total fixed overhead variance £5,000 (A) → Fixed overhead expenditure variance £5,000 (F) → ← Fixed overhead volume variance £10,000 (A) ← Fixed overhead capacity variance £13,750 (A) Fixed overhead efficiency variance £3,750 (F) →						

Figure 16-11: Variance Analysis Workings Sheet for Band Books showing the fixed overhead variances. (A means Adverse, F means Favourable.)

Look at the labour efficiency variance in the earlier section 'Finding direct labour variances efficiency and rate' and the fixed overhead efficiency variance: both are favourable. It must always be true that both are favourable or both are adverse. The labour efficiency and the fixed overhead efficiency variances both show the difference in hours taken (3,600 – 3,450 = 150 hours). The labour variance is 150 hours at £12 per hour = £1,800, and the fixed overhead efficiency is the same 150 hours, this time at £25 per hour = £3,750.

The *total fixed overhead variance* is the difference between the overhead absorbed and the actual overhead incurred. The *fixed overhead expenditure variance* is the difference between the budgeted overhead cost and the actual overhead cost.

As the fixed overhead expenditure variance was favourable, certain costs were lower than the budget had expected, possibly due to external factors.

Beware managers who made a decision to cut certain discretionary expenditure, such as maintenance contracts for machinery. Doing so cuts the fixed overhead expenditure and might even lead to the fixed overhead expenditure variance being favourable, but it doesn't reflect improved operating performance. It was caused by cutting out a budgeted cost. As it was budgeted it can be expected that it is necessary for the effective running of the machines. Such a cut might be a sign that a manager is trying to give an impression of improving performance, but this action is very risky and might cause much higher costs to be incurred later if the machines breakdown.

The fixed overhead volume variance is caused by one thing only: volume produced. Look at the two values of £100,000 and £90,000 and you see that they're different because the volume produced was 900, which only absorbed £90,000, whereas the original budgeted overhead was £100,000 based on 1,000 units.

In terms of variances, output was below budget for two reasons: the capacity (or total hours worked) and the efficiency (or output per hour).

In this example, hours worked were 3,450, which is far lower than the budget of 1,000 × 4 hours per unit (4,000 hours). Because this figure has contributed to the lower output than budget, capacity is an adverse variance.

This point can sometimes take time to digest. But if total hours worked are lower than the budgeted hours, the capacity variance must be adverse (and must be favourable when more hours are worked than budgeted).

To produce 900 cases takes a standard time of 3,600 hours. To produce 900 in 3,450 hours shows efficiency at a higher level than the standard.

Viewing the full worksheet – cost variances

In this section, we show you how to complete the whole worksheet, because all three sections fit together and give a complete picture of a business's performance.

In an exam, a full worksheet can generally fit on a single sheet of A4 paper. For this example, however, we abbreviate the longer titles for each column in Figure 16-12.

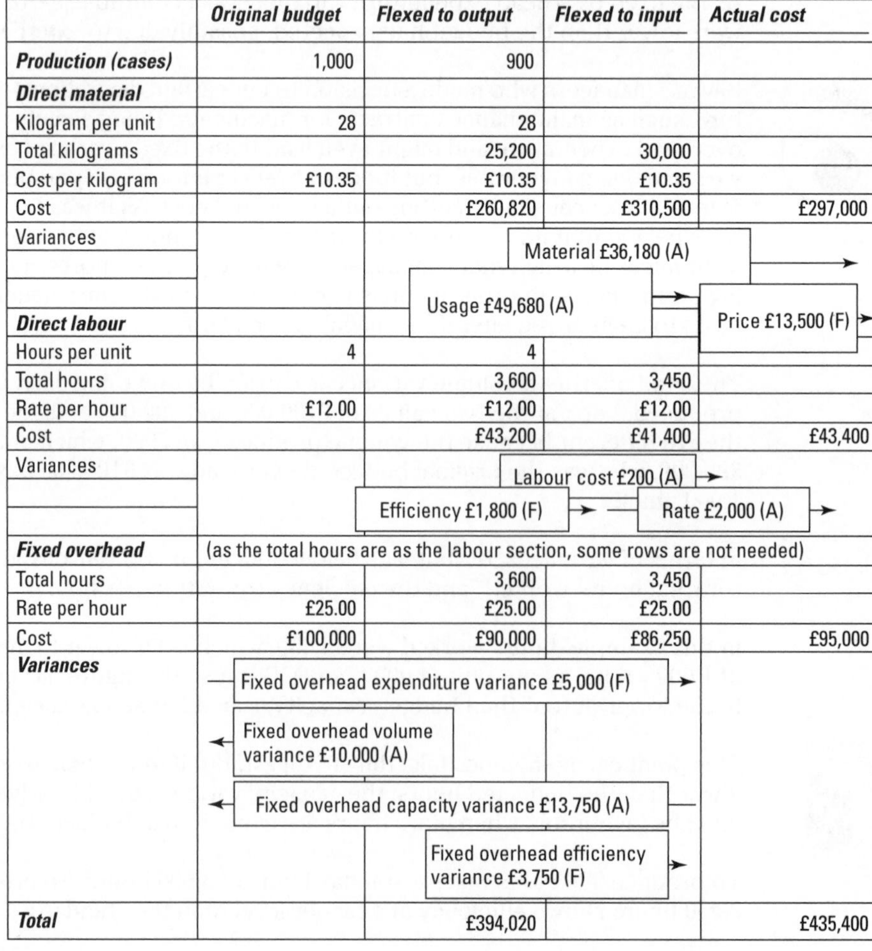

	Original budget	*Flexed to output*	*Flexed to input*	*Actual cost*
Production (cases)	1,000	900		
Direct material				
Kilogram per unit	28	28		
Total kilograms		25,200	30,000	
Cost per kilogram	£10.35	£10.35	£10.35	
Cost		£260,820	£310,500	£297,000
Variances			Material £36,180 (A)	
		Usage £49,680 (A)		Price £13,500 (F)
Direct labour				
Hours per unit	4	4		
Total hours		3,600	3,450	
Rate per hour	£12.00	£12.00	£12.00	
Cost		£43,200	£41,400	£43,400
Variances			Labour cost £200 (A)	
		Efficiency £1,800 (F)	Rate £2,000 (A)	
Fixed overhead	(as the total hours are as the labour section, some rows are not needed)			
Total hours		3,600	3,450	
Rate per hour	£25.00	£25.00	£25.00	
Cost	£100,000	£90,000	£86,250	£95,000
Variances	Fixed overhead expenditure variance £5,000 (F)			
	Fixed overhead volume variance £10,000 (A)			
	Fixed overhead capacity variance £13,750 (A)			
		Fixed overhead efficiency variance £3,750 (F)		
Total		£394,020		£435,400

Figure 16-12: Variance Analysis Workings Sheet for Band Books showing all the variances.

This approach shows an examiner the method of finding the variances clearly, which helps the examiner award 'workings' marks even if there's an error in your final answer. It also helps you as a candidate, because you use a shorter period of time to generate the variances compared to other approaches.

The complete variance analysis worksheet (Figure 16-12) includes an extra row showing the total costs for all three expenditure types, which are used in management reporting.

Reporting variances to management: Operating Statement

The Operating Statement enables the management accountant to present all the variances in a format that reconciles the standard cost of the units produced with the actual cost.

Figure 16-13 presents the Operating Statement in the format widely used by examiners.

The two actual costs values reconcile (agree). This report shows management the difference in the cost and the variances that have caused the difference.

Remembering key facts that are always true

In variance analysis, certain key points are worth looking for.

- Fixed overhead volume variances are always favourable when production is more than budgeted.
- Fixed overhead capacity variances are always favourable when the hours worked are more than the hours budgeted.
- If labour hours are used to absorb overheads, the labour efficiency variance and the fixed overhead efficiency variance are always both adverse or both favourable.

Operating Statement Band Books Company			
			£
Standard cost of actual production *(900 x £437.80 per case) or the total value from the flexed to output column*			394,020
	***Adverse* £**	***Favourable* £**	
Material usage	49,680		
Material price		13,500	
Labour efficiency		1,800	
Labour rate	2,000		
Fixed overhead expenditure		5,000	
Fixed overhead capacity	13,750		
Fixed overhead efficiency		3,750	
	65,430	24,050	41,380
Actual cost (calculated)			435,400
Actual cost (from the Variance Analysis Workings Sheet)			435,400

Figure 16-13: Operating Statement for Band Books.

Watching out for other things

The following aspects aren't always true, but are often linked:

- When cheaper than standard materials are purchased, look for adverse variances in usage and favourable variances for price. Also look to see whether the cheaper material led to more hours being worked, and so to an adverse labour efficiency variance.
- When inexperienced staff are used, look for adverse variances on efficiency, because they take longer to carry out the work, but also for favourable variances for rate, because they're likely to have a lower hourly rate to reflect their inexperience.

We don't address the topics of mix and yield variances where more than one type of material or more than one grade of labour is used in production in this book, or the separation of operational and planning variances. These subjects are covered in more advanced cost-accounting courses.

Teasing Out Variances

In your business, variance analysis helps you identify problem areas that require attention, such as:

- Poor productivity
- Poor quality
- Excessive costs
- Excessive spoilage or waste of materials

Identifying and working on these problems helps management improve production flow and profitability. Managers and management accountants often talk about *management by exception* – using variance analysis to identify *exceptions* (problems) where actual results significantly vary from standards. By paying careful attention to these exceptions, managers can root out and rectify manufacturing problems and inefficiencies, thereby improving productivity, efficiency and quality.

Focusing on the big numbers

Management by exception directs managers to investigate closely the largest variances. For example, the two largest variances for the earlier Band Books example (which we introduce in the 'Establishing direct materials standards' section) are the direct materials usage variance (£49,680 adverse) and the direct materials price variance (£13,500 favourable). Band Books' managers need to focus on how the company buys and uses its direct materials.

The direct materials usage variance resulted because the company should have used 18,000 kilograms of paper but actually used 20,000 kilograms of paper. Here are a few possibilities as to why:

- The paper was poor quality, and much of it needed to be scrapped.
- The company underestimated the amount of paper needed (the standard quantity needs to be changed).
- Someone miscounted the amount of paper used; 2,000 kilograms of paper is sitting in the back of the warehouse (oops!).

- A new employee misused the machine, shredding thousands of kilograms of paper.

Management by exception directs managers to where the problem may have occurred so that they can investigate what happened and take corrective action.

Here are some questions to ask regarding the favourable direct materials price variance of £13,500:

- How did the purchasing department come to purchase direct materials for only £9.90 a kilogram, rather than the £10.35 standard?
- Did the purchased materials meet all the company's quality standards?
- Should the company reduce its standard price in the future?

Companies sometimes set *control limits* to determine which items are sufficiently large to investigate. Variances exceeding the control limit require more investigation than those under the control limit.

Tracing little numbers back to big problems

Be careful! Don't focus exclusively on the big numbers and ignore the little numbers. Big problems can also hide in the small numbers. For example, although many frauds (such as stealing raw materials) may trigger large variances, a well-planned fraud can be designed to manipulate variances so that they stay low, below the radar, where managers don't notice them.

Knowing that the standard price of a raw material is £100 per unit, a crooked purchasing manager arranges to purchase the units for exactly that price – £100 per unit – while receiving £10 per unit as a kick-back gratuity from the supplier. This scheme results in a direct material price variance of zero, but it doesn't reflect what should be the company's actual cost of doing business. A more scrupulous purchasing manager would have arranged a purchase price of £90, resulting in a large positive direct material price variance.

To avoid these problems, managers still need to investigate all variances, even while focusing most of their time and effort on the largest figures.

Chapter 17

Establishing Accountability with Responsibility Accounting

In This Chapter

- Organising to implement strategy
- Handing over authority and establishing accountability
- Evaluating the performance of responsibility centres

Ah, teenage driving: one of the great rites of passage. The teenager reaches legal driving age, passes the driving test and then asks for the car keys. Along with the keys comes authority – not only to drive a car, but also to go to more places and take family and friends there, too.

Of course, with this new authority comes responsibility (to drive carefully, follow the law and obey other parental rules) and limits (driving the old banger is okay, but keep away from the MG). When the young driver oversteps these limits, it becomes time for accountability.

Just as a parent can't hand over the keys to the car without setting some degree of accountability, a manager can't delegate authority over a division of the company without also establishing accountability.

Responsibility accounting is the primary tool to establish accountability throughout an organisation; it involves ensuring that subordinates receive the authority to perform tasks and are held accountable for their performance. Organisations usually have a hierarchical structure in which individual managers report to more senior managers, who in turn report to top managers.

In this chapter, we look at how a company's strategy ties to its corporate organisation and delve into how divisions are classified based on what they're held responsible for.

Linking Strategy with an Organisation's Structure

Companies and other organisations establish *goals* that they plan to meet, such as benchmarks for sales, profitability, new products and even employee satisfaction. Ideally, all employees know the organisation's goals and understand their roles in meeting them. The plan to meet the company's goals is called the *strategy*.

Allocating responsibility

Managers need to structure the company's operations to support its strategy for meeting its goals. Doing so usually means breaking the strategy down into smaller tasks that different managers and departments can take responsibility for performing. In the typical chain of command for a small company, a number of directors report to a managing director, each overseeing a different aspect of executing the company's strategy. A separate group of employees reports to each director. The organisational structure requires the managing director to delegate tasks to individual directors, who in turn delegate tasks to their employees.

Suppose that the NNW Company has a goal to earn £100,000 in profit. Part of its strategy is to advertise in social media outlets to encourage more teenagers to buy its leading product, the MacGuffin. The company hopes that the ads will lure more teenagers to MacGuffins, increasing the company's sales and profit.

To implement this strategy, NNW needs to prepare a master budget (which we discuss in Chapter 14) to provide a kind of map for outlining how exactly the company plans to sell more MacGuffins and increase its profits. This budget breaks up the strategy into different tasks and objectives, assigning them to managers and departments throughout the company. For example, in the case of NNW:

- The advertising department takes responsibility for creating a social media campaign.
- Sales staff are responsible for identifying new distribution channels for MacGuffins (which in turn increases sales and profitability).
- Factory workers produce MacGuffins (increasing sales and profitability).
- Maintenance workers keep the factory running so that other employees can work effectively and efficiently to increase MacGuffin sales while keeping costs down.

The management controls in this chapter (and in Chapters 15 and 18) help managers identify weaker and stronger areas within the organisation and understand how performance in those areas affects the implementation of the overall strategy.

For example, suppose that NNW senior managers budget £50,000 for the advertising department to spend on the new MacGuffin social media campaign. When examining the advertising budget report, senior managers notice that the department only spent £30,000 on the campaign, a favourable variance of £20,000 (*favourable* because it increases income; refer to Chapters 15 and 16 for more on variances). Managers now need to ascertain why the department spent so little on its social media campaign even though the social media angle is such an important part of its growth strategy.

When delegating tasks, managers have to give authority and accountability to complete those tasks:

- **Authority:** The subordinate must receive authority to perform the task.
- **Accountability:** The subordinate must be accountable to the manager for performing the task.

For example, at NNW:

- A saleswoman is given the office space, samples and computer software needed to serve customers, but she's also accountable for sales made to those customers.
- A factory worker receives a workstation and job responsibilities to produce goods and is made accountable for the amount and quality of goods produced.
- A maintenance worker receives the supplies and equipment needed to keep the equipment running.
- A supervisor checks to make sure that all cleaning procedures were followed.

The following sections look at a couple of important points to consider about organisation structure and accountability: decentralising and designating authority over and responsibility for costs.

Decentralising decision-making

Decentralisation is the process of moving decision-making powers down the chain of command. In a highly *decentralised* organisation, frontline managers and staff often make important decisions. On the other hand, in a highly *centralised* organisation, senior managers at the top of the organisation chain make the decisions.

Decentralisation offers several benefits:

- Helps top-level managers in large corporations, who may need to oversee many diverse subsidiaries and can't possibly call all the shots.
- Enables frontline employees, who usually have closer access to the information needed to make decisions, to respond more quickly than senior managers can.
- Empowers employees to make more independent decisions with less red tape from senior managers, often improving employee morale.
- Facilitates speedy customer service because it doesn't require employees to wait for supervisor approvals.

As an example of decentralisation, many supermarkets train and empower customer service staff to decide which customer returns to accept and which to reject. After all, these people ought to know which returns appear reasonable, and anyway, the value of each return is low. A more centralised organisation would impose stricter requirements on which returns a customer service employee can or can't accept, leaving very little to the employee's own judgement.

Decentralisation does involve some problems, however, and isn't for every organisation:

- Organisations often have to devote duplicate assets and duplicate efforts to get things done.
- Senior managers often have difficulty in fully monitoring and controlling a large number of frontline employees making decisions. As such, more scope exists for poor or self-interested decisions, which can lead to errors and the potential for fraud.

For example, when issuing home mortgages, most banks require that a central department approve every mortgage applicant. Although this process delays the application process (and damages the perception of customer service), it also reduces the proportion of bad loans.

Distinguishing controllable from non-controllable costs

Authority and accountability go together, and so you can only hold individuals and units in your organisation accountable for those things that they have the authority to control. If you don't give subordinates authority to do something, you can't hold them accountable for doing it.

Suppose that Eve asks Alfred to walk her dog for a week. But she refuses to give Alfred the keys to her flat and so he has no access to the dog. Eve doesn't give Alfred the authority to do his job and so can't possibly hold him accountable for not walking the dog (or for the resulting mess in her apartment).

Given the organisation's goals and strategies, every required task and decision needs to be under someone's watch. Responsibility accounting allows you to hold subordinates responsible for all tasks over which they have control.

In the realm of budgets and costs, therefore, the budget needs to carefully designate which departments have authority over and are responsible for which costs:

- **Controllable costs:** Those costs that a department has authority over and responsibility for.
- **Non-controllable costs:** Those costs that a department doesn't have authority over and can't change.

Overhead absorption, which we describe in Chapter 6, is usually inconsistent with the idea of controllable costs. Overhead absorption uses absorption rates to assign overhead costs based on number of units, direct labour hours or other cost drivers to individual departments. Each production department then has to include a portion of overhead costs such as head office administration or general maintenance overhead as a cost in its own budget, even though these production departments usually have little or no say over how money is spent for this overhead. Even when a production department closes completely, these company-wide overhead costs often remain and are reassigned to the remaining departments.

The allocation of such overhead costs bear no relation to the extent to which each department has caused them. Such arbitrary overhead allocations force departments to accept responsibility for overhead costs that they have little or no control over – for them these are non-controllable costs.

Identifying Different Kinds of Responsibility Centres

Responsibility centres are identifiable segments within a company for which individual managers have accepted authority and accountability. Responsibility centres define exactly what assets and activities each manager is responsible for.

As we describe in this section, companies have four basic kinds of responsibility centres:

- Revenue centres
- Cost centres
- Profit centres
- Investment centres

Classifying any given department depends on which aspects of the business the department has authority over.

Managers prepare a *responsibility report* to evaluate the performance of each responsibility centre. This report compares the responsibility centre's budgeted performance with its actual performance, measuring and interpreting individual variances. Responsibility reports need to include only controllable costs so that managers aren't held accountable for activities over which they have no control. Using a flexible budget, which we cover in Chapter 15, or an Operating Statement of variances (see Chapter 16), can be helpful for preparing a responsibility report.

Revenue centres: Scoring on sales only

Revenue centres usually have authority over sales only and have very little control over costs. To evaluate a revenue centre's performance, you look only at its revenues and ignore everything else.

Think about a sports arena concession stand owned by BIG Concessions and run by a man called Al. BIG Concessions' senior management sets the prices and the purchasing department buys food products at the lowest possible cost. Therefore, Al, as manager of the concession stand, can influence only one factor: how many greasy hot dogs, juicy hamburgers and sticky soft drinks he sells during an event. This set-up means that the concession needs to be classified as a revenue centre.

This season, BIG Concessions budgeted for Al to sell 100,000 hot dogs for £5 each. At this price, he and his concession stand in fact sell 105,000 hot dogs. Take a look at the responsibility report in Figure 17-1.

BIG Concessions
Stand No. 347 (run by Al)
Responsibility Report
For the Year Ended 31 December, 2014

Sales	Budget	Actual	Favourable / Adverse
No. of units	100,000	105,000	
Price	£5.00	£5.00	
Total revenues	£500,000	£525,000	£25,000 Favourable

Figure 17-1: A revenue centre's responsibility report.

Here, a £25,000 favourable variance makes Al look good.

Revenue centres have drawbacks. Their evaluations are based entirely on sales, and so revenue centres have no reason to control costs. This kind of free rein encourages Al to hire extra employees or to find other costly ways to increase sales (giving away salty treats to increase drink purchases, perhaps).

Therefore, sales centres need to keep tight restrictions over costs. In this example, BIG Concessions probably institutes rules that the concession manager can't hire additional employees without approval from BIG Concessions' managers.

Cost centres: Counting costs

Cost centres usually produce goods or provide services to other parts of the company. They make goods or services only and so have no control over sales prices; therefore they can be evaluated based only on their total costs.

Suppose that the farm department of fictional company Grey Gardens Florist grows flowers. To evaluate this department, the managers' focus is strictly on its costs.

Such an approach may encourage the farm department to produce fewer goods. After all, one easy way to reduce costs is to make and do less. As we explain in Chapter 15, flexible budgets take into account how unexpected increases or decreases in volume affect total costs. Therefore, a flexible budget holds the department accountable for its costs at the actual volume level rather than at a hypothetical budgeted volume level.

Figure 17-2 provides a responsibility report for Grey Gardens' farm department. This analysis includes only the costs that Judy, supervisor of the farm department, can control. It doesn't include any non-controllable overhead allocated from other departments (check out the earlier section 'Distinguishing controllable from non-controllable costs' for more details).

Grey Gardens
Farm Department
Responsibility Report (based on Flexible Budget)
For the Year Ended 31 December, 2014

Controllable Cost	Flexed Budget	Actual	Favourable / Adverse
Units of production	300,000 flowers	300,000 flowers	
Direct materials	£200,000	£207,000	£7,000 Adverse
Direct labour	£80,000	£83,000	£3,000 Adverse
Overhead	£300,000	£340,000	£40,000 Adverse
Total costs	£580,000	£630,000	£50,000 Adverse

Figure 17-2: Responsibility report for a cost centre.

Figure 17-2 reveals that Judy has a lot of explaining to do. For this level of production, the flexible budget predicts that the farm department needs to have costs of £580,000. However, costs went up to £630,000, causing an adverse variance and much concern.

One way for a cost centre to reduce costs is to buy inferior materials, but doing so hurts the quality of finished goods and can lead to lost sales in the future as customers seek better value for their money. When dealing with cost centres, always carefully monitor the quality of goods.

Profit centres: Controlling revenues and expenses

Profit centres are businesses within a larger business, such as the individual stores that make up a shopping centre. Managers of profit centres enjoy control over their own revenues and expenses. They often select the merchandise to buy and sell, and they have the power to set their own prices.

Profit centres are evaluated based on *controllable profit margin* – the difference between controllable revenues and controllable costs. You exclude all non-controllable costs, such as allocated central overhead or other indirect fixed costs, from the evaluation. The beautiful thing about running a profit centre is that doing so gives managers an incentive to do exactly what the company wants: earn profits.

When a company makes and sells a particular good, the manufacturing and retail departments aren't automatically classified as profit centres. Unless the company uses *transfer pricing* (which establishes the prices for goods bought and sold between departments of the same company; refer to Chapter 13), the manufacturer is just a cost centre and the retailer is treated as a revenue centre (see the two preceding sections). You can see this set-up in Figure 17-3a.

Figure 17-3b, however, shows that a transfer price allows the manufacturing department to record sales to the retail department, transforming manufacturing from a cost centre to a profit centre. Similarly, the same transfer price sets a cost for the retail department, transforming retail's status from a revenue centre to a profit centre.

Without transfer price

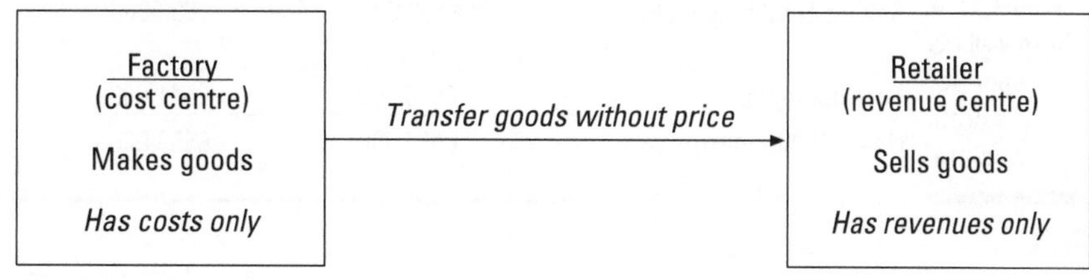

With transfer price

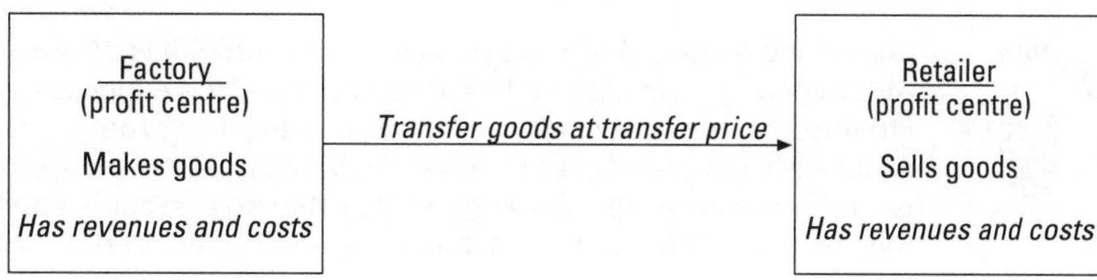

Figure 17-3: Transfer pricing can turn revenue and cost centres into profit centres.

Consider Blake, a company that makes and sells the Replicon fashion line. Blake's manufacturing department makes Replicon swimsuits for the company's own retail department, and so the company's responsibility centres can be classified in either of the two different ways. For this example, assume that Blake's retail department is a profit centre (this is the profit centre section, after all). Figure 17-4 provides a responsibility report for Blake's retail department.

Blake
Retail Department
Responsibility Report (based on Flexed Budget)
For the Year Ended 31 December, 2014

	Flexed Budget	Actual	Favourable / Adverse
Sales	£1,000,000	£1,100,000	£100,000 Favourable
Controllable costs:			
Cost of goods sold	£450,000	£445,000	£5,000 Favourable
Selling & administrative	£100,000	£96,000	£4,000 Favourable
Total expenses	£550,000	£541,000	
Controllable margin	£450,000	£559,000	£109,000 Favourable

Figure 17-4: Responsibility report for a profit centre.

As you can see, the retail department had an excellent year, reporting a £109,000 favourable variance. Note that the responsibility report covers only controllable costs.

Classifying responsibility centres as profit centres has disadvantages. Although they're evaluated based on revenues and expenses, no one pays attention to their use of assets. This scenario gives profit centre managers an incentive to use excessive assets to boost profits. The upside for them is clear – increases in sales and profits – and no downside applies as far as they're concerned, because managers of profit centres aren't held accountable for the assets they use.

You can address this flaw in the evaluation of profit centres by carefully monitoring how profit centres use assets or by simply reclassifying a profit centre as an investment centre, as we explain in the next section.

Investment centres: Being responsible for the lot

Investment centres are the luxury cars of responsibility centres because they feature everything. Managers of investment centres have authority over – and are held responsible for – revenues, costs and investments made in their centres. *Return on investment* (ROI) is often used to evaluate their performance, as follows:

$$\text{Return on investment} = \frac{\text{Controllable profit}}{\text{Average operating assets}}$$

In this formula, controllable profit is the difference between controllable revenues and controllable costs. To improve ROI, the manager can increase controllable profits or decrease average operating assets (improve productivity). The operating assets are effectively the investment the company has made in the investment centre.

Suppose that Blake's retail department (from the preceding section) is budgeted to have £2,000,000 in average operating assets. Its budgeted controllable profit is £450,000, as shown in the earlier Figure 17-4. You calculate the department's budgeted ROI as follows:

$$\begin{aligned}\text{Budgeted ROI} &= \frac{\text{Controllable profit}}{\text{Average operating assets}}\\ &= \frac{450{,}000}{2{,}000{,}000}\\ &= 22.5\%\end{aligned}$$

Now imagine that the company dramatically increases its inventory and other operating assets, driving up average operating assets all the way to £3 million. Actual controllable profit is £559,000 (from Figure 17-4). You calculate the department's actual ROI as follows:

$$\begin{aligned}\text{Actual ROI} &= \frac{\text{Controllable margin}}{\text{Average operating assets}}\\ &= \frac{559{,}000}{3{,}000{,}000}\\ &= 18.6\%\end{aligned}$$

Even though the retail department's controllable profit had a very favourable variance (see Figure 17-4), its actual ROI fell below the budget to just 18.6 per cent because of excessive investments in operating assets. In future periods, the retail department needs to increase its controllable profit to justify the increase in operating assets or decrease its operating assets to become more productive.

Using ROI to evaluate investment centres addresses many of the drawbacks involved in evaluating revenue centres, costs centres and profit centres. However, classification as an investment centre can encourage managers to emphasise productivity over profitability – to work harder to reduce assets (which increases ROI) rather than to increase overall profitability. This approach can lead to managers being reluctant to invest in new equipment, even when the investment centre needs such equipment. The remedy lies in changing the way that senior managers measure these investment managers' performance.

Chapter 18

The Balanced Scorecard: Reviewing Your Business's Report Card

In This Chapter

- Juggling the four important perspectives of a business
- Using the balanced scorecard to implement strategy
- Considering balanced scorecard exam questions

As much as we love numbers and accounting, we have to admit that they don't tell the whole story. Take profitability. We like to know a company's profit – the difference between income and expenditure. To us, this figure is accounting's be-all and end-all, the ultimate and final buck-stops-here measure of the company's performance.

Yet profit doesn't say much about the company's future prospects. It may be profitable this year but unprofitable for the next five years. Furthermore, profit can come from good actions (such as selling products with a nice mark-up) or bad actions (selling off successful parts of a business, anyone?).

For this reason, many companies evaluate their own performance by using a tool called the balanced scorecard. This assessment of a business uses several different measures, some of which accountants and managers are used to seeing (such as Sales Revenue and Operating Profit) and others that help predict future success (such as research and development spending, the number of new customers or employee satisfaction).

In this chapter, we explain and explore the balanced scorecard and how you can use it to give a comprehensive view of a company or organisation's future performance. We use the example throughout of a small cornershop business.

Introducing the Balanced Scorecard: Key to Strategy

Do you have big dreams? That's great, but you're not likely to get anywhere without a plan. You have to know how you're going to reach your business goal. What's your strategy? How are you going to exploit emerging possibilities and gain an advantage over the competition?

Don't confuse strategy with budgeting:

- **Strategy** defines how you're going to get your customers to pay good money for your products. A master budget (which we describe in Chapter 14) is also a plan with the financial details. It shows how the strategy is to be put into action.
- **Budgeting** follows on from an agreed strategy. It shows you how much you're going to make, when you're going to make it, how much it will cost to make this money, where the money is going to come from, and how you're going to spend it so that you end the year with a profit and a sound statement of financial position, and you achieve your strategic goals.

The *balanced scorecard* is a report card for your company that indicates not only how profitable you were last year, but also how well you're implementing your strategy in order to stay profitable for many years into the future.

The balanced scorecard concept was developed and introduced by Robert Kaplan and David Norton to help management accountants provide more information about companies' success in implementing strategies. When following the balanced scorecard, management accountants do much more than predict profits (as part of budgets) or provide information for decisions about pricing products or buying new equipment; they also provide information to help managers and investors assess how closely a company is moving towards meeting a broad range of goals and objectives.

Kaplan and Norton argue that a successful strategy has to include four perspectives, which we cover in the following four sections:

- **Financial:** Incorporates traditional measures of performance, such as profit and revenues.
- **Customer:** Considers customer satisfaction and how well the company stacks up against its competitors.
- **Internal business:** Considers how well the company develops, makes, delivers and services products.

- **Learning and growth:** Evaluates the ability of the company and its employees to change and improve.

Although some attributes, such as sales, are fairly easy to measure with figures and numbers, more subjective aspects – such as customer satisfaction – are tougher nuts to crack. You can't count these measures and create a solid list of numbers for appraisal. As a result they require special attention so that you can capture this information and present it in a meaningful way.

For example, you can use market surveys or the percentage of customer returns to measure customer satisfaction. Or you can get creative. One fast-food chain knows that customers demand a speedy drive-through experience, and so it times electronically how long each car takes to get its food and whizz out the drive-through.

Making money: The financial perspective

Like it or not, most businesses are in it for the money – cash flow, profits and maximising shareholder value. This fact means that no balanced scorecard is complete without considering the return generated for the shareholder.

Perhaps you're wondering if that always applies. After all, nonprofit organisations and governmental entities are explicitly set up with goals that reach beyond making money. For example, a child-welfare agency may be created to ensure that every child has a home, a political organisation sets out to win elections, and a local fire station is established to put out fires. These organisations can ignore profits or finances, can't they?

No, not really. You can't eradicate homelessness, win elections or put out fires without money. Even if these organisations don't try to buy and sell products at a profit, they still need funding in order to accomplish their goals. The financial perspective applies to every organisation, whether the entity is set up to earn a profit or not.

That said, different types of businesses need to consider the financial perspective in different ways. Nonprofit organisations have to look to increase donations or the number or amount of project grants. For-profit corporations usually want to earn profits to maximise shareholder value, but they may develop this profitability in different ways. Some companies, such as Fortnum and Mason or Tiffany & Co., rely on a market differentiation strategy that allows them to charge high prices while selling a fairly low volume of merchandise. When a company opts for differentiation it wants the products that customers buy to be perceived as better than their competitors. Because the customers perceive the products as superior, they're prepared to pay higher prices. Other companies, such as Kia Motors or Lidl, use a competitive price strategy with low profit margins but very high sales volume. The strategy of selling at lower prices than competitors charge for similar products is the opposite strategy to differentiation. Although market differentiators may try to focus on increasing sales prices and Gross Profit (that's Sales less Cost of Goods Sold), competitive-price companies focus on selling more goods: increasing the total number of units sold, number of sales outlets or sales per outlet.

Here are some examples of performance measures from a financial perspective for different kinds of companies and organisations:

- Credit rating
- Donations received
- Net sales
- Profit available to be distributed to shareholders of ordinary shares
- Profit per employee
- Return on assets
- Return on investment
- Return on sales
- Same-store sales
- Share price
- Subscription income

Managers and stakeholders need to think carefully about their company's priorities in order to identify which performance measures most closely align with the strategies and goals of the company. They then have to select those indicators that are the most significant for the specific businesses they run.

A company focusing on growth probably homes in on net sales as one of the factors to add to its balanced scorecard. A retail chain may also include *same-store sales,* which compare the Sales Revenue of established shops from one accounting period to another (it excludes any shops acquired or closed during the period, making it a like-for-like comparison). To round things out, managers may want to use a measure of profitability such as return on assets. This approach focuses the company on growing net sales, same-store sales and return on assets.

In contrast, a company trying to boost the profitability of existing sales may select return on sales as one of its financial measures. This figure measures how much profit the company can squeeze out of its sales. A retailer may focus on profit per employee, reflecting a goal of earning as much profit as possible from the existing workforce. For micro-businesses, including those with no employees, profit per hour worked is an excellent financial measure to identify those activities earning the business the best return on the owner's time.

Some balanced scorecard measures may be appropriate considerations for more than one perspective. For example, profit per employee can probably fit into any one of the four perspectives depending on the business and its strategy.

Ensuring your clients are happy: The customer perspective

Customers are the stakeholders who give you Sales Revenue, and so the balanced scorecard considers the customer perspective as a critical aspect of strategy. After all, customers who like your business keep buying things; they're your key to future Sales Revenue.

Unhappy customers patronise your competitors, and so the balanced scorecard forces you to keep tabs on your customers as carefully as you keep tabs on your profits.

Some typical measures of performance from the customer perspective include the following:

- Results of customer surveys
- Numbers of new customers
- Response time to customer enquiry
- Market surveys of brand recognition
- Tracking customer complaints
- Market share
- Product returns as a percentage of sales
- Percentage of repeat customers
- Same-store sales

As with all measures on the balanced scorecard, customer perspective measures need to reflect the company's strategy towards customer satisfaction. Discount retailers usually try to satisfy customers with a wide selection and low prices. They may survey customers to make sure that they've found what they're looking for in the shop and then include the results on their balanced scorecard. They may also develop a sample shopping list and then compare the cost of buying the items on this list in their shop with the cost of buying the stuff from key competitors.

Upmarket retailers trying to attract wealthy clientele, however, may choose to focus on consumer profiles, such as the average family income of customers.

Keeping the clock ticking: The internal business perspective

Companies rely on an operating cycle, in which they work continuously through the following steps:

1. **Buy raw materials.**
2. **Pay for raw materials.**
3. **Put raw materials into production (Work-in-Progress – flip to Chapters 4 and 7 for details).**
4. **Complete Work-in-Progress (becomes Finished Goods Inventory).**
5. **Sell Finished Goods Inventory.**
6. **Deliver sales to customers.**
7. **Collect payment from customers.**

This process is continuous. As the company collects cash payments, it purchases more inventory. As it purchases more inventory, it puts it into production to complete it and sell it to customers, who give the company more cash payments.

A company typically has other important processes, too, such as new product cycles and customer service. The internal business perspective considers how well the company works its way through these processes. The company needs to identify those processes most critical to its success and find ways to measure how successfully it works through these processes. For example, here are some typical measures of the internal business perspective:

- Amount of inventory spoilage
- Cost of quality control
- Customer satisfaction with service calls
- Development time needed for new products
- Inventory turnover

- Number of *stockouts* (when your business runs out of inventory to sell)
- Number or percentage of product defects
- Raw materials inventory as a percentage of sales
- Set-up time
- Variance analyses (refer to Chapter 16)
- Work-in-Progress inventory as a percentage of sales

As an example of identifying and measuring the most critical aspects, a fast-food restaurant may well focus on how quickly it can make and sell different food products or on minimising spoilage. A more expensive restaurant, on the other hand, may focus on the number of stars it earns from the critics. As always, the measures need to reflect the strategy.

Appraising the ability to change and improve: The learning and growth perspective

People who sit around and talk cleverly about how to make money instead of actually making it (like business professors) theorise that a business is nothing more than a *nexus of contracts,* a huge bundle of relationships between different stakeholders. Employees work for their salaries and wages. Suppliers deliver merchandise and raw materials in exchange for payments. Customers buy finished goods and pay the company for them. Shareholders invest in the company and expect dividends.

Any company or organisation is a huge set of different people working together to make things happen for themselves and for each other.

These relationships need to work like clockwork. However, this complex bundle of relationships has to be flexible enough to change along with the external business environment. Therefore, employees' ability to learn, grow, anticipate change and react to the external environment is absolutely critical to a company's success.

Throughout this chapter we use the example of a local cornershop, Arkwright's, that you've been asked to help by producing a balanced scorecard. Suppose that Arkwright's sells soft drinks. The trend in soft drinks right now is leaning towards offering consumers a wide variety of different products to choose from – carbonated colas, energy drinks, protein shakes, drinks infused with vitamins, sugary drinks and sugar-free drinks. Customers want to choose between high-caffeine, caffeine-free and stress-reducing drinks. They can even choose among different sizes of bottles and cans. In short, customers expect to be able to walk into Arkwright's and select from a multitude of different beverages.

Is this local shop aware of this trend? Is it ready?

Motivated and well-trained employees know what's going on and anticipate these sort of changes. They find ways to squeeze more varieties of soft drinks into their refrigerated display cases and think about creative new offerings that may appeal to customer niches. Without these motivated, well-trained, proactive employees, the entire bundle of contracts falls apart. A poor selection of products turns customers off, sales drop, suppliers focus on your competitors, profits drop and before you know it, shareholders start missing out on dividends.

Here are some measures that a business like Arkwright's can use to better understand the learning and growth perspective:

- Average employee earnings per year
- Average hours of training per employee
- Employee turnover
- Number of employees with professional qualifications
- Number of employees with undergraduate or advanced degrees
- Percentage of employees who own company shares

The learning and growth perspective requires managers to consider carefully which employee skills most benefit the organisation. A school, where learning and growth are key to the success of the organisation, may want to measure the percentage of teachers with postgraduate degrees. They may also count the number of in-service days, when teachers become the students and the students stay home.

If you read about the *innovation and learning perspective* in newspaper articles about companies, this means exactly the same as the *learning and growth perspective*.

Demonstrating the Balanced Scorecard in Action

Management accountants (and the other chapters in this book) focus almost exclusively on costs and profits. Part of the beauty of the balanced scorecard is how it considers a variety of different perspectives as critical parts of the company's strategy. To be successful, your company needs to:

- Be profitable, *liquid* (have enough money in the bank to pay debts as they fall due) and *solvent* (be able to pay its debts in the long term).
- Have happy customers who'll continue to buy from it in the future.
- Have internal operations that are functioning well – in other words, the company knows how to make, sell and deliver products and services productively and at a profit.
- Be ready to adapt to future circumstances; employees have to be quick to learn new things and prepared for change. At Arkwright's, employees may be learning about the relationship between the weather and likely cola sales; another day learning what has been tried at a rival shop; and on yet another day learning why no staff are allowed to take a break during the half-hour after the local school closes for the day!

If all these perspectives are in shape and working properly, the company is likely to thrive. If even just one of these perspectives falls short, the company needs to prepare for challenges ahead.

In this section you discover how to ensure that your business policy covers all four of the perspectives that we define in the preceding sections (financial, customer, internal business, and learning and growth) and the items that you want to feature on your scorecard.

After you develop your balanced scorecard, collect the necessary information and update it regularly. Then use the balanced scorecard much like you use the dashboard in your car – to see how fast you're going, how much fuel is in the tank and to estimate when you're going to reach your destination.

For the cornershop example in the preceding section, you discover that customers expect to find an increasing variety of alternative drinks in addition to the sandwiches, sundry snacks, newspapers and magazines that they've always offered.

Up until now the owner, Arkwright, has been managing his shop like any well-meaning accountant:

- He watches sales and profits.
- He prepares a master budget before each month, projecting future profits and cash flows (check out Chapter 14).
- He compares these budgets to actual results, flexing when necessary (as we describe in Chapter 15).
- He designates carefully the standard costs (see Chapter 16) of sandwiches and coffee made in the shop and uses this information to set prices (read Chapter 12 for more).
- He even prepares a capital budgeting spreadsheet (flip to Chapter 11 for details) before buying so much as a new coffee pot.

However, Arkwright's shop has a few problems:

- The employees hate working at the shop and don't like Arkwright.
- Customers often have to wait several minutes to get a sandwich.
- Customers don't seem to like the coffee or the bland, generic-brand beverages on sale.
- Low profits and weak cash flow are threatening to close the business.

The following sections detail how you can implement the balanced scorecard to address these issues.

Sketching a strategy that incorporates all four perspectives

To start you have to set a goal, which for Arkwright is to make money: good cash flow, plain and simple.

You come up with a strategy to meet that goal and address all four perspectives from the earlier section 'Introducing the Balanced Scorecard: Key to Strategy'. The strategy is to have happy and friendly employees (learning and growth perspective) who think about, understand and meet customer needs (customer perspective). Satisfied customers become regular customers, who pay premium prices for the wide selection of quality merchandise that they're looking for (internal business perspective). If everything goes right, the result is healthy profits and cash flow (financial perspective).

As Figure 18-1 shows, this strategy considers all the key perspectives and how they relate to each other.

Identifying measures for the balanced scorecard

You have to figure out how to quantify progress for each perspective, using a combination of historic measures (that look back at the past) and predictive measures (that drive future results).

The historic isn't a problem, because most accounting information is historic and looks at what happened in the past. This rear-view is inevitable because the only way you can measure sales or profit is if it has happened already. The balanced scorecard, by its very nature, must include some of this retrospective information.

But the scorecard also needs to include predictive and forward-looking information that decision-makers can use to predict future events. Items such as the number of new customers or advertising expense drive future sales and profits. Make sure that your balanced scorecard includes a healthy dose of these predictive measures.

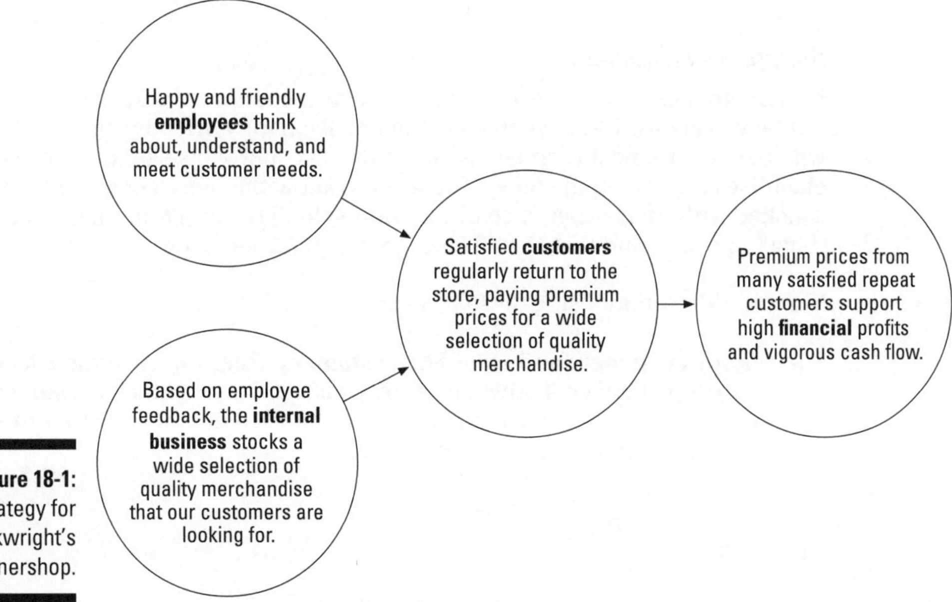

Happy and friendly **employees** think about, understand, and meet customer needs.
Based on employee feedback, the **internal business** stocks a wide selection of quality merchandise that our customers are looking for.
Satisfied **customers** regularly return to the store, paying premium prices for a wide selection of quality merchandise.
Premium prices from many satisfied repeat customers support high **financial** profits and vigorous cash flow.

Figure 18-1: Strategy for Arkwright's cornershop.

Making money

Like all for-profit enterprises, Arkwright's cornershop isn't a charity. You need to keep an eye on the bottom line: the profit. To evaluate financial performance, you use some of the measures in Chapter 17 and add others that focus on the strategy:

- **Profit after tax:** Calculated as revenues less all expenses. Alternatively, you can try *controllable profit* (revenues less controllable expenses) if you want to look at, say, a chain of shops treated as profit centres.
- **Return on investment (ROI):** As we explain in Chapter 17, you measure ROI by dividing controllable profit by average operating assets:

  $$\text{Return on investment} = \frac{\text{Controllable profit}}{\text{Average operating assets}}$$

  Accountants use a range of different formulas to measure return on investment. Instead of controllable profit, you can use operating profit or profit available for distribution to the shareholders; in place of average operating assets, you can use shareholders' equity.
- **Dividends:** How much profit is Arkwright himself taking home?
- **Hours worked by owner:** Arkwright's personal strategy is to stop working on the business 24/7 (he's already 'open all hours'!). Therefore, the actual number of hours that he works may be a useful measure of the financial success of the strategy

Satisfying customers

In order to make money, Arkwright has to keep customers satisfied. The strategy in Figure 18-1 says that customers like happy, friendly employees who're eager to meet their needs. They also like a broad selection of merchandise and hot, fresh coffee. You need to know that customers are truly satisfied with their experience of the shop – that you aren't missing something important and that they'll keep coming back for more.

You can think about using these measures:

- **Survey customers and would-be customers.** Offer the customers a hot, fresh cup of coffee if they complete a survey. Better yet, mail a survey out to likely customers in the neighbourhood to find out whether they visit the shop (and if not, why).

- **Ask for customer suggestions and complaints.** If something is bothering a customer, Arkwright needs to find out exactly what it is, and quickly. Slow service? Warm cola? A stomach-turning smell coming from the back room? Whatever it is, placing suggestion and complaint forms where customers can find them, fill them out and drop them in a box provides the feedback that Arkwright can act on.
- **Track the average spend per customer visit.** Satisfied customers buy things. Therefore, you recommend that Arkwright invests in a gadget that counts the number of customers who come in and out of the shop. You then divide total sales each day by the number of customer visits.
- **Compute Gross Profit margin.** *Gross Profit* is the difference between Sales Revenue and Cost of Goods Sold. This figure measures your profit – how much you make, on average, from each product you sell. To calculate the Gross Profit margin, just divide Gross Profit by Sales Revenue:

  $$\text{Gross profit margin} = \frac{\text{Net sales revenue} - \text{Cost of goods sold}}{\text{Net sales revenue}} \times 100\%$$

  For example, suppose that Arkwright's buys a bag of crisps for £0.40 that sells for £0.99:

  $$\begin{aligned}\text{Gross profit margin} &= \frac{£0.99 - £0.40}{£0.99} \times 100\% \\ &= 59.6\%\end{aligned}$$

  For these crisps, 59.6 per cent of each sale goes to profits. You can also calculate the Gross Profit margin for all the products you sell in total.

Because the strategy requires customers to pay premium prices, keeping an eye on the Gross Profit margin is a good idea; it indicates whether customers are willing to put up with the high mark-ups.

Mark-up is the difference between the cost of sales for a product and the selling price. In the example of Arkwright's shop, the crisps are *marked-up* by 59 pence from 40 pence to find the selling price. This is an increase of

$$\frac{59}{40} \times 100 = 147\%$$

Margin is the approach shown. It's the difference between the price and the cost of sales.

The value of a mark-up is exactly the same as the value of a margin, but you divide that value by Cost of Sales for mark-up and by Sales Revenue for margin.

Some exams specifically test the understanding of this difference; others assume that you know it.

Stocking merchandise that customers want

The internal business strategy dictates that Arkwright's has to stock the wide selection of quality merchandise that customers are after. Therefore, you need a few measures to see how well Arkwright is implementing that strategy. Consider using the following measures:

- **Total number of products stocked:** If customers are looking for a wide selection, counting the actual number of different products in stock makes sense; the more variety the better.
- **Inventory holding period (sometimes called *the number of days* inventory):** The inventory holding period is calculated as follows and measures how many days' worth of inventory are held in stock:

$$\text{Inventory holding period} = \frac{\text{Inventory of finished goods}}{\text{Cost of goods sold}} \times 365$$

The definition of inventory is the one used for most exams: *the closing value of inventory.* In business this works well too, but you can also use an alternative: *the average value.* If this measure is used in an exam, you're expected to add together the opening and closing values and divide by 2. In many businesses, where the inventory value is broadly the same from one time period to another, this gives a very similar number of days' worth of inventory to the closing value approach.

Carrying the right amount of inventory

You use the inventory holding period to determine whether a business is holding the right amount of inventory. Having too much inventory can require exorbitant financing (increasing interest payments) and also lead to unnecessary spoilage, damage and obsolescence. But having too little inventory can cause stock to run out, resulting in lost sales and, worse still for your strategy, dissatisfied customers.

According to this balanced scorecard plan, the inventory holding period needs to be just right. The company may want to set a standard benchmark or target for this measure based on previous experience. This way, a measure that's too high above the company's benchmark indicates that the inventory may be getting old and may deteriorate. On the other hand, a measure that's too low indicates that the company may not be stocking enough inventory to satisfy customer demand:

- **Number of new products stocked because of customer requests:** You want to make sure that Arkwright's is listening to its customers, and so you keep track of the feedback and ask the owner to count the number of new products that have been added to the inventory based on their requests. If the number of new products is too low, Arkwright needs to find new ways to get customers to tell him what they want.
- **Average coffee life:** Customers want their coffee hot and fresh; nothing tastes worse than two-hour-old, lukewarm coffee. To ensure that the shop is providing the freshest coffee possible, you set up a timer to measure and keep track of the average time between when coffee is brewed and when it's served to customers.
- **Percentage of off-brand products:** Some customers insist on buying off-brand or generic products, but anecdotal feedback and consumer surveys indicate that most customers are turned off by these products. They say that it makes the shop seem cheap. Therefore, Arkwright makes a strategic decision to keep only 6–10 per cent of the total product items in the shop as off-brand.

Producing happy and friendly employees

This whole grand scheme can't possibly work without an employee team that thinks about, understands and meets customer needs. The following measures put this strategy into practice:

- **Average employment period:** On average, how long have the employees worked here? To understand and meet customer needs, employees require a lot of experience working in Arkwright's. Plus, happy employees are less likely to quit.
- **Amount of employee training:** Training helps employees to know how to present a friendly face to customers and understand and meet their needs. Therefore, you can measure how many hours of training each employee receives.

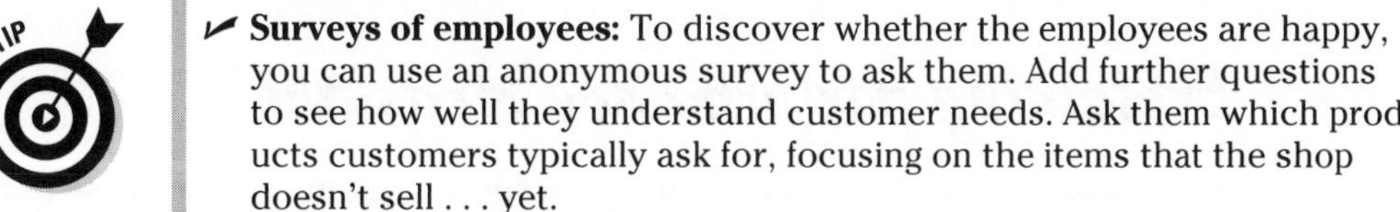

- **Surveys of employees:** To discover whether the employees are happy, you can use an anonymous survey to ask them. Add further questions to see how well they understand customer needs. Ask them which products customers typically ask for, focusing on the items that the shop doesn't sell . . . yet.
- **Employee compensation:** Good wages and benefits make employees happy and keep them from leaving, and so measure the average employee compensation per hour to confirm that the workers are satisfied on this front.

Testing Times: Exam Advice

The balanced scorecard is tested on ACCA F5 and CIMA P2, although in earlier formats it appeared in other exams and the aspect of non-financial as well as financial performance measures is widely examined.

Typical questions tend to test the knowledge of the four perspectives we discuss in the earlier section 'Introducing the Balanced Scorecard: Key to Strategy': financial; customer; internal business; learning and growth.

Measuring performance

As a candidate, you're expected to demonstrate how the balanced scorecard measures performance, most probably in the context of a specific organisation. This request demands that you apply the details of, say, a bus operator, home audio manufacturer or whatever business is chosen when you write your answer.

Contributing towards improved profits

You're told to 'answer the question asked' time and again. We don't need to repeat the mantra. If a question asks how a named company can use the balance scorecard to improve profits it demands an answer about the scorecard's use.

You need to answer this sort of a question within about 7 minutes during an exam. Instead of defining the scorecard perspective in detail, focus on the conversion of broad strategic ambitions into specific and measureable targets, how the future prospects focus on the non-financial measures and how it coordinates so many aspects of the business in a way that's easy to communicate and easily measured on key dates.

Explaining performance measures

Some tasks ask for an explanation of how a specific organisation can use performance measures (which you have to select) to assess how well it has performed. These questions are rarely numerical; they require an explanation.

Such a task typically expects you to devise a measure to suit the organisation and to classify which perspective of the balanced scorecard this would apply to. You're expected to state what it measures and why measuring it is so important to the business. In this area you need to *understand* what the balanced scorecard is used for; not merely know what it is.

Targets are very valuable in helping to bring everyone who works for an organisation together for a common goal. But when you use your balanced scorecard at work you need to think very carefully about the measures you use. As soon as people know the measures that are used for their performance, these measures become their targets and other things are treated as less important. When the targets are the right ones, this is excellent: everyone has the priorities that can move the business forward. If the measures set targets that aren't the most important ones to contribute to the overall business success, however, they're still used: What You Measure Is What You Get (WYMIWYG)!

Chapter 19

Squeezing Out of a Tight Spot with the Theory of Constraints

In This Chapter

- Identifying constraints that choke up a system
- Following the five steps of managing and reducing constraints

Creeping to work every morning on the motorway gives people an awful lot of time to think about constraints. On a typical day, drivers encounter at least one bottleneck where everybody slows down – sometimes because the police are cautioning a driver for speeding, or road works are blocking the road or everyone's rubbernecking at an intriguing accident. And then, of course, some people just feel like slowing down for no apparent reason.

The problem with a bottleneck is that it slows down all the traffic behind it. After all, when one car moves at 2 miles per hour through a bottleneck every car behind must also slow down to that speed (or else). A truly theatrical accident can back traffic up for miles in both directions. To get traffic moving again, the police need to manage the constraint – in other words, open up the bottleneck so that traffic can move again.

Manufacturing – and even services – often work a lot like the motorway. As we discuss in this chapter, to improve production you need to focus on and then break the bottleneck.

Understanding the Nature of Constraints

Constraints are anything that limits a system from achieving higher performance. On the motorway, accidents that prevent you from driving at 70 miles per hour to work in the morning are constraints. Constraints can occur in any process, whether in manufacturing or service industries.

Identifying manufacturing constraints

In a manufacturing plant, constraints slow down assembly line production, gumming up the works so that you can't produce as many units as you need.

Consider the pork-processing plant at Pam's Canned Hams. (Try saying *that* five times fast.)

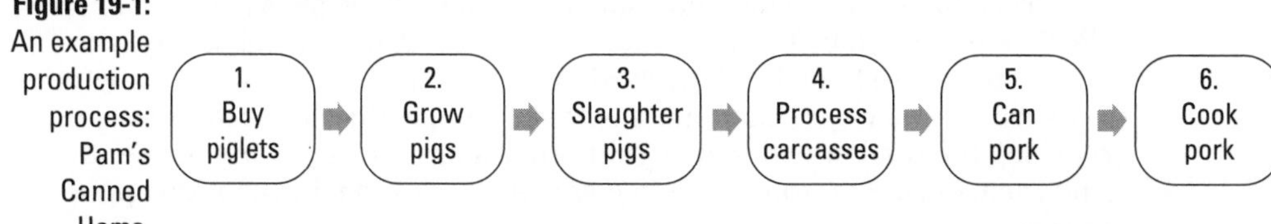

Figure 19-1: An example production process: Pam's Canned Hams.

Figure 19-1 illustrates Pam's production process:

1. **Department 1 buys the direct materials: in this case, piglets.**
2. **Department 2 takes the materials and combines them ready for further processing: the farm feeds and grows the piglets over a 12-month period.**
3. **Department 3 takes the processed materials and adds time and effort to take them one step further towards a finished product: in this case, the abattoir slaughters the pigs.**
4. **Department 4 carries out further processing: the butchery processes the carcasses.**

5. **Department 5 processes the product further still: the canning department cans the meat to make ham.**
6. **Department 6 completes the process: in this case, the kitchen cooks the canned ham, resulting in the Finished Goods Inventory.**

Figure 19-2 shows how many units of production each department can process during a single day.

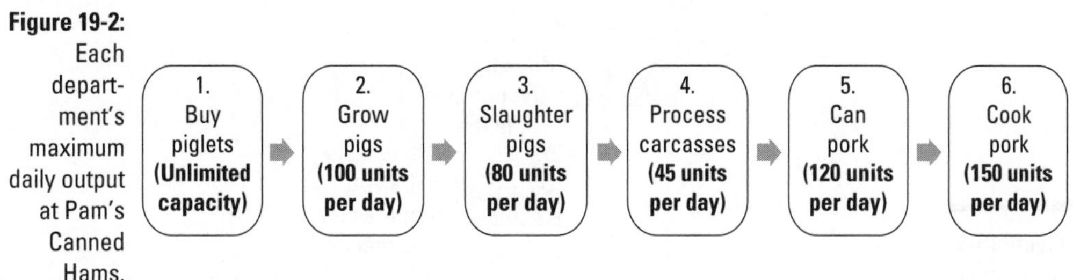

Figure 19-2: Each department's maximum daily output at Pam's Canned Hams.

As the figure shows, Pam's constraint is in Department 4 (butchery), which can handle only 45 units per day. This constraint limits Pam's entire production capacity to just 45 units per day. All the additional capacity in the other departments is completely wasted as a result; the fact that Department 2 (the farm) has enough employees, space and equipment to grow 100 units a day or that Department 5 (canning) is capable of canning 120 units of pork per day doesn't matter. Department 4 (butchery) slows every department down to just 45 units per day.

Considering service constraints

The constraint phenomenon isn't limited to manufacturers – it can also occur in service businesses.

Consider a surgeon's office, where every patient has to go through certain steps before and after surgery, as Figure 19-3 illustrates.

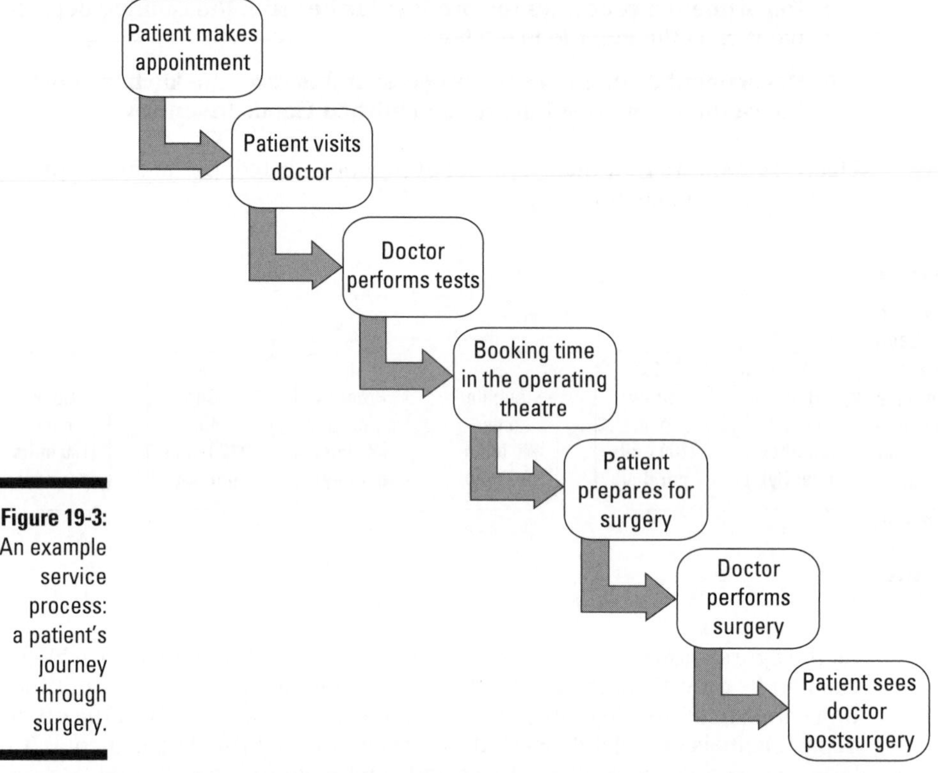

Figure 19-3: An example service process: a patient's journey through surgery.

In order to maximise the chance of a successful surgical procedure, each patient needs to go through a series of steps:

1. **The patient makes his first appointment with the doctor.**
2. **The doctor orders a series of tests and reviews the results.**
3. **The doctor deems surgery necessary and so her office needs to book operating theatre time.**
4. **The patient is prepared for surgery.**
5. **The patient needs a post-operative visit.**

Here, constraints can risk the health of patients. For example, if the doctor can handle only a limited number of patient visits per week, every step that requires her involvement is slowed down, or constrained. Delays in booking operating theatre time have a similar effect.

In order to meet patient needs, managers in the doctor's office need to manage these steps carefully.

Managing Processes with the Theory of Constraints

According to its creator Dr Eliyahu Goldratt, the *theory of constraints* features five steps for managing processes, as follows:

1. **Identify system constraints.**

   Find the bottleneck that slows down the process.

2. **Exploit the constraints.**

   Make sure that you get the most out of constrained resources.

3. **Subordinate everything to the constraints.**

   Rearrange other processes so that they work at the same pace as the constraint.

4. **Break the constraints.**

   Find ways to increase the capacity of the constraint.

5. **Go back to Step 1.**

   After the constraint is broken, go back to Step 1 to identify another constraint to work on.

We run through the five steps in the following sections, illustrating these with the example of the Axiamm Company's hot sauce production.

Step 1: Identifying system constraints

Inevitably, in any process, something slows everything else down; a weakest link always exists (hint: it's not always Anne Robinson!). For example, a family hike typically has to travel at the speed of the slowest member of the family, possibly the youngest child, who has the shortest legs. In a production process, the weakest link is usually the department with the slowest output.

A number of factors can cause constraints. They can include:

- Poorly-trained people who lack the skills to do their jobs.
- Inefficient equipment that has insufficient capacity to meet production needs.
- Company policies (written or unwritten) that prevent people or equipment from accomplishing more.

According to the theory of constraints, every system has at least one constraint.

If every step in the process is operating below capacity, the constraint is product demand.

Goldratt calls the constraint the *drum,* because it sets the tempo that the entire production process needs to follow.

Suppose that the fictional Axiamm Company manufactures Tex's Hot Sauce. Production requires five production steps, as shown in Figure 19-4:

Figure 19-4: Production steps needed to make Tex's Hot Sauce.

1. **The purchasing department buys the freshest and spiciest raw materials.**
2. **The preparation department prepares these ingredients, pureeing and/or cooking.**
3. **The blending department measures the ingredients into a giant blender so that each batch can be mixed together.**
4. **A quality control inspector tastes every batch.**
5. **The packaging department bottles each batch and packs it into cases.**

Alice, the plant manager, is concerned about the quality control department, which always seems backlogged. On any given day, six or even seven batches of hot sauce are waiting for inspection. This backlog blocks up the blending department, forcing it to pause production while quality control catches up.

Alice identifies quality control as a constraint, primarily because of the lack of taste experts. The company has always had difficulty hiring well-qualified tasters who can verify that each product tastes right.

Step 2: Exploiting the constraint

After you identify the process that slows down the system, carefully consider how you can optimise the use of this constraint.

For example, in a traffic jam you'd go to the bottleneck and try to get the vehicles to drive through it as quickly as possible. When hiking with small children, you'd offer the youngest one incentives to move more quickly (snacks ahead, bears behind).

In a production process, you may be able to save time by setting up a buffer behind the constraint. A *buffer* is a stockpile of inputs, ready and waiting for the constrained step in the process so that your constraint never needs to stop working in order to wait for more inputs. In the Pam's Canned Hams example from the earlier section 'Identifying manufacturing constraints', the company keeps a buffer of slaughtered pigs so that the carcass process never stops.

Also, you may be able to exploit the constraint by maximising contribution per unit of constrained resource, as we explain in Chapter 10. For example, consider how the Axiamm Company can use this technique. When making hot sauce, the quality control department already has a buffer waiting to get tested – the backlog of batches that stretches all the way back to the blending department. Suppose that Tex's Hot Sauce comes in three different flavours, each of which provides a different throughput contribution margin:

- Tex's Very Hot Sauce: Throughput contribution of £1,000 per vat
- Tex's Super Hot Sauce: Throughput contribution of £700 per vat
- Tex's Atomic Hot Sauce: Throughput contribution of £500 per vat

The definition of contribution is modified when dealing with the theory of constraints and is called *throughput contribution*: sales revenue per vat less material costs only. In Chapter 9 we consider contribution where the calculation is sales revenue less all the variable costs. In modern manufacturing plants the materials are the only variable costs, making throughput contribution more appropriate. The only costs saved if a sale is lost are the materials not used.

To exploit this constraint, Alice has quality control first test the Very Hot Sauce; this strategy brings in the most contribution: £1,000 per vat. After the tasters get through the Very Hot Sauce, they move on to the Super Hot Sauce, which has a lower contribution: just £700 per vat. Finally, if they have any time left, they test the Atomic Hot Sauce, which provides only £500 of contribution per vat.

In this example, the quality control time is the same for each of the three types of hot sauce. But sometimes constraint times are different for different products. If the bottleneck time differs, you have to divide throughput contribution by the time in the bottleneck (a similar process to the limiting factor analysis in Chapter 10).

For example, if Very Hot Sauce requires 3 minutes, Super Hot requires 2 minutes and Atomic Hot requires 1 minute, the entire order is changed around, as Table 19-1 shows.

Table 19-1 Ranking Products Based on Throughput Contribution Per Minute Spent Going Through the Bottleneck

Hot Sauce Type	*Very*	*Super*	*Atomic*
Throughput contribution per vat	£1,000	£700	£500
Minutes in quality control (per vat)	3	2	1
Throughput contribution per minute	£333	£350	£500
Ranking (priority for time in bottleneck)	3	2	1

Now the Atomic Hot Sauce is identified as the product which earns the highest throughput contribution for the time it spends going through the bottleneck and is ranked number one. The Super Hot Sauce is second best and the Very Hot Sauce comes third. The business should prioritise Atomic production.

By exploiting the constraint based on contribution per minute in the bottleneck, the tasters are sure to test the most profitable products before they work on the less profitable products.

Step 3: Subordinating everything to the constraint

In Step 3, you rework your entire production schedule so that it moves at the same pace as the drum. Any processes going faster than the drum produce unnecessary units. Goldratt calls this pacing of processes the *rope,* such that goods move through production like a single rope – all at the drum's pace.

In the example of motorway traffic, subordinating everything to the constraint means getting all the cars to drive at the same speed – the maximum speed that they can drive through the bottleneck. When hiking with small children, it means getting the older children to slow down. For the Axiamm Company, it means purchasing, preparing and blending the raw materials to make as much Very Hot Sauce as it can sell, because this product has the highest contribution margin (see the preceding section).

Step 4: Breaking the constraint

Breaking the constraint means creatively thinking about alternative ways around the constraint. In traffic, you can get off the motorway and take side streets. In hiking, maybe the little one can keep up by taking a shortcut.

At the Axiamm Company, Alice and her colleagues are thinking about how to increase capacity in quality control. They've tried recruiting more workers, to no avail. They've also tried forcing the tasters to test more vats of hot sauce each day. That didn't turn out well, either.

Then Alice has a great idea. The blending department usually blends 50 litres of hot sauce at a time and then sends them to quality control in 50-litre vats. However, the blenders have the capacity to handle 100-litre loads. Therefore, she suggests that they blend 100 litres at a time and replace the 50-litre vats with 100-litre vats. This increase can cut the required number of quality control tests in half.

Problem solved. Now the quality control department can handle a full production load.

Step 5: Returning to Step 1

After you break the constraint in Step 4, start over again. Take a look at the production process to identify new constraints, exploit them, subordinate everything to them and then break them.

Putting you to the test: Exam tip

ACCA F5 exams have included a 20-mark question based on three types of surgical procedures within a private hospital and the identification of the best use of surgeon time. CIMA P1 exams tend to test the theory of constraints and throughput accounting using multiple choice and 5-mark questions.

Here's an example of a multiple choice question. Company X operates a throughput accounting system. The following details apply to one unit of F:

Selling price	£34.00
Material cost	£10.50
Labour cost	£6.80
Overhead costs	£6.20
Time on bottleneck resource	8 minutes

Is the throughput contribution per hour for product F:

a. £188.00?

b. £176.25?

c. £133.60?

d. £57.50?

The recommended approach is:

1. **Find the throughput contribution per unit.**

   £34.00 – £10.50 = £23.50.

2. **Divide the throughput contribution per unit by the minutes and convert to hours.**

   £23.50 ÷ 8 minutes × 60 minutes per hour = £176.25 (answer b).

Part V

The Part of Tens

Visit `www.dummies.com/extras/managementcostaccountinguk` to enjoy an additional management and cost accounting Part of Tens chapter 'Ten Ratios to Know for Management Accountants', including exam practice.

In this part . . .

- Discover a quick reference to key formulas used in managerial accounting.
- Consider career options open to management accountants.
- Know the salary you might be able to receive as a management accountant.

Chapter 20

Ten Key Management Accounting Formulas

In This Chapter

- Understanding accounting ratios
- Using contribution margin
- Analysing price and quantity variances
- Computing time value of money

As a management accountant, you work out and provide information within a company. Your reports provide managers with up to date information about the organisation.

Management accounting information is, of course, number-based and calculated using certain formulas. This chapter provides a quick guide to some of the most important formulas used in management accounting. Pop to this chapter whenever you need to jog your memory about a formula. Without a doubt, you're going to find these equations extremely helpful.

The Accounting Equation: Working with Assets and Liabilities

The *accounting equation* equates assets with liabilities and owners' equity:

Assets = Liabilities + Owners' equity

Assets are things owned by the company – such as cash, inventory and equipment that will provide some future benefit. *Liabilities* entail future sacrifices that the company must make, such as paying bills or other kinds of debts. *Owners' equity* (or *book value*) represents the portion of the company that belongs to the owner.

Understanding the accounting equation is easier with numbers. Suppose that Jasobo Co., owned by Jason Bone, has £1,000,000 in assets and owes £200,000 in debt. Jason's share of the company is worth £800,000:

Assets = Liabilities + Owners' equity

£1,000,000 = £200,000 + Owners' equity

£800,000 = Owners' equity

A basic rule of accounting is that the accounting equation must always balance. If assets exceed the sum of liabilities and owners' equity, the company holds things that don't belong to anyone. If the sum of liabilities and owners' equity exceeds assets, owners and creditors lay claim to things that don't exist.

Profit: Focusing on the Bottom Line

Profit is called the *bottom line* because in many ways it's the sum total of accountants' work. To calculate profit, you subtract expenses from revenues:

Revenues – Expenses = Profit

Revenues are inflows, for example sales to customers. *Expenses* are costs associated with making sales. When these are the only expenses, the profit is called *profit from operations.*

Accountants also sometimes need to add gains or subtract losses in the profit before tax; these gains and losses come from miscellaneous events that affect stockholder value, such as selling equipment at a gain or getting your factory destroyed by a mutated prehistoric survivor of the dinosaurs.

Suppose that the fictional *Daily Planet* newspaper had £100,000 in revenues, £80,000 in expenses, £5,000 in gains and £4,000 in losses. What was its profit before tax?

£100,000 – £80,000 + £5,000 – £4,000 = £21,000 profit before tax

Investors love profit because it provides a simple measure of a company's performance that's easy to understand. In a limited company, the profit value investors tend to look for is the *profit available for distribution.* This long-winded description is also called the *profit for the year* and it is, quite literally, the bottom line: no other line appears below it on an Income Statement or Profit and Loss Account. It's the profit earned *after* tax has been taken off.

Cost of Goods Sold: Handling Inventory

For manufacturers and retailers, *Cost of Goods Sold* measures how much the company paid – or will need to pay – for inventory items sold.

To compute a retailer's Cost of Goods Sold, you put the following formula to use:

> Opening Value of Inventory + Cost of Purchases – Closing Value of Inventory = Cost of Goods Sold

Here, a retailer's *inputs* are the cost of the purchases it makes. The *outputs* are the goods that were sold (recorded at cost, of course).

Suppose that The English Channel Swimming Shop started the season with £100,000 worth of inventory. The company purchased an additional £200,000 worth of inventory. At the end of the season, the inventory was worth £50,000. The following equation reveals the Cost of Goods Sold:

Opening value of inventory	+	Cost of Purchases	–	Closing value of inventory	=	Cost of Goods Sold
£100,000	+	£200,000	–	£50,000	=	£250,000

You can adapt this formula to different scenarios. For example, suppose that your company makes, rather than purchases, the goods that it sells. To compute Cost of Goods Sold, you replace the Cost of Purchases with the Cost of Goods Manufactured:

Opening value of finished goods inventory	+	Cost of Production	–	Closing value of finished goods inventory	=	Cost of Goods Sold

Contribution: Measuring the Impact of Decisions on Profit

REMEMBER

Contribution measures how selling one item, or a group of items, increases total profit. To calculate contribution, you subtract variable costs from sales:

Total sales revenue – Total variable cost = Total contribution

Contribution helps managers by explaining the impact that decisions have on profit. For example, should you prepare a special order with a contribution of £100,000? Yes, because doing so increases profits by £100,000. Should you prepare another special order with a contribution of *negative* £50,000? No, because it decreases total profit.

To compute contribution per unit, you divide the total contribution by the number of units sold. If the business has only one product, you can calculate sales price less variable cost per unit:

Price per unit – Variable cost per unit = Contribution per unit

For example, if a given product sells for £12 and has a variable cost per unit of £9, its contribution per unit equals £3. In other words, every unit of this product sold increases total profit by £3.

To calculate the contribution to sales (CS) ratio, you divide contribution by sales, either in total or per unit:

$$\text{Contribution to Sales (CS) ratio} = \frac{\text{Total contribution}}{\text{Total sales revenue}}$$

or

$$\text{Contribution to Sales (CS) ratio} = \frac{\text{Contribution per unit}}{\text{Price per unit}}$$

For example, if a given product sells for £12 and has a contribution per unit of £3, its CS ratio is 25 per cent (£3 ÷ £12). This result means that every £1 of sales increases net profit by £0.25.

Cost-Volume-Profit Analysis: Considering the Effects of Changing Volume

Cost-volume-profit (CVP) analysis helps you understand how changes in volume affect costs and profit. If you know sales price, variable cost per unit, volume and fixed costs, this formula predicts your profit:

Net profit = ((Sales price – Variable cost per unit) × (Volume)) – Fixed costs

To help understand where this formula comes from, consider how production volume affects total costs:

Total cost = (Variable cost per unit × Volume) + Fixed costs

As we explain in Chapter 8, variable cost per unit is the additional cost of producing a single unit. *Volume* is the number of units produced and sold and *fixed cost* is the total fixed cost for the period. Profit is just the difference between total sales and total cost:

Profit = (Selling price × volume) – Total cost

Combining these two equations gives you the super-useful formula for understanding how volume affects profits:

Profit	=	(Selling price × volume)	–	Total cost		
	=	(Selling price × volume)	–	[(Variable cost per unit × volume) + Fixed costs]		
	=	(Selling price × volume)	–	(Variable cost per unit × volume)	–	Fixed costs
	=	[(Selling price – variable cost per unit) × volume]			–	Fixed costs

Not coincidentally, a critical part of this formula equals contribution – remember that selling price less variable cost per unit equals contribution per unit:

Price per unit – Variable cost per unit = Contribution per unit

This formula lets you further simplify the CVP formula:

Profit = (Contribution per unit × Volume) – Fixed costs

Suppose that Caroline's Dairy Ice Cream Company expects to sell 10,000 ice cream cones next year, each with a contribution margin of £1. Caroline's Dairy pays £4,000 for fixed costs a year. How much profit is the company going to earn next year?

Profit = (£1 × 10,000 ice cream cones) – £4,000 = £6,000

CVP analysis reveals that Caroline's Dairy probably earns £6,000 next year.

Break-Even Analysis: Ensuring You Don't Make a Loss

Break-even analysis helps you determine how much you need to sell in order to break even – that is, not make a loss. To figure out this break-even point, use the following formula:

$$\text{Break-even volume} = \frac{\text{Fixed costs}}{\text{Sales price} - \text{Variable cost per unit}}$$

Perhaps you recognise contribution margin in the denominator (Sales price – Variable cost per unit), allowing you to further simplify this formula:

$$\text{Break-even volume (units)} = \frac{\text{Fixed costs}}{\text{Contribution per unit}}$$

To figure out the number of units needed to break even, just divide total fixed costs by contribution margin per unit.

The Apple Pie Company incurs £30,000 worth of fixed costs each year. Each pie sells for £11 and requires variable costs of £5 to make. Contribution per pie equals £6 (£11 – £5):

$$\text{Break-even volume (units)} = \frac{£30{,}000}{£6.00} = 5{,}000 \text{ units}$$

In order to break even – not make a loss – The Apple Pie Company needs to sell 5,000 pies.

Calculating the Effect of Direct Materials Price Variance on Total Cost

The *direct materials price variance* tells you how an unexpected change in the cost of direct materials affects total cost. Figure 20-1 shows you how to calculate the price variance.

		Standard Cost per Unit of Input Flexed to Actual Quantity Purchased		*Actual Cost*
Direct Materials				
Total litres		Actual litres purchased		Actual litres purchased
Cost per litre	×	Standard cost per litre	×	Actual cost per litre
Cost	=	Standard cost of material purchased	=	Actual cost of purchases
Variance		Material Price Variance (Standard cost of actual material less actual cost)		

Figure 20-1: The Variance Analysis Worksheet (the Materials Price Variance).

Standard price is the amount you originally expected to pay, per unit, of direct materials. *Actual price* is the real price you paid, per unit, for direct materials. The *actual quantity* is the number of units purchased and used in production.

Suppose that the Pig's Head Tavern made and sold 2,000 pints of lager last month. It expected to pay 80 pence per pint, but the actual price was 90 pence per pint. You simply plug in these numbers to find the price variance, as shown in Figure 20-2.

		Standard Cost per Unit of Input Flexed to Actual Quantity Purchased		*Actual Cost*
Direct Materials				
Total pints		2,000 pints		2,000 pints
Cost per pint	×	£0.80	×	£0.90
Cost	=	£1,600.00	=	£1,800.00
Variance		Material Price Variance £200 adverse		

Figure 20-2: The Variance Analysis Worksheet for The Pig's Head Tavern.

This unexpected price increase hurts profits by £200 and so is called an adverse variance (flip to Chapter 15 for more on variances).

Although the price variance formula focuses on the direct materials variance, you can adapt it easily to figure out the direct labour rate variance. To do so, replace standard cost per unit of input with the standard rate per hour of direct labour; replace actual cost per unit of material with the actual rate per hour; and then replace the actual material used with the actual number of hours worked.

Determining the Effect of Direct Materials Usage Variance on Total Cost

The *direct materials usage variance* measures how using too much or too little in direct materials affects total costs. Stinginess in using direct materials usually decreases your costs, but wasting direct materials increases costs. See Figure 20-3 for the layout.

		Standard Cost per Unit of Output Flexed to Actual Units Produced		***Standard Cost per Unit of Input Flexed to Actual Quantity Used***
Production		***Units Produced***		
Direct Materials				
Litres per unit	×	Standard material per unit		
Total litres	=	Standard materials for actual production		Actual litres used
Cost per litre	×	Standard cost per litre	×	Standard cost per litre
Cost	=	Standard cost of material (for actual production)	=	Standard cost of material used
Variance		Material Usage Variance →		
(Standard cost of material for actual production less standard cost of material used)				

Figure 20-3: The Variance Analysis Worksheet (the Materials Usage Variance).

Standard price is how much you originally expected to pay, per unit, of direct materials. *Standard quantity* is the number of units of direct materials that you expected to use. *Actual quantity* is the number of units of direct materials that you actually used in production.

Future Value: Computing the Value of a Cash Investment

Future value measures how much a present cash flow is going to be worth in the future. For example, if you put £1,000 into the bank today, earning 6 per cent interest a year, how much are you going to have ten years from now?

To solve such problems, you can use tables printed in textbooks or financial calculators. But you can also solve these problems using the time value of money formula:

Future value	=	Present value	×	(1 + interest rate)$^{\text{number of years}}$

Present value measures how much money you receive or pay now. Make this figure positive if you're receiving the money and make it negative if you're paying the money out. Future value is how much you can expect to receive or pay in the future (again, positive for incoming cash, negative for outgoing cash). Enter the interest rate as the *annual* interest rate (rather than daily, monthly or quarterly). The number of years is for the period of time between the date of the present value and the date of the future value, in years.

Therefore, if present value equals £1,000, the interest rate is 6 per cent and the number of years is 10 (see Figure 20-4):

Future value	=	Present value	×	(1 + interest rate)$^{\text{number of years}}$
	=	£1,000	×	(1 + 0.06)$^{\text{10 years}}$
	=	£1,000	×	(1.06)$^{\text{10 years}}$
	=	£1,000	×	1.791
	=	£1,791		

Figure 20-4: Working out the future value.

The number of years, 10 in this case, is a 'to the power of' value. Effectively, you're multiplying 1.06 by itself 10 times.

Most accountancy exams require you to calculate values to the power. Investing in a good scientific calculator near the beginning of your course gives you the opportunity for plenty of practice before the exam.

The future value indicates that if you put £1,000 away now, earning 6 per cent per year, you can expect to receive £1,791 at the end of ten years.

Present Value: Deciding How Much to Invest

Okay, we admit it: the chapter title is a bit of a lie! We really mean *nine* key formulas, not ten, because *present value* uses the same formula as future value in the preceding section. If you're trying to memorise these formulas, we're sure you aren't going to mind having to remember one fewer.

Future value	=	Present value	×	(1 + interest rate)$^{\text{number of years}}$

Here's how you can use this formula to compute the present value of a cash flow (see Figure 20-5). Suppose that, four years from now, you want to have £5,000 (that's the future value). How much do you need to put into the bank today, earning 5 per cent interest?

Future value	=	Present value	×	(1 + interest rate) $^{\text{number of years}}$
£5,000	=	Present value	×	(1 + 0.05) $^{\text{4 years}}$
£5,000	=	Present value	×	(1.05) $^{\text{4 years}}$
£5,000	=	Present value	×	1.216
£5,000 / 1,216	=	Present value		
£4,112	=	Present value		

Figure 20-5: Working out the present value.

So if you put £4,112 into the bank today, earning 5 per cent interest, in four years' time you have £5,000 to take out.

Here's a version of the formula to calculate present value more directly:

Present value	=	$\dfrac{\text{Future value}}{(1 + \text{interest rate})^{\text{number of years}}}$

On CIMA and on ACCA F9 exam papers the following formula is shown above the present value table:

> *Present value of £1, that is* $(1+r)^{-n}$ *where r = interest rate; n = number of periods until payment or receipt.*
>
> Future value × $(1 + r)^{n}$ = Present value

The two different arrangements of the formula give exactly the same present value:

Present value	=	$\frac{\text{Future value}}{(1 + \text{interest rate})^{\text{number of years}}}$
Present value	=	Future value × $(1 + \text{interest rate})^{-\text{number of years}}$

If you use the second formula, make sure that you put the minus sign in front of the number of years.

Chapter 21

Ten Careers in Management Accounting

In This Chapter

- Climbing the management accounting ladder
- Running effective finance operations
- Managing and controlling a company's costs

Most of our students choose accounting careers because of the consistent high demand for hiring accountants. The starting salaries aren't bad either, according to the Salary Guide published by finance staffing specialists Robert Half International (see `www.roberthalf.co.uk/salary-guide`).

All the salaries we cite in this chapter are the salaries of accountants working for large companies, but these salaries vary by location. Local labour markets influence the actual salaries paid. Robert Half quantify this using an index. For example, national rates are inflated by over 25% for London, whereas northern England rates are just over 90% of the national rate.

A common reason for the difference in salaries is the role carried out. Many firms struggle to set job titles, often because the job role has changed over a period of time. This leads to the job title not actually being the best indication of the role. When considering advertised job vacancies, look beyond the job title to the job description. This description gives the details and what you need to do to earn the advertised salary.

The salaries given in this chapter are guidelines, correct at the time of writing in 2013. There are always variations in salaries between people with the same job titles.

Corporate Treasurer

The coveted position of *treasurer* is the career summit that management accountants aspire to. Treasurers take responsibility for all financial activities within a corporation, including managing liquidity risk, managing cash, issuing debt, hedging foreign exchange and interest rate risk, securitising, overseeing pension investments and managing capital structure.

The corporate treasurer typically sits on the corporation's board of directors and chairs its finance committee but is usually not involved in day-to-day operations. A treasurer of a large company can expect to earn in excess of £150,000 per year.

Chief Financial Officer

The *chief financial officer*, or CFO, runs all corporate finance functions on a day-to-day basis. The CFO acts as steward of the company's assets, minimising risk and making sure that the books and financial statements are correct. The CFO also needs to run an effective and efficient finance operation within the company. The CFO installs a financial mindset throughout the organisation so that all parts of the business perform better. A CFO of a large company can anticipate earning between £75,000 and £130,000+.

Financial Controller

Financial controllers collect and maintain information about all aspects of a company's finances. They prepare financial statements, budget reports, forecasts, cost-analysis reports, profit and loss statements and recommendations for spending or cost cuts. They also supervise other accountants in the company. They work to ensure that internal controls are in place and working properly, that the financial statements are prepared accurately, and that all of the company's finances are properly documented. They also make sure that monies owed to the company are collected and that bills for the company's expenses get paid.

In a large company, a typical financial controller can expect to earn between £54,000 and £80,500.

Group Accountant

The *group accountant* prepares fiscal and budget reports for internal management, and financial statements and other reports to stockholders and other external stakeholders. He or she also oversees the development of master budgets and other projections in order to make recommendations to management. A group accountant at a large company can expect to earn between £40,500 and £64,250.

Financial Analyst

Financial analysts help to prepare budgets, monitor task performance, keep track of actual costs, analyse different kinds of variances, review contract completion reports and assist other executives in preparing forecasts and projections. Starting salaries for recent graduates starting as financial analysts with large companies are expected to range between £35,500 and £60,000. More experienced financial analyst managers can anticipate earning between £38,250 and £61,750.

Cost Accountant

Cost accountants accumulate accurate data about the cost of raw materials, work-in-progress, finished goods, labour, overhead and other related manufacturing costs. They also set cost standards, such as how many hours of direct labour or direct materials manufacturing a widget requires. Experienced cost accounting managers are projected to earn between £39,500 and £60,250.

Budget Analyst

The *budget analyst* prepares and administrates the master budget and then compares master budget projections with actual performance. To prepare this information, the budget analyst needs to become intimately familiar with all the operations in the budget and work closely with both cost accountants and production managers working on the plant floor. Experienced budget analyst managers can expect to earn between £38,250 and £61,750.

Internal Auditor

Internal auditors ensure that controls over cash and other assets and various other procedures are working as they should. Internal auditors are often called on to investigate budget variances and are typically the first to look for – and identify – poor work quality, waste materials, fraud, theft and deliberate acts of industrial sabotage.

Unlike external auditors, the internal auditors work for the very company that they audit. Therefore, they typically report to executives at a very high level in the organisation (such as the treasurer). Starting salaries for recent college graduates entering the workforce as internal auditors with large companies are expected to be about £34,750. Internal audit managers with more experience can anticipate earning between £34,750 and £56,500.

Fixed-Assets Accountant

A *fixed-assets* accountant is responsible for keeping records related to a company's property, plant and equipment. These folks inspect the property, the plant and the equipment to verify the accuracy of the books. Furthermore, they oversee the computation of depreciation, as reported in financial statements and tax filings. Salaries for fixed-asset accountants generally range in the same area as for financial analysts, which we cover earlier in this chapter.

Cash-Management Accountant

The *cash-management accountant* is responsible for cash-related financial operations, including transfers between accounts, monitoring deposits and payments, reconciling cash balances, creating and following cash forecasts and abiding by the company's system of internal controls. Salaries for cash-management accountants are generally in the same range as those we list for financial analysts earlier in the chapter.

Index

• A •

• C •

• D •

• E •

• F •

• G •

• H •

• I •

• J •

• N •

• P •

• Q •

• R •

• S •

• T •

• U •

• V •

• W •

• Z •

About the Authors

Mark Holtzman is chair of the Department of Accounting and Taxation at Seton Hall University in South Orange, New Jersey, where he teaches financial accounting and managerial accounting courses to both graduate and undergraduate students.

In addition to authoring articles and other research materials, Mark is coauthor of *Interpreting and Analyzing Financial Statements* with Karen Schoenebeck, now in its 6th edition (Pearson).

In his spare time, Mark enjoys spending time with his family, hiking, camping and studying ancient Hebrew texts.

Sandy Hood is CIMA course tutor at Chichester College. He has been an accountancy lecturer since 1990. He regularly provides advice and guidance to the AAT discussion forum and contributes articles to *PQ Magazine*.

Dedications

To my family: Rikki, who stoically endures living with a curmudgeon accounting professor, and my astonishing kids, David, Aaron, Levi and Esther.

– Mark

For my beloved and fantastic wife Maureen who died of pancreatic cancer on 16th May 2013.

– Sandy

Authors' Acknowledgements

I would like to thank all of the wonderfully dedicated professionals at Wiley who helped make this book a reality in spite of my best attempts to the contrary.

Thank you, too, to my colleagues and students at Seton Hall. It is a privilege and joy to learn and work with you.

– Mark

Many thanks go to Rachael Chilvers and Claire Ruston at Wiley and Andy Finch for their patience and help. My thanks to those students who have studied with me over the years; many of the ideas in this book have grown from their classes. Thanks also to my colleagues at Chichester College who put up with me with tremendous forbearance. Particular thanks to my family who have rallied round following Maureen's diagnosis in March and been a wonderful support. You have *all* been lovely and I'm sure you know that without needing a list here. Thank you.

– Sandy

Publisher's Acknowledgements

Project Editor: Rachael Chilvers

Commissioning Editor: Claire Ruston

Associate Commissioning Editor: Ben Kemble

Development Editor: Andy Finch

Proofreader: Kerry Laundon

Production Manager: Daniel Mersey

Publisher: Miles Kendall

Cover Photos: © iStockphoto.com/Laura Flugga

Project Coordinator: Kristie Rees

For Dummies®

Making Everything Easier!™

UK editions

BUSINESS

978-1-118-34689-1

978-1-118-44349-1

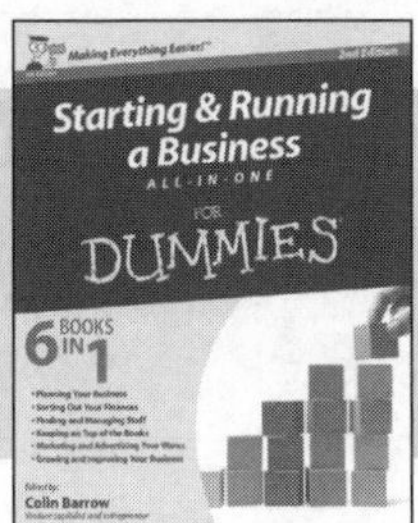

978-1-119-97527-4

MUSIC

978-1-119-94276-4

978-0-470-97799-6

978-0-470-66372-1

HOBBIES

978-1-118-41156-8

978-1-119-99417-6

978-1-119-97250-1

Asperger's Syndrome For Dummies
978-0-470-66087-4

Basic Maths For Dummies
978-1-119-97452-9

Body Language For Dummies, 2nd Edition
978-1-119-95351-7

Boosting Self-Esteem For Dummies
978-0-470-74193-1

Business Continuity For Dummies
978-1-118-32683-1

Cricket For Dummies
978-0-470-03454-5

Diabetes For Dummies, 3rd Edition
978-0-470-97711-8

eBay For Dummies, 3rd Edition
978-1-119-94122-4

English Grammar For Dummies
978-0-470-05752-0

Flirting For Dummies
978-0-470-74259-4

IBS For Dummies
978-0-470-51737-6

ITIL For Dummies
978-1-119-95013-4

Management For Dummies, 2nd Edition
978-0-470-97769-9

Managing Anxiety with CBT For Dummies
978-1-118-36606-6

Neuro-linguistic Programming For Dummies, 2nd Edition
978-0-470-66543-5

Nutrition For Dummies, 2nd Edition
978-0-470-97276-2

Organic Gardening For Dummies
978-1-119-97706-3

12-47776-187x234mm

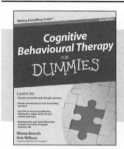

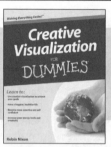

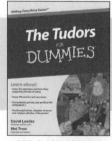

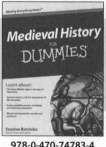

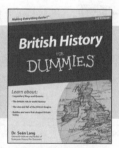

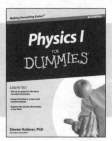

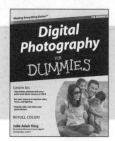

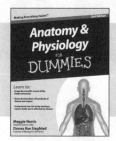

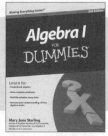